PME 707

Environmental Management Quick and Easy

Also available from ASQ Quality Press:

The Management System Auditor's Handbook
Joe Kausek

*ANSI/ISO/ASQ E14001-2004: Environmental management systems—
Requirements with guidance for use (e-standard)*
ANSI/ISO/ASQ

*ANSI/ISO/ASQ QE19011S-2004: Guidelines for quality and/or
environmental management systems auditing—U.S. Version with
supplemental guidance added*
ANSI/ISO/ASQ

*ANSI/ASQ E4-2004: Quality systems for environmental data and
technology programs—Requirements with quidance for use*
ANSI/ASQ

*ANSI/ISO/ASQ E14064-1:2006 Greenhouse gases—Part 1: Specification
with guidance at the organization level for quantification and reporting of
greenhouse gas emissions and removal*
ANSI/ISO/ASQ

*ANSI/ISO/ASQ E14064-2:2006 Greenhouse gases—Part 2: Specification
with guidance at the project level for quantification, monitoring and
reporting of greenhouse gas emission red.*
ANSI/ISO/ASQ

*ANSI/ISO/ASQ E14064-3:2006 Greenhouse gases—Part 3: Specification
with guidance for the validation and verification of greenhouse gas
assertions*
ANSI/ISO/ASQ

Effective Implementation of ISO 14001
Marilyn R. Block

The ASQ Auditing Handbook, Third Edition
J.P. Russell, editing director

*Process Driven Comprehensive Auditing: A New Way to Conduct
ISO 9001:2000 Internal Audits*
Paul C. Palmes

To request a complimentary catalog of ASQ Quality Press publications,
call 800-248-1946, or visit our Web site at http://qualitypress.asq.org.

Environmental Management Quick and Easy

Creating an Effective ISO 14001 EMS in Half the Time

Joe Kausek

ASQ Quality Press
Milwaukee, Wisconsin

American Society for Quality, Quality Press, Milwaukee 53203
© 2007 by American Society for Quality
All rights reserved. Published 2006
Printed in the United States of America
12 11 10   5 4 3 2

Library of Congress Cataloging-in-Publication Data

Kausek, Joe, 1957–
    Environmental management quick and easy : creating an effective ISO 14001
    EMS in half the time / Joe Kausek.
        p. cm.
    Includes bibliographical references and index.
    ISBN-13: 978-0-87389-705-1 (hard cover : alk. paper)
    1. Industrial management—Environmental aspects.   2. Environmental
    management.   I. Title.

    HD30.255.K38   2006
    658.4'083—dc22

                                                                2006032728

Publisher: William A. Tony
Acquisitions Editor: Matt Meinholz
Project Editor: Paul O'Mara
Production Administrator: Randall Benson

ASQ Mission: The American Society for Quality advances individual, organizational, and community excellence worldwide through learning, quality improvement, and knowledge exchange.

Attention Bookstores, Wholesalers, Schools, and Corporations: ASQ Quality
Press books, videotapes, audiotapes, and software are available at quantity
discounts with bulk purchases for business, educational, or instructional use. For
information, please contact ASQ Quality Press at 800-248-1946, or write to ASQ
Quality Press, P.O. Box 3005, Milwaukee, WI 53201-3005.

To place orders or to request a free copy of the ASQ Quality Press Publications
Catalog, including ASQ membership information, call 800-248-1946. Visit our
Web site at www.asq.org or http://qualitypress.asq.org.

Quality Press
600 N. Plankinton Avenue
Milwaukee, Wisconsin 53203
Call toll free 800-248-1946
Fax 414-272-1734
www.asq.org
http://qualitypress.asq.org
http://standardsgroup.asq.org
E-mail: authors@asq.org

AMERICAN SOCIETY
FOR QUALITY™

∞ Printed on acid-free paper

Contents

Part II   EMS Design and Deployment **41**

Chapter 3   The Planning Phase. **43**

Chapter 4   The Design and Development Phase **59**

CD-ROM Contents

The following resources are available on the CD-ROM accompanying this book. To access them, you will need word processing software such as Microsoft Word, spreadsheet software such as Microsoft Excel, Microsoft Project, and PDF-viewing software such as Adobe Acrobat Reader.

Environmental Planning Workbook Example.xls

Audit Checklists and Tools

EMS Management System Audit Checklist.doc

Environmental Aspects Identification Checklist.doc

Environmental Briefing Survey.doc

Environmental Bulletin.doc

Environmental Planning Workbook Example for Book.xls

Generic Project Plan for 14001.mpp

Management Review Agenda Blank.doc

Project Charter.doc

Project Communication Plan.doc

EPA Resources

15 Best Practices for Buildings.pdf

Climate Leaders Program Guide.pdf

Climate Leaders GHG Program Guide.pdf

Combined Heat Power Technologies Catalog.pdf

DfE Brochure.pdf

DfE Lead Free Solder Fact Sheet.pdf

DfE Lead Life Cycle Report.pdf

DfE Putting DfE in Your Policy Statement.pdf

DfE PWB.pdf

DfE PWBs.pdf

Energy Star and Manufacturers Presentation.pdf

Energy Star Lighting.pdf

Energy Star Program Guide.pdf

EPA building manual upgrade for energy reduction.pdf

EPA DfE Program Guide.pdf

EPA DfE Surface_Finishing for PWB.pdf

EPA Green Power Purchasing Guide.pdf

EPA Prioritizing Env Aspects.pdf

Fan Systems Upgrades.pdf

Green power.pdf

Greenscape.pdf

Heating and Cooling Upgrades.pdf

How to Recycle Program Guide.pdf

Putting DfE in Your EMS.pdf

Resource Conservation Challenge.pdf

Source Reduction Manual.pdf

Supplemental Load Reductions.pdf

Surface_Finishing PCB.pdf

WasteWise Elec and Computer Fact Sheet.pdf

WasteWise Motor Vehicles Fact Sheet.pdf

WasteWise Update.pdf

Water Conservation Fact Sheet.pdf

Procedures

Document & Record Control.doc

Environmental Policy Manual.doc

Identification and Control of Sign Env Aspects.doc

Internal Audits.doc

Nonconformities, Corrective and Preventive Action.doc

List of Figures

Preface

The current concern for the environment has never been greater. Turn on any newscast, read any newspaper, or scan any of the top stories on your favorite Internet site and you're likely to find at least one article discussing global warming, the change in climate, the rising price and scarcity of oil, or the need for alternative energy sources. When I first got involved in developing and implementing environmental management systems (EMSs) back in the 1990s, much of the debate centered on whether global warming was real. Now, however, while almost all scientists agree that humans are impacting on the environment, the debate now centers on what the effects of this impact will be. Interesting enough, most scientists also agree that these effects, in whatever form they take, will for practical purposes be irreversible if we do not act quickly.

But what can we do right now? Passing stricter environmental regulations may be part of the answer, but these are typically costly and have great economic impact. In addition, many of the current environmental issues have developed over the past 30 years despite the passage of a multitude of laws. Although stricter regulations in certain key areas are needed, clearly we will not be able to regulate our way out of our current dilemma.

The answer is voluntary environmental performance improvement beyond compliance. The goal is to achieve sustainable development, which is economic development that meets the needs of today's generation without impacting on the ability of future generations to meet their own needs. It was for this reason that the international community developed ISO 14001. The ISO 14001 standard provides a model for companies to use in developing a management system that moves beyond compliance toward sustainable development. The real benefit of ISO 14001 is that it can significantly improve an organization's environmental performance while greatly improving its bottom line at the same time. Unfortunately, most companies that have implemented ISO 14001 have not yet moved beyond compliance and have not yet realized these dual benefits.

My motivation in writing this book was to demonstrate that the design and implementation of an ISO 14001 EMS need not be complicated or costly. The focus is on getting a basic yet effective EMS in place with minimal effort so that the organization can move quickly toward the environmental performance improvements that will be needed to meet the growing international demand for corporate environmental stewardship. Throughout this book, the focus is on the actions needed to generate corporate-wide support for and involvement in environmental performance improvement. It is my wish that readers understand not only what they need to do and how to do it but also why they should do it and how to infuse this passion to others within their company.

In order to support the goal of fast and easy ISO 14001 implementation, I have provided dozens of tools, checklists, procedure templates, and spreadsheets I have developed and used during dozens of ISO 14001 implementations in organizations of all sizes. These tools not only speed the design and implementation of the EMS, they also provide for efficient and effective ongoing maintenance of the system. The goal is to minimize the overhead needed to manage and maintain the system so that more time and resources are available for actions that actually benefit the environment.

By no means do the chapters in this book or the tools on the CD represent the only or, in some cases, even the best way to implement an EMS in any specific company. I would be very grateful for any feedback or suggestions on this book or the tools provided. I can be contacted through authors@asq.org.

Part I
EMS Overview

Part I examines the structure and intent of the ISO 14001 management system standard. Chapter 1 looks at what any management system should do and then briefly reviews the structure of ISO 14001.[1] Of particular note is the section that discusses management system evolution from conformance through effectiveness and toward improvement.

Chapter 2 builds on Chapter 1 by examining the ISO 14001:2004 model in more detail. The structure, interactions, and basic principles of environmental management as defined by ISO 14001:2004 are explored along with some of the important environmental factors driving organizations to implement comprehensive EMSs.

1

Management Systems Overview

In general, any management system is composed of three primary processes:

- The *core processes,* which focus on the primary purpose or outputs of the system and the processes that produce them. In the EMS it is the identification of significant environmental aspects along with the methods and means to control their related activities and to minimize or eliminate any adverse environmental impacts. The processes used to determine, assign, and monitor environmental improvement objectives would also classify as core processes in that they directly contribute to the core purpose of the EMS.

- The *key supporting processes,* which provide direct inputs into the core processes or measure the results of the outputs. These include the processes used to maintain an awareness of legal and other requirements, ensure competency and awareness of employees, provide an adequate infrastructure, communicate important EMS information, and monitor and evaluate environmental performance.

- The *management system supporting processes*, such as document control, record control, and internal auditing.

For a management system to be effective, these three components must be aligned and must perform as intended. While most of the attention is given to the core processes, failure to adequately monitor or control any of the supporting processes will impact on the effectiveness of the overall system. Now we will look at what a management system is supposed to do.

THE PURPOSE OF A MANAGEMENT SYSTEM

One can say that the primary purpose of any management system is to implement the chosen strategy of an organization by focusing resources on areas critical for organizational success. For an ISO 14001 management system, this means meeting the commitments stated in the organization's policy statement. These commitments could include reducing or eliminating the negative environmental impacts of its products, services, and activities and/or increasing their positive effects.

To meet this purpose, all management systems establish requirements and guidelines that, when followed, should provide reasonable assurance that the outputs from the system will be as expected (that is, minimal negative environmental impact and improved environmental performance). The purpose of the ISO 14001 management system standard is to provide these general requirements. It should be noted that the ISO 14001 standard is non-prescriptive; that is, it details what should be done, not necessarily how to do it. Organizations then develop and implement internal systems, processes, and procedures that provide more detail on how these general requirements are met within their unique operating environment.

The general trend in management systems is to reinforce this need to align processes into integrated systems of processes, all focused on providing the highest value to the customer. In this sense, the primary customer of the EMS is the local, regional, and global environment. Secondary customers may include the organization's owners or shareholders, customers, government agencies, and employees. Effective EMSs provide significant benefits to each of these customer groups. Conversely, poor environmental management can present significant risk (negative value) to these same customers. Those charged with developing, implementing, and maintaining these systems must understand and be able to articulate these benefits and risks in order to enlist the support of both management and employees in the common goal of creating an effective and efficient management system. These potential benefits and risks are examined next in order to prepare the reader for the consensus building needed to develop an effective management system.

THE CASE FOR ISO 14001

The History of ISO 14001 and Global Environmental Concerns

The ISO 14001 standard is published by the International Organization for Standardization. It is somewhat unique from other ISO standards in that it was not developed to facilitate international trade, as was ISO 9001, but rather as a response to international concerns for the environment. The principle behind the development of ISO 14001 is that organizations in general, and industry in particular, need to move beyond regulatory compliance toward sustainable development. *Sustainable development* is defined as development that meets the needs of the present without compromising the ability of future generations to meet their own needs. Sustainable development is seen as necessary because global environmental degradation continues despite the introduction and enforcement of a multitude of environmental laws and regulations. Consider the following:[2]

- The earth's temperature is predicted to increase between 2.5°F and 10.4°F by the end of this century if the current rate of greenhouse gas emissions continues. The impact on rising sea levels and on climate change brought about by these gases is somewhat uncertain, but it is generally accepted by the world's scientific community to be serious, adverse, and possibly irreversible.

- About 25 percent of the world's population is exposed to potentially harmful amounts of sulfur dioxide, ozone, and particulate matter in smog. Globally, some 50 percent of cases of chronic respiratory illness are now thought to be associated with air pollution. Estimates of U.S. deaths related to outdoor air pollution range from 50,000 to 188,000 per year. Healthcare costs associated with indoor and outdoor air pollution are estimated at more than $150 billion annually.

- In the 1980s, acid rain was identified as a major international environmental problem, moving from heavily industrialized areas of both Europe and North America into prime agricultural areas that lay downwind. Mountain regions suffered the most because their higher rainfall increased the volume of acid deposition and their often thin soils could not neutralize the acid. Lakes and streams in pristine parts of Scandinavia and Scotland became acidified, and fish populations were decimated in some areas. Although significant progress has been made in controlling acid-forming emissions in some countries, the global threat from acid precipitation still remains. In fact, the problem is rapidly growing in Asia, where 1990s-level sulfur dioxide emissions could triple by 2010 if current trends continue.

- During the past century, the world population has tripled. Over roughly the same period of time, water use worldwide has increased sixfold. Experts predict that by 2025 global water needs will increase even more, with 40 percent more water needed for cities and 20 percent more water needed for growing crops. Yet while needs increase, the amount of fresh water available worldwide is dwindling. Over the next two decades, it is estimated that the average supply of water per person will drop by one-third. Annually, the lack of clean drinking water can be linked to roughly 250 million cases of water-related disease and between 5 million and 10 million deaths worldwide. Thus, water shortages indirectly condemn millions of people to an avoidable premature death each year. At the same time that global water supplies are declining, so is the quality of the water that remains. Unless corrective and conservative measures are taken, it is estimated that by 2030 global demands for fresh water will exceed the supply.

- Despite increases in food production, the earth seems to be approaching the limits of global food production capacity based on present technologies. At the same time, environmental damage caused by agricultural practices is continuing, and in many parts of the planet it's intensifying. Worldwide, enormous areas of forests and grasslands have been converted to cropland. Every year, water and wind erode an estimated 2500 million metric tons of topsoil from the world's croplands. All told, about 85 percent of the world's agricultural lands contain areas now degraded to some degree by erosion, salinization, compaction, nutrient depletion, biological degradation, or pollution. The extent of cropland degradation raises questions about the long-term capacity of agro-ecosystems to produce food. At the same time, some of the world's best farmland is being withdrawn from food production and put to other uses, including urbanization. One of the most urgent problems facing the world today is the damage to and loss of arable land, which has a direct impact on global food production.

- Oceans represent one of the greatest sources of food on the earth as well. Global fish production exceeds that of cattle, sheep, poultry, or eggs. It represents the largest source of wild or domestic protein in the world. Marine fish catches rose from 51 million metric tons in 1975 to nearly 70 million metric tons in 1999. In 1995, studies reported that 52 percent of the oceans' wild-fish stocks were being exploited at the maximum sustainable limit, 16 percent were already overexploited, and 7 percent were depleted. Only 23 percent will be able to sustain further expansion. Coral reefs are particularly vulnerable to environmental change and damage from human activities. Nearly two-thirds of all the world's coral reefs are deteriorating.

- It is estimated that about 8000 years ago, forests occupied 50 percent of the earth's land surface. Today, less than 28 percent of that total remains. This reduction in forest cover continues: from 1990 to

2000, the global net rate of deforestation was approximately 36,294 square miles per year. In addition, deforestation is responsible for approximately 30 percent of the world's annual carbon emissions into the atmosphere.

- Most of the world's meat comes from animals that forage on grasslands. Worldwide, the quality of surviving grasslands is declining. It is estimated that 73 percent of the world's grazing land has so deteriorated that it has lost at least 25 percent of its animal-carrying capacity.

What is especially significant is that these conditions have occurred and are getting worse despite the rise in environmental regulations over the past 40 years. Clearly, adherence to environmental laws and regulations is not enough. The United States, with only 5 percent of the world's population and the toughest environmental regulations, contributes between 20 percent and 25 percent of the earth's greenhouse gases. Add to this the estimated increase in the world's population from the current 6 billion to an estimated 10.5 billion by 2100 and you can understand the need to move more quickly toward sustainable development.

If one looks at environmental progress in the United States, it is apparent that this is the direction in which industry is heading. Figure 1.1 shows that in the 1950s and 1960s, the focus was on increasing the nation's industrial

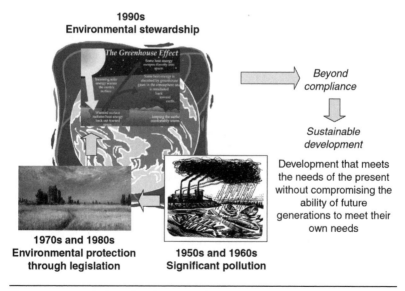

Figure 1.1 Evolution of environmental management in the United States.

capacity. Little thought was given to the environmental impacts of industry. In the late 1960s and 1970s, however, several significant events occurred that brought to the forefront the need to balance industrial activities with protection of the environment. These events include:

- Love Canal, New York, where the legal (at that time) burial of toxic wastes was shown to contribute to significant increases in the adverse and serious health effects of the community built over the toxic waste dump (hazardous waste disposal).

- The Cuyahoga River in Ohio caught fire and burned for several days as a result of the heavy concentration of industrial pollutants released into the river (water pollution).

- The accidental release of cyanide gas in Bhopal, India, which killed thousands and left a community devastated (air pollution and chemical hazards).

- The release of the book *Silent Spring,* by Rachel Carson, which presents the results of the studies on the bioaccumulation of chemicals and toxins (especially DDT, the "wonder" pesticide of the 1960s) throughout the ecosystem and their potential effects on humans.

The result of these and other events was the formation of the U.S. Environmental Protection Agency (EPA) and the issuance of most of the current environmental regulations, including the Clean Air Act, the Clean Water Act, and the Resource and Conservation Recovery Act. The impact of these and many other regulations was significant. The pollution of lakes, rivers, and streams was significantly reduced, the air is cleaner, and the contamination of soils and groundwater from hazardous wastes is much reduced.

What has become clear, however, is that compliance to these regulations is not enough. New and serious environmental issues have surfaced and are in many cases accelerating despite the improvements that have been driven by environmental regulations. One of the most prominent issues is the increase in greenhouse gas emissions and the subsequent concerns for global warming. Other concerns include ozone depletion in the earth's upper atmosphere (which has been stabilized due to the global ban on chlorofluorocarbons, or CFCs), acid rain, desertification, and the other concerns cited earlier in this chapter. Even with the passage of environmental laws, these issues have continued, and in many cases grown, driving industry toward environmental stewardship and the adoption of the principles of sustainable development. ISO 14001 was created to provide a model that organizations can use to move beyond compliance.

Economic Benefits of Good Environmental Stewardship

Clearly the focus on moving beyond regulatory compliance embedded in ISO 14001 provides sufficient justification for its adoption and implementation. ISO 14001 can provide significant economic benefits as well:

- *Corporate reputation and image.* Customer goodwill can be permanently damaged by a single incident. A properly designed EMS should lower the risk of environmental accidents. If you don't believe that, take a minute to think about Exxon. What's the first image that pops into your head? If you're like most people, you create an image of oil-soaked seagulls off the Alaskan coast. The monetary cost of such an incident goes far beyond the cost of the cleanup.

- *Lower environmentally related costs and fees.* A properly implemented EMS should significantly lower the costs associated with licenses, disposal fees, and permits and the administrative costs associated with manifesting and reporting once the organization starts focusing on source reduction versus treatment and disposal.

- *Increased access to new customers.* Many large companies now require their suppliers to be ISO 14001 certified. For example, the Ford Motor Company, DaimlerChrysler, and General Motors all require certification for their direct suppliers. Obtaining certification can open new markets for the organization.

- *Direct savings through environmental source reduction.* The real economic benefits arise from environmental improvement projects undertaken as part of the organization's commitment to continual improvement and pollution prevention. Consider the following two case studies drawn from the automotive industry.

CASE STUDY

DAIMLERCHRYSLER STERLING HEIGHTS ASSEMBLY PLANT

Description of the Opportunity Being Addressed

Cleaning chemicals used in an electro-deposition paint system showed minimal cleaning efficiency and required frequent material dumps to drain. As a result, a team was formed to examine alternative cleaning methods.

Description of the Improvement

Anolyte, a mild acid by-product and waste stream in the process, was found to produce better results than the previously used cleaning chemicals. The anolyte waste stream was diverted to the skid washer and is now used to clean the skids, prior to going to drain.

Results

The new method eliminated 7.3 tons of volatile organic compounds per year by utilizing an existing waste stream as a direct replacement for a cleaner that was a hazardous chemical, eliminated the handling and disposal of more than 22,000 gallons of hazardous material to waste treatment, and eliminated the handling and disposal of more than 400 55-gallon drums per year.

Savings (Operational)

> $300,000/year

C A S E   S T U D Y

FORD MOTOR COMPANY WOODHAVEN STAMPING PLANT

Description of the Opportunity Being Addressed

Twenty-five percent of electrical energy consumption was being used to produce compressed air.

Description of the Improvement

Assigned an air leak detection/correction team—saved 2500 standard cubic feet per minute (SCFM)

Replaced leaking seals on the stamping press die automation valves—saved 1000 SCFM

Lowered the air header pressure by 5 psig—saved 2,300,000 kWh

Replaced flow-measuring orifice plates with low-loss venturis

Results

Average flow reduced from 25,000 to 20,500 SCFM

One 800-hp reciprocating compressor taken completely off-line

Energy usage saved ~7,900,000 kWh

Equivalent reduction in nitrous oxide emissions ~60,000 lb

Equivalent reduction in sulfuric oxide emissions ~85,000 lb

Savings (Operational)

~$400,000/year

Clearly, as both of these examples show, improving your environmental performance can also improve the bottom line. The regulatory control system seeks to establish a balance between corporate profitability and environmental performance . . . ISO 14001 seeks to improve both at the same time.

MANAGEMENT SYSTEM EVOLUTION

Management systems, like other systems, must evolve. Initially when an organization puts in a management system, the focus is on implementation of and conformance with the new procedures and practices. Corrective action is taken when nonconformances are found. The focus is on getting a basic system in place. I call this the *compliance phase*.

The benefits realized at this initial level of maturity depend on how well the informal practices that existed prior to implementing the management system worked and how consistently they were followed. If a company had reasonably good management practices in the past, then just "saying what we do" in the form of procedures is unlikely to significantly improve its environmental or health and safety performance unless the procedures were not being consistently followed. These companies make up a large share of the organizations that complain that they have not benefited from implementing ISO 9001, ISO 14001, and/or OHSAS 18001. Organizations with good preexisting practices must rapidly move to the next level of maturity to benefit from their management system.

On the other hand, organizations without good preexisting systems or practices should realize significant improvements in environmental conformance during the compliance phase. The goal should be to move rapidly through the compliance phase toward the effectiveness phase. Unfortunately, many companies never leave the compliance phase, and after realizing the initial benefits, they complain that the management system no longer adds value. This phase is characterized by internal audits with numerous conformance deficiencies. For EMSs, this phase normally focuses on compliance with regulatory requirements.

As the management system matures and conformance becomes less of an issue, more attention is focused on the results. This is termed the *effectiveness phase*. In this phase both process owners and internal auditors focus more attention on the results produced by the system and by the internal processes that make up the system. In any large system with multiple interdependent processes, it is inherent that some processes or improvement objectives will not produce the results they should. The key to improving the overall performance of the system is to improve the results of each of the interdependent processes that feed into the system. In this phase the management team and process owners will develop more robust systems of metrics to measure how well these internal processes are performing. Areas where results are not obtained are targeted for improvement. Internal auditors will spend more time looking at process effectiveness and less at conformance. Internal audits will uncover more findings relating to effectiveness and opportunities for improvement. Nonconformances are primarily associated with processes that are not performing adequately. Organizations in this phase will see improvements in their environmental performance, productivity, and bottom-line profitability.

The final level of maturity is the *continual improvement phase*. In this phase there is a complete system of metrics on all important processes, and these processes have been optimized to produce results. Although effectiveness and conformance continue to be monitored, more attention is placed on source reduction and deriving additional value out of existing processes. This is the level at which innovation, creativity, and the implementation of best practices become widespread throughout the organization. At this phase all the primary benefits will be realized, with significant improvements in profitability. This evolutionary model of management system development is illustrated graphically in Figure 1.2.

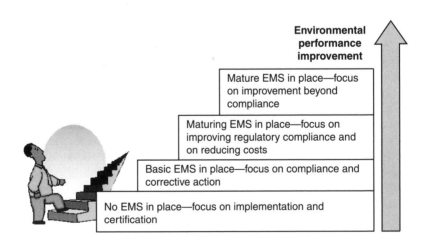

Figure 1.2   Management system evolution.

The bottom line is that the management system is what you make it. If you are not realizing the expected benefits from your management system, ask yourself what level of maturity you are currently at, and then take the steps needed to proceed to the next level. The ISO 14001 standard is a nonprescriptive minimal standard. It does not tell you exactly what to do or how to do it. It is minimal in that it provides the minimum requirements for environmental management; it is up to you to go beyond the minimum in areas of importance to your company and the environment.

2

EMSs and the
ISO 14001:2004 Standard

ISO 14001 BASICS

The ISO 14001 EMS standard is a model of environmental stewardship that combines regulatory compliance with sustainable development initiatives. The standard was developed to help address the rash of environmental issues that generated global concerns in the 1980s, such as greenhouse gas emissions (global warming), ozone depletion in the upper atmosphere, the loss of biodiversity, deforestation, and depletion of the earth's natural resources. The standard embraces the concept of sustainable development, which is development that meets the needs of the present without compromising the ability of future generations to meet their own needs. To achieve this, the standard requires that an organization commit to environmental performance that goes beyond compliance, or beyond the minimum required to satisfy regulatory and legal requirements.

The ISO 14001 standard is developed around W. Edwards Deming's famous Plan-Do-Check-Act model of improvement. Its planning elements consist of the development of an environmental policy that must include the organization's commitments to the environment. Of note, a commitment to comply with regulatory and legal requirements is mandatory, as are commitments to continual improvement and the prevention of pollution. As part of planning its EMS, the organization must also identify those products, services, and activities that could have an impact on the environment. These are called *environmental aspects*. The organization then evaluates these aspects to determine those that could or do impact the environment in a significant way. It then identifies controls and methods to minimize the harmful impacts or to expand on those that benefit it. This typically includes substitution of environmentally friendly materials for hazardous materials, resource conservation, reuse, recycling, and process modifications. Planned improvements, in the form of environmental objectives and targets, must also be established along with methods on how to achieve them.

The "doing" component is titled implementation and operation, and in this phase the organization implements the controls and methods identified in the planning phase. In addition, the standard requires that operators be trained in performing environmental duties and be made aware of their impact on the environment, that the roles and responsibilities be defined and communicated, that the documents used to support the EMS be controlled, and that emergency plans be developed, maintained, and tested.

The checking and corrective action elements represent the "check" component of the PDCA cycle. Here the organization monitors how well its environmental controls are working, along with how well its management system is performing. Records of actions and performance must be maintained and controlled. Compliance to regulatory and legal environmental requirements must also be reviewed. If deficiencies or nonconformances are identified, corrective action is initiated to restore the performance of the system.

The "act" component of the PDCA cycle is represented by the management review requirements, which need senior level review of the overall performance of the EMS and its related components. The output of this review should lead to actions and decisions to correct or improve performance.

It has been shown that a mature ISO 14001 EMS leads not only to improved environmental performance but also to improved profitability. Significant cost reductions in the handling and disposal of hazardous materials and solvents, reductions in energy costs, and increased revenues from recycling and the sale of by-products are commonly cited by companies that have learned that it pays to go beyond compliance.

The ISO 14001:2004 EMS model is shown in Figure 2.1. The standard was recently revised and includes some major changes. The requirements for objectives, targets, and management programs in clauses 4.3.3 and 4.3.4 were combined, and the requirements for environmental performance monitoring in clause 4.5.1 were separated into two clauses: 4.5.1, monitoring and measurement, and 4.5.2, evaluation of compliance. The core requirements and intent of the standard have essentially remained intact.

In this chapter we examine each of the major clauses in the ISO 14001:2004 standard, including the specific requirements and their intent. It will be helpful to have a copy of the standard handy as we walk through the requirements.

INTRODUCTORY INFORMATION

The introductory material in the front of the ISO 14001 standard contains some important information that will help you structure your EMS. It notes

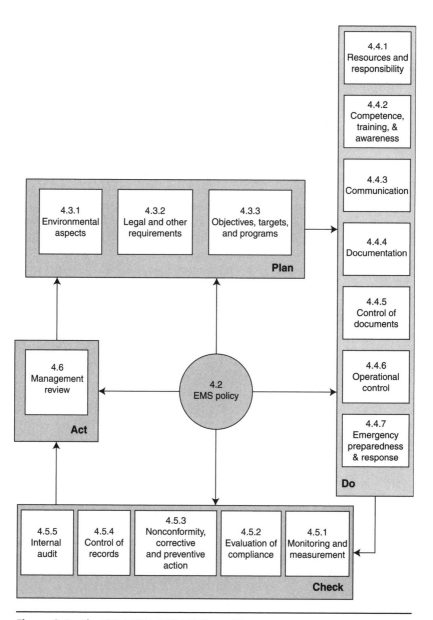

Figure 2.1 The ISO 14001:2004 EMS model.

that adoption of the standard by itself will not guarantee optimal environmental performance. As discussed in Chapter 1, ISO 14001, like other standards, sets minimal requirements for environmental management. It is up to the organization to go beyond the minimum in areas of high environmental importance.

The introductory material also states that ISO 14001 does not include specific requirements for occupational health and safety (OH&S). This is important because humans are included in the standard's definition of the environment. While the standard does not require the coverage of health and safety issues, I strongly recommend that the organization seriously consider doing so because health and safety management encounters similar risks, and a comprehensive OH&S management program can provide significant benefits, as discussed in Chapter 1. Also, the standards are closely aligned, which makes managing a combined program easier and more efficient than managing two completely separate programs.

Finally, the standard points out that the detail and complexity of the EMS and the amount of documentation required to implement it depend on the organization and the nature of its operations. In other words, the standard gives you the flexibility to build a system that meets your needs. You can make it very simple and straightforward, or you can make it incredibly detailed. My preference, and the premise embedded in Part II, is that it is normally best to start simple and add detail only where needed.

SCOPE

Section 1 of the standard presents the scope, which defines the intended coverage of the standard. Of particular interest is subitem c, which indicates how the standard can be used for demonstrating an organization's compliance. It states that organizations can use the standard for certification, for second-party verification of an organization's compliance, or for self-declaration of compliance. This last option, self-declaration, allows an organization to implement and verify its conformance to ISO 14001 and self-declare its conformity, thereby avoiding the costs of certification. While this option may be attractive to some companies, keep in mind that self-declarations normally will not satisfy those customers who require suppliers to be ISO 14001 certified. Certification brings with it a certain amount of rigor to the process and can provide the driver for further improvement. Unless the organization has a lot of discipline and the full and sustained commitment of all employees and its senior management team, I would not recommend this option.

NORMATIVE REFERENCES

Normative references relate to other documents that must be used in support of the standard. For ISO 14001 there are none. The ISO 14004 standard is the companion document to ISO 14001, but it is not required for certification.

TERMS AND DEFINITIONS

Section 3 of the standard contains terms and definitions used throughout the standard. The most important of these are as follows:

- *Document*—The standard provides a very liberal definition of a document (see Note 1 in the standard). It states that a document can be in the form of a hard-copy paper document, an electronic document, or even a photograph or sample. This definition is important because in Part II we see how an electronic spreadsheet can be used to replace traditional hard-copy documentation. It is worth mentioning at this time, however, that the requirements for mandatory documents in ISO 14001 are very minimal.

- *Environment*—The standard defines the environment as the surrounding air, water, land, natural resources, plant life (flora), animal life (fauna), humans, and the interaction between these categories. Just about everything is considered to be part of the environment except for perhaps the organization's buildings and equipment. Even with these, natural resources come into play. Note that humans are defined as part of the environment, which, although obvious, does open the door to including health and safety within the scope of the EMS. Indeed, in a few areas it is almost impossible to separate the two.

- *Environmental aspect*—The standard defines an environmental aspect as an element of the organization's products (what it makes), services (transactional companies), or activities (the core and support processes the organization uses to make its products or deliver its services) that could interact with the environment. I generally like to narrow this definition down to products and activities because services are basically a form of activity. To simplify the definition we can state that an environmental aspect is an element of those things we make or things we do that could interact with the environment. Needless to say, organizations have hundreds or thousands of environmental aspects within the scope of their operations because almost everything we make or do could interact with the environment in some way.

- *Environmental impact*—An environmental impact is defined as an actual change to the environment as a result of those things we make or things we do (that is, environmental aspects). Note that the standard clarifies that environmental impacts can be beneficial or harmful. While most organizations focus on the harmful impacts, going beyond compliance also means looking for ways in which the organization can benefit the existing environment. An example might be the restoration of a wetlands area on part of the company's property.

- *Environmental management system*—The standard simplifies the definition of an EMS to that part of the management system used to implement the environmental policy and manage its environmental aspects. It's that simple. The value of this definition is that it clearly focuses on the overall intent of the EMS and what's important. Note that the environmental policy statement and the identification and control of environmental aspects are at the heart of the EMS, a concept that is expanded on later in this chapter and in Part II.

- *Environmental objective*—An environmental objective is an overall environmental goal the company sets for itself. The standard clearly indicates that the goal should be consistent with the environmental policy. Objectives are clearly linked to the commitments that form the heart of the policy. Note that the objective is an overall or broad goal. The targets (defined next) focus on specific performance requirements associated with this overall goal.

- *Environmental target*—The standard defines an environmental target as a detailed performance requirement that must be met in order to achieve its environmental objectives. Later we will see how the objectives are related to the policy commitments, while the targets are related to the organization's significant environmental aspects.

- *Nonconformity*—Failure to meet a requirement. The requirement may be a regulatory requirement (hope not), an ISO 14001 requirement, or a local requirement specified by the organization.

- *Corrective action*—Action to address the cause of a nonconformity (failure to meet a requirement).

- *Preventive action*—Action to address the cause of a potential nonconformity. Both preventive and corrective action deal with nonconformities or failures to meet requirements. Continual improvement, on the other hand, deals with performance that currently meets requirements but that could be improved. Taking action to address a violation of regulatory requirements is not improvement, it's corrective action. Taking action to address a likely regulatory violation is not improvement, it's preventive action.

- *Procedure*—The standard defines a procedure as a specified way to carry out an activity. Of greater interest is Note 1 to this definition, which states that procedures may or may not be documented. Unless the standard requires a documented procedure, the need to develop written guidance is left up to you.

- *Prevention of pollution*—The ISO 14001 definition includes processes, practices, materials, techniques, or anything else used or done to avoid, reduce, or control the creation, emission, or discharge of any type of pollutant or waste. This definition is important in that it includes treatment as a form of pollution prevention. I point this out because the EPA's definition of pollution prevention does not include treatment as a form of prevention (that is, it focuses on source reduction). ISO 14001's inclusion of treatment in the definition gives the organization more choices for how it meets its commitment to the prevention of pollution.

Now that we've examined the definitions, it's time to turn our attention to the requirements (see Figure 2.1).

CLAUSE 4.1 GENERAL REQUIREMENTS

Clause 4.1 says that the organization must develop a systematic EMS that meets the requirements of the ISO 14001 standard. It also states that the company must define and document the scope of its EMS. By "scope," we mean what is included and what is not included. An organization may choose to cover only certain operations, facilities, products, or services within the scope of its EMS. I do not generally exclude products or operations strictly because they have serious environmental liabilities associated with them, as this negates the purpose of the standard. What is more common is to exclude certain operations performed at remote sites. Sometimes an organization will include only certain products and their supporting processes due to a customer requirement to certify to ISO 14001. With few exceptions, however, the wisest course is to include the entire organization and all products, services, and/or activities in the scope of the EMS. The scope of the EMS is normally documented in the organization's environmental policy manual.

CLAUSE 4.2 ENVIRONMENTAL POLICY

Clause 4.2 requires that the organization develop an environmental policy. The importance of the policy statement cannot be overemphasized. Everything done within the EMS should be consistent with and aligned with the policy statement. The standard requires that the policy statement:

- Be defined by top management

- Be consistent with the nature of the organization's scale and scope of operations (activities, products, and services)

- Be documented, implemented, and maintained

- Be communicated throughout the organization (including temporary or agency employees or other individuals working on behalf of the organization)

- Be made available to the public

In addition to these basic requirements, the implementation of which is discussed in Part II, the standard also includes certain content requirements for the policy statement. In particular, ISO 14001 requires that the policy statement:

- Include commitments to comply with legal and other requirements related to its environmental aspects, to the prevention of pollution, and to continual improvement

- Provide a framework for setting and reviewing environmental objectives and targets

"Other requirements" refers to voluntary requirements the company has adopted, either through its own commitment to environmental performance improvement or through implementation of customer requirements. Examples of the former include the International Chamber of Commerce's Business Charter for Sustainable Development, which includes a set of principles for businesses to follow in order to demonstrate good environmental stewardship. It could also include industry standards like the Responsible Care program, used within the chemical industry, or it may be as simple as a commitment to follow the guidelines set forth in the EPA's Green Lights or Energy Star programs. Examples of the latter include customer requirements specifying prohibited or restricted materials or the marking of polymeric parts (plastics) with the appropriate ISO symbol to aid recycling and reuse.

Many companies include only the three mandatory commitments required by the standard in their policy statements. While this is acceptable, it does not provide a solid framework for setting environmental objectives and targets that are focused and meaningful to the organization. These mandatory commitments are simply too broad to serve as the basis for setting objectives and targets. This issue is further discussed in Part II.

CLAUSE 4.3.1 ENVIRONMENTAL ASPECTS

If the policy statement forms the heart of the EMS, then the determination of the organization's significant environmental aspects is the mind. The standard requires that the organization maintain a process (not necessarily documented) to:

- Identify its environmental aspects (those things that we do or make that could interact with the environment)

- Determine which aspects have or could have a significant impact (those that could change the environment in a significant way)

The standard requires that the organization focus on those aspects it can influence or control, including those associated with new or modified products, services, activities, or other developments. Before going further, let's make sure we understand what we mean by environmental aspects and impacts.

Assume your organization manufactures computer systems. A general picture of some of your product's environmental aspects might be as shown in Figure 2.2.

In essence, you can see that the majority of a product's environmental aspects are associated with its materials, wastes, and use considerations. Manufacturing considerations are also important, but they are normally addressed as part of the review of an organization's activities (that is, manufacturing processes). They are included here, however, because a product's design does influence, or limit, the manufacturing options available to production. We can simplify this even further by stating that the major environmental aspects associated with a product involve the material choices that are made (which will in turn dictate the waste streams generated during disposal); how those materials are designed for assembly, or disassembly upon end of life; and the design features related to use considerations such as energy consumption, radiation, noise emissions, and/or ergonomics.

All these aspects evidence themselves as design choices made when the products are developed or modified. Influencing these design decisions requires the organization to control its design process to include considerations such as the hazardous or nonhazardous nature of the materials going into the product; the ability and ease with which the product can

Product

Computer and monitor

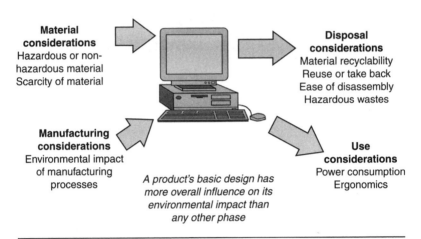

**Material
considerations**
Hazardous or non-
hazardous material
Scarcity of material

**Disposal
considerations**
Material recyclability
Reuse or take back
Ease of disassembly
Hazardous wastes

**Manufacturing
considerations**
Environmental impact
of manufacturing
processes

*A product's basic design has
more overall influence on its
environmental impact than
any other phase*

**Use
considerations**
Power consumption
Ergonomics

Figure 2.2   Computer system environmental aspects.

be disassembled, recycled, or reused; and the impact on the environment resulting from the product's use (for example, power consumption). This is generally termed "design for the environment," or DfE. In general, the product's basic design has more overall influence on its environmental impact than does any other phase such as manufacturing, storage, and sale because the basic design limits or determines to a large extent the impacts that will be generated during all these other phases. It is somewhat sad but true that many organizations that implement an EMS devote almost all their attention to the environmental aspects of their manufacturing process and almost none to their product design and development processes.

Let's now look at the environmental aspects associated with an organization's activities (or processes). A typical process—in this case, printing—is shown in Figure 2.3.

Like a product, the majority of a process's environmental aspects are associated with its materials and waste streams. An easy way to look at this is to identify the inputs into a process (materials, solvents, energy, water, inks, pigments, and so on) and the outputs from a process (waste products, emissions, and scrap materials). When viewed as inputs and outputs, the environmental aspects of the activity are usually fairly easy to identify. Keep in mind that activities include not only manufacturing operations but also clerical activities. These activities use ink, toner, paper, and energy for computers

Activity

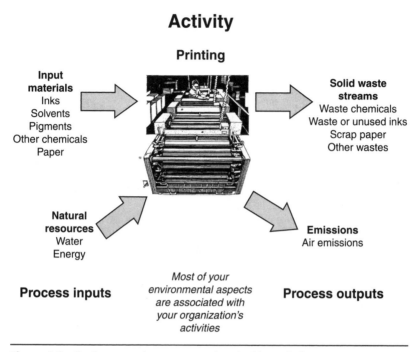

Printing

Input materials
Inks
Solvents
Pigments
Other chemicals
Paper

Solid waste streams
Waste chemicals
Waste or unused inks
Scrap paper
Other wastes

Natural resources
Water
Energy

Emissions
Air emissions

Process inputs

Most of your environmental aspects are associated with your organization's activities

Process outputs

Figure 2.3   Environmental aspects associated with a printing process.

and other consumables and produce waste paper, used toner cartridges, and other outputs that can be recycled, reused, or must be disposed of.

As a final example we will look at a service—in this case, a janitorial service (see Figure 2.4).

As in the case of the printing activity, using the inputs and the outputs from the process is normally the easiest way to identify the environmental aspects of a service. We will now look at the environmental impacts of these aspects.

Figure 2.5 shows some of the potential environmental impacts associated with our product example. Environmental impacts normally fall into about a dozen broad categories. Examples include air pollution, water pollution, groundwater or soil contamination, loss of habitat, natural resource depletion, and landfill usage. Many more specific impacts could be identified within each broad category, but that is not normally required. What is most important is that employees appreciate at least the general impact their activities have or could have on the environment.

Another way of looking at aspects and impacts is through cause and effect. In this sense the environmental aspect is the cause, and the

Service

Janitorial

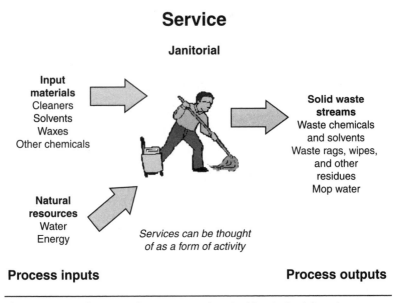

Input materials
Cleaners
Solvents
Waxes
Other chemicals

Solid waste streams
Waste chemicals and solvents
Waste rags, wipes, and other residues
Mop water

Natural resources
Water
Energy

Services can be thought of as a form of activity

Process inputs   **Process outputs**

Figure 2.4   Environmental aspects associated with a janitorial service.

Product

Computer and Monitor

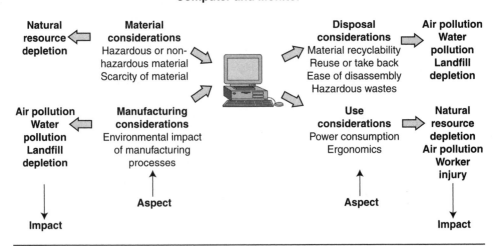

Natural resource depletion

Material considerations
Hazardous or non-hazardous material
Scarcity of material

Disposal considerations
Material recyclability
Reuse or take back
Ease of disassembly
Hazardous wastes

Air pollution
Water pollution
Landfill depletion

Air pollution
Water pollution
Landfill depletion

Manufacturing considerations
Environmental impact of manufacturing processes

Use considerations
Power consumption
Ergonomics

Natural resource depletion
Air pollution
Worker injury

Aspect   **Aspect**

Impact   **Impact**

Figure 2.5   Potential environmental impacts associated with a computer system (product).

environmental impact is the effect. The long-term value of identifying environmental aspects and impacts becomes apparent when one asks the question, What are some things that the designers could do to improve the environmental performance of this product, given the environmental aspects and their related impacts shown earlier? Hopefully it is obvious that the overall impacts could be lessened through a careful selection of nonhazardous materials where possible; through the planned design to allow disassembly, recycling, and reuse; through the incorporation of efficient power components and the power management routines; and through the use of other DfE methodologies.

If we look at the potential environmental impacts associated with our printing operation, we see a list of impacts that looks very similar to those for the computer system. These are shown in Figure 2.6.

In this instance, as in the computer example, the long-term value of identifying environmental aspects and impacts becomes apparent when one asks the question, What are some things that the process engineers could do to improve the environmental performance of this activity, given the environmental aspects and their related impacts shown earlier? A search for nonhazardous inks, solvents, and/or pigments may be conducted; a water filtration and reuse system could be installed; and energy efficiency

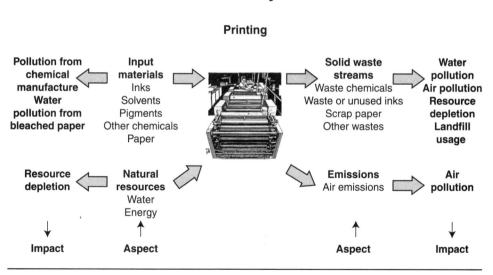

Figure 2.6 Potential environmental impacts associated with a printing operation (activity).

improvements could be made. Improved treatment of the wastes and emissions could also be considered, although this is clearly a second-best solution when compared with source reduction actions on the inputs. Finally, quality process improvement actions that reduce the amount of first-off scrap could be initiated to reduce the amount of scrap paper.

Fortunately, the standard requires only that we identify those aspects that could have a *significant* impact on the environment. As previously noted, every organization has literally hundreds if not thousands of environmental aspects, but we need consider only those that have changed or could change the environment in a significant way. It also allows us to disregard those that we cannot control or influence, keeping in mind that these two conditions are not equivalent. There may be many environmental aspects that we cannot control but that we can influence in some manner. Finally, only those aspects associated with the scope of our EMS need be considered. A straightforward, simple strategy for identifying our significant aspects is presented in Part II.

We are now ready to complete our review of this important clause. The standard says that the organization must keep the information regarding our significant environmental aspects up to date. Facility modifications, process changes, material substitutions, and product engineering changes occur on a frequent basis. A process must be in place to determine which, if any, of these changes affect an organization's significant aspects, and if so, by how much. We discuss how to do this in Part II. Finally the standard requires that you consider your significant environmental aspects during EMS design, maintenance, and improvement.

CLAUSE 4.3.2 LEGAL AND OTHER REQUIREMENTS

ISO 14001 requires that the organization maintain a process to:

- Identify the legal and other requirements that apply to the organization

- Access these requirements

- Define how these requirements apply to the organization's environmental aspects

Essentially, the requirements are directed at answering the following questions: What requirements apply to us, where do I find them and what do they say, and how do they apply to us? Once you've determined what requirements apply to you, the standard instructs you to consider these requirements during EMS design, maintenance, and improvement.

Although the requirements themselves look fairly straightforward, identifying the exact federal, state, and/or local regulatory environmental requirements that you must meet can be very difficult if your organization does not have environmental specialists on staff. Many small-to-medium-sized organizations simply limp along from year to year, complying with the regulations they are aware of and ignoring those they are not. Be careful, however, because ignorance is no excuse in the world of environmental compliance. Owners and operators can be cited and heavily fined for violations of regulations they were not even aware existed. Establishing once and for all exactly what applies to you and what does not is the first step toward fulfilling the mandatory environmental policy commitment for compliance to legal and other requirements.

CLAUSE 4.3.3 OBJECTIVES, TARGETS, AND PROGRAMS

Clause 4.3.3 was consolidated from two separate clauses in the 1996 version of ISO 14001. The essential requirements remain the same. The organization must set *documented* environmental objectives and targets at relevant levels and functions of the organization. The clause also says that these objectives *and* targets should be measurable wherever practicable.

There are essentially two ways to look at objectives and targets. The first is to define the objective in global terms (for example, "reduce air emissions") and the target in terms of amount (for example, "by 20 percent"). Many organizations develop their objectives and targets this way. In the second way, and the way that I prefer, the target is the actions that must be accomplished in order to support the overall objective. For example, the objectives and targets to improve energy conservation might be as follows:

Environmental Objective: Reduce energy usage by 25 percent over 2003 levels by the end of 2005. (The objective is measurable and has a timeframe associated with it.)

To accomplish this objective, the organization may target the following activities:

Target 1: Relamp the production area with high-efficiency lighting by June 2004 (this target is also measurable and has a timeframe)

Target 2: Install motion sensors in all conference rooms by March 2004

Target 3: Conduct an energy survey of the facilities in the first quarter of 2004

Target 4: Evaluate, select, and install an energy management system for the main building by June 2004

Target 5: Evaluate the use of variable speed motors for the oil transfer system during the first quarter of 2004

Target 6: Provide refresher training on the energy conservation guidelines to all personnel in January 2004

I prefer this method of defining objectives and targets because it provides more specific measurable goals that must be met by the various functions and levels of the organization. Each target would then have its own set of required actions. Taken together, achieving the targets should allow the organization to meet or even exceed its overall objective of a 25 percent reduction in energy usage. When defined as suggested here, the objective is derived from the policy commitments, and the targets focus on the activities related to the significant aspects that must be improved to meet the objective. This alignment of policy, objectives, targets, and aspects looks something like Figure 2.7.

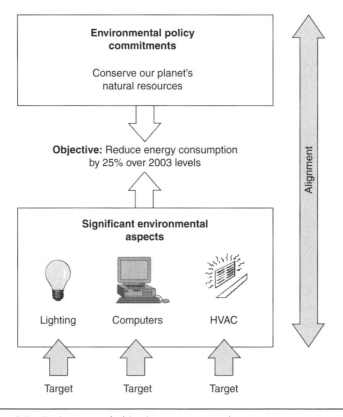

Figure 2.7   Environmental objectives, targets, and aspects.

The key is to keep the environmental objectives, targets, policy commitments, and environmental aspects aligned and supportive of each other. The standard requires that the organization consider its policy commitments, its legal and other requirements, and its significant environmental aspects when it sets its objectives and targets. Essentially, the standard is saying to align your objectives with what's important (your policy commitments and significant environmental aspects).

When setting these objectives and targets, the standard also requires the organization to consider:

- Financial, business, and operational requirements

- The views of interested parties

Interested parties include employees and shareholders, the local community, regulatory agencies, or anyone else who has a stake in the organization's environmental performance. Part II examines techniques to ensure these parties are considered during the setting of objectives and targets.

Once the organization decides on its objectives and the targets needed to accomplish them, it must develop management programs to ensure their achievement. Management programs are nothing more than action plans. The standard says that the programs must define who is responsible for achieving the objectives and targets, the means (and resources) needed, and the time frame by which they will be achieved. In essence, an action plan.

CLAUSE 4.4.1 RESOURCES, ROLES, RESPONSIBILITY, AND AUTHORITY

Everyone must understand his or her roles and responsibilities for operation of the EMS. The standard requires that roles, responsibilities, and authorities be defined, documented, and communicated.

In addition, it requires that a management representative be appointed by top management. The management representative's responsibilities include ensuring that the EMS is established, implemented, and maintained. In addition, the management representative must also report to top management with recommendations for improvement.

Finally, this clause also addresses resources. Resources needed to implement and maintain your EMS must be identified and provided. Management demonstrates its commitment to the EMS by providing the necessary resources, which include:

- Human resources

- Infrastructure

- Technological resources

- Financial resources

CLAUSE 4.4.2 COMPETENCE, TRAINING, AND AWARENESS

ISO 14001 requires that all personnel working on behalf of the organization who could significantly impact the environment must be competent. You must identify the training needed to properly perform tasks that could impact your environmental performance, along with the other skill sets needed to competently perform the activity. You must then provide the necessary training and maintain records. Competency can be determined by appropriate education, experience, and/or training.

The standard also requires that environmental *awareness* training be provided to all those working for or on the behalf of the organization. Organizations have traditionally been very good at telling employees *what* to do and *how* to do it. This requirement instructs that we inform employees *why* they need to comply. People are much more inclined to support the EMS if they understand the environmental consequences of not complying. Awareness training must include:

- The importance of complying with policies, procedures, and the requirements of the EMS

- The significant environmental aspects and potential impacts of employees' activities and the environmental benefits of improved personal performance

- Employees' individual roles and responsibilities

- The potential consequences of failing to follow specified operating procedures

CLAUSE 4.4.3 COMMUNICATION

You must develop procedures to communicate information relating to your EMS, including your environmental aspects. This system must include both internal communications and external communications with interested parties. External communications include government agencies, shareholders, suppliers, customers, contractors, and the local community. For external parties the standard requires that you document and respond to the communication.

Clause 4.4.3 also requires that the organization decide whether it will communicate information about its significant environmental aspects to the outside world and document its decision. While the environmental policy statement does have to be made public (reference clause 4.1), the standard does not require you to share information about your significant aspects beyond your four walls. The advantages of doing so include better public relations and a higher level of trust with the community. Most importantly it will put more accountability on the senior management team to follow through on its commitments to improve its environmental performance. A higher and much more public level of accountability should result in more dedication to provide the resources and effort needed to develop an effective EMS. The main disadvantage is the same: it puts more accountability on senior management to perform. If the organization does not see itself investing in its EMS to drive improvement in areas relating to its significant environmental aspects, it may be best not to make its aspects public. In addition, it can also open up the organization to criticism or community concerns it might otherwise have avoided had its significant environmental aspects remained below the local radar screen. In the United States most organizations elect not to share this information.

CLAUSE 4.4.4 DOCUMENTATION

Clause 4.4.4 simply summarizes what has to be documented and what does not. It requires documentation of:

- The environmental policy

- Environmental objectives and targets

- The scope of the EMS

- An overall description of the main elements of the EMS, how these elements interact, and references to any documents that describe these activities in more detail (this is normally accomplished in an environmental policy manual)

- Any documents *required* by the standard

- Any other documents and records the organization determines are necessary for the operation or control of processes relating to its significant environmental aspects

The only documents absolutely required by the standard are those listed in the first four bullets (records are expanded on later). While almost every clause requires the development of a procedure, as was noted earlier, Note 1 in the definition of a procedure states that procedures do not have to be documented. While I certainly recommend documenting procedures, the decision rests with the organization (which is essentially what the last bullet says). Later on you will see that clause 4.4.6 essentially repeats this requirement when discussing the need for documented procedures relating to operational control.

The organization must therefore carefully weigh the advantages of documentation versus the disadvantages. On the plus side, documentation helps ensure consistency, provides a repository for operating criteria and other hard-to-remember information, and is a valuable aid when training new team members. Just as important, and often overlooked in written procedures, is that documentation also provides a place to describe nonroutine activities and explains how to respond to unusual situations. Finally, documented procedures form the basis for continual process improvement in that they describe and communicate the baseline set of actions that serve as the best current way of performing an activity. This allows others to study, challenge, improve, and subsequently communicate more efficient and more effective ways of performing the task. This improvement, or modification of processes, can be accomplished in a controlled manner through the document control process (discussed next), which prevents the infusion of ill-advised and possibly disastrous "improvements."

The disadvantage of documentation is that you must develop, review, approve, issue, and control it. This requires some level of overhead effort. While some would argue that documentation also brings inflexibility with it, I would counter that this is the case only in situations where the documentation was not well written. In the final analysis, it is up to the organization to determine whether a documented procedure would add value. If so, develop a written procedure. If not, review and strengthen your training and other controls and move on. It is a judgment call the organization must make. Internal auditors will help evaluate whether the company made the right decision as part of its management system audits, as will be discussed in Chapter 7.

CLAUSE 4.4.5 CONTROL OF DOCUMENTS

The organization must control those documents it determined it needed, along with external documents and forms. Document control as required by ISO 14001 includes:

- Uniquely identifying the document to eliminate possible confusion.

- Reviewing and approving documents prior to issue and as needed to keep them updated.

- Identifying revision status so that the current version of the documents is known.

- Identifying any changes to documents so that users can quickly see what is different in how they should perform their tasks.

- Making documents available where they are needed by users.

- Ensuring that documents are and remain legible.

- Removing or otherwise ensuring that obsolete documents, including those kept for historical value, are identified as obsolete and otherwise safeguarded to prevent their unintentional use.

- Identifying and controlling the distribution of external documents used by the organization. This would include external consultant's reports, regulatory requirements, permits, environmental equipment, technical manuals, or any other outside document needed to operate the EMS.

CLAUSE 4.4.6 OPERATIONAL CONTROL

If the policy statement forms the heart of the EMS, and identification of significant environmental aspects the head, then the operational control clause is the body. Operational control consists of all those methods used to control your significant environmental aspects identified during the planning phase.

The standard requires that the organization identify, plan, and control those operations associated with its significant environmental aspects and consistent with its policy, objectives, and targets. Operational controls are established for activities (or processes) that relate to your significant aspects. Establishing realistic, effective controls is an essential step toward improving your environmental performance.

Control means carrying out these activities under specified conditions, which include:

- Establishing and maintaining *documented* procedures where their absence could lead to deviations from your environmental policy commitments or your ability to achieve your objectives and targets

- Stipulating *operating criteria* in these procedures where needed

- Identifying the significant environmental aspects of the goods and services used by the organization, and establishing, maintaining, and communicating relevant procedures and requirements to your suppliers and contractors

Although the emphasis is on developing documented procedures where needed, the organization will also use other controls to minimize any adverse environmental impact of its significant aspects. These may include maintenance practices, engineering controls, and training programs. The identification and deployment of appropriate operational controls is discussed in more detail in Part II. Note that controls on suppliers, contractors, and subcontractors must also be established and communicated to these external parties.

CLAUSE 4.4.7 EMERGENCY PREPAREDNESS AND RESPONSE

You must identify potential accident and emergency situations and develop appropriate procedures to prevent and/or mitigate any adverse impacts that may result. Because of the regulatory structure in the United States, most companies already have plans and procedures to address emergency situations they may face. You should review these procedures to ensure they include responses to any new potential situations that may have been identified as part of your initial environmental review.

Your emergency preparedness and response procedures must be periodically reviewed and revised where necessary, including after accidents or emergencies. They must also be periodically tested where practicable. This is where most companies have weaknesses.

CLAUSE 4.5.1 MONITORING AND MEASUREMENT

In clause 4.4.6 you established operational control of your significant operations and activities. In clause 4.5.1 you ensure that your controls work. Your organization must monitor and measure on a regular basis key characteristics of its operations that could significantly impact the environment.

Procedures for this monitoring must include:

- Documentation of the information needed to monitor performance

- Operational controls

- Methods to ensure monitoring of conformity with your environmental objectives and targets

The organization's monitoring and measurement equipment must be calibrated or verified and maintained. Monitoring equipment may include pH meters, gas spectrometers, and emissions-control equipment. Calibration and maintenance records must be retained.

CLAUSE 4.5.2 EVALUATION OF COMPLIANCE

The standard requires that environmental compliance reviews be periodically conducted to evaluate compliance to relevant environmental regulatory and other requirements. Compliance reviews are not management system audits. They specifically evaluate your environmental compliance to the regulatory requirements you identified in clause 4.3.2. Records of these reviews must be retained.

CLAUSE 4.5.3 NONCONFORMITY, CORRECTIVE AND PREVENTIVE ACTION

An EMS does not guarantee you won't have problems, but you must be able to react appropriately when they occur. ISO 14001 requires that the organization establish and maintain a process for dealing with actual and potential nonconformities and for taking corrective and/or preventive action. This process must provide for:

- Identification and correction of nonconformities

- Appropriate action to mitigate any adverse environmental impacts that result from the nonconformity

- The need to take preventive action to avoid the occurrence of potential nonconformities or the recurrence of actual nonconformities

- Recording the results of the actions taken

- Verification of the effectiveness of these actions

The standard also notes that the corrective and preventive action taken should be appropriate to the magnitude of the problem and the risk presented by the problems associated with the environmental impacts. The standard also requires that the organization update any documentation affected by the actions taken.

CLAUSE 4.5.4 CONTROL OF RECORDS

The organization is required to develop processes to maintain records, demonstrating that it is complying with the ISO 14001 standard and its local procedures and policies, and that it is achieving results. This process must address:

- The identification of records
- Records storage
- Protection of records
- Record retrieval
- Record retention and disposal

Records must remain legible, identifiable, and traceable.

CLAUSE 4.5.5 INTERNAL AUDIT

An internal environmental audit program must be established. Audits must be conducted at planned intervals to determine whether the EMS conforms to the ISO 14001 standard and other planned arrangements and whether the EMS has been properly implemented and is being maintained.

The environmental audit program must be based on the environmental importance of the operations concerned and past audit results. The process must also ensure that auditors and audits are objective and impartial. The audit process must also address:

- Responsibilities and requirements for planning and conducting audits, reporting results, and maintaining audit records
- The determination of audit criteria, scope, frequency, and methods

Finally, the results of audits must be reported to management.

CLAUSE 4.6 MANAGEMENT REVIEW

Top management must perform periodic reviews of the EMS to ensure the system's continuing:

- Suitability (does the system address the requirements of ISO 14001 and the organization's needs and policy commitments?)
- Adequacy (are the resources sufficient to maintain and improve the EMS?)
- Effectiveness (is the system getting results?)

In order to determine this, the standard requires that certain items be considered during the review. These mandatory inputs include:

- Internal audit results and the results of reviews of compliance to regulatory and other requirements

- External communications (including complaints)

- Environmental performance (monitoring and measurement results)

- Performance in achieving objectives and targets

- Status of corrective and preventive actions

- Follow-up from previous reviews

- Changes in regulatory and other requirements

- Recommendations for improvement

The output from the management review should be in the form of decisions and actions needed to address weaknesses in the EMS or to improve the system or its environmental performance. As a minimum, the following are required to be considered throughout the management review:

- Needed changes to the environmental policy

- Needed adjustments to environmental objectives and targets

- Any other changes to the EMS needed to meet the organization's commitment to continual improvement

The focus of the management review is on monitoring and action. If your management reviews do not result in actions, they are not effective. Note that the review must be documented and records retained.

SUMMARY

The purpose of reviewing the ISO 14001 EMS standard is to equip the reader with an understanding of the requirements that must be met before launching into system design and deployment. To summarize this section, we should note that the ISO 14001 standard is broken up into five major sections or clauses, which can be recombined into five operational components as follows:

- *A planning component.* In ISO 14001 planning is represented by the initial and ongoing identification of significant environmental aspects and legal requirements associated with the organization's products, services, and activities and the identification of appropriate methods to control them. Planning for unexpected events is captured by the emergency preparedness and control requirements.

Planning is centered around the establishment of an organizational policy that declares the company's commitments for environmental performance.

- *An operational component.* In ISO 14001, requirements focused on operation and maintenance of the system are specified in the requirements for operational control.

- *A monitoring and corrective action component.* In ISO 14001 these activities are defined in monitoring and measurement, evaluation of compliance, nonconformance and corrective and preventive action, and the EMS audit clauses.

- *An improvement process.* Improvement is embedded in the requirements for the setting of environmental objectives and in the conduct of management reviews.

- *Key support processes.* These activities support the overall EMS and include document and record control, structure and responsibility, communication, and training, awareness, and competence.

Part II focuses on the steps needed to develop an effective EMS. Various strategies and tools are presented that allow the organization to develop an EMS in the fastest, most efficient manner possible.

Part II

EMS Design
and Deployment

This part focuses on the design and deployment of an EMS based on the ISO 14001 standard. The goal is to create a system that is simple, effective, and easy to maintain. The emphasis is on getting the system up and running as soon as possible so that it can start providing benefits right away. By keeping the EMS simple, administrative overhead will be reduced and more attention can be spent on improvements that go beyond compliance. Tools and methods are provided to help the organization meet these goals.

3

The Planning Phase

This chapter focuses on the initial steps required to develop an EMS based on the ISO 14001 standard. The emphasis is on organizing and planning. One of the goals is to move quickly through this phase so as to maintain the momentum generated after the initial decision to create an EMS.

PROJECT OVERVIEW

In any management system deployment, the first steps involve getting organized and developing a project plan. The general sequence of steps for designing and rolling out the EMS is shown in Figure 3.1.

The time frames shown in the flowchart represent the general time frame for each phase, assuming a moderate level of effort is applied to the project. Adhering to this plan would result in a fully functional EMS in six months. Unless your organization is unusually complex or has a large number of significant environmental aspects, I do not recommend extending the time for ISO 14001 implementation much beyond six months, because doing so often results in a loss of the momentum generated when the project was announced and the initial training was provided.

Although each of these phases is shown in a series sequence, in reality many of the actions in the individual phases occur simultaneously. These concurrent actions will be reflected in greater detail in the project plan.

The rest of this chapter walks through each of these phases step by step.

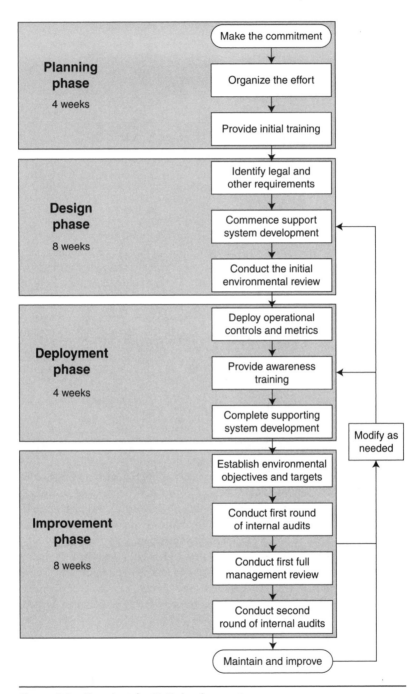

Figure 3.1   Flowchart for EMS development.

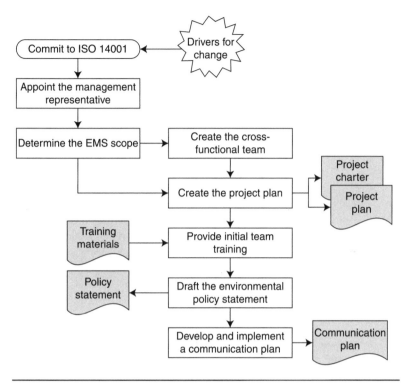

Figure 3.2 The planning phase.

PLANNING YOUR EMS

In the planning phase the initial steps needed to develop the EMS are taken, and the project is organized. A detailed flowchart for this phase is shown in Figure 3.2.

MAKE THE INITIAL COMMITMENT

The first step in the planning phase is to obtain a commitment to develop and deploy an EMS. Note that a commitment is not the same as a decision. A commitment reflects a strong belief in the need for and the benefits of good environmental stewardship. While a decision to implement ISO 14001 can lead to a certified EMS, a commitment will be needed to produce the meaningful results envisioned by the standard's creators.

Obtaining Top Management and Organizational Support

The key to obtaining the commitment needed for an effective EMS is to convince senior management that such a system is truly needed and can provide significant benefits for the organization and the environment as a whole. The need should stem from more than just a customer requirement. I recommend reviewing with the management team the information and statistics provided in Chapter 1, supplemented by current local or national issues or reports. Case studies that illustrate the possible environmental and cost savings from implementation should also be shared. Two such case studies, along with the benefits of an effective EMS, were presented in Chapter 1.

Any discussion of top management support would be incomplete without a section detailing the role that senior management plays in the success or failure of the management system. These responsibilities go far beyond providing resources in the form of personnel, time, and money, to providing and reinforcing a culture that drives environmental performance improvement throughout the organization. Some of management's most important responsibilities are discussed in the following sections.

Providing Resources

The most fundamental of management's responsibilities is to provide resources in the form of personnel, time, and training for the EMS. Personnel resources include the assignment of cross-functional team (CFT) members and a management representative. Perhaps even more important, management must be willing to provide the time for the CFT to conduct the initial environmental review and to design the system. A minimal CFT requires several individuals representing key operating areas within the company. Money is also required to support the training that will be needed. Even if the training is conducted internally there is an opportunity cost associated with the time away from work for the trainees.

Direction and Vision

Another responsibility of senior management is to provide vision and direction to the management system. Senior management must be involved in the shaping and operation of the management program through the development and communication of a meaningful environmental policy statement, and it must ensure that the EMS moves quickly through the compliance phase into the effectiveness and improvement phases. Senior management must demand accountability for performance from process owners. Establishing a culture of performance and accountability goes a long way toward ensuring that all managers and supervisors take the management system seriously.

System Metrics

One of the most important actions that management can take to speed the transition from conformance toward effectiveness is to implement a robust system of metrics that monitors the organization's progress in improving its environmental performance. Criteria and related metrics should be developed at the individual activity level, to be used by supervisors and midlevel managers on an ongoing basis to measure how well they are controlling their significant environmental aspects. System metrics should be implemented at the senior management level to monitor overall system performance in areas important to the environment and the organization's environmental objectives. The identification and assignment of metrics will be a primary focus of the deployment phase.

Communicating Commitment

It can be argued that the most important responsibility of senior management is its active communication of the significance of environmental stewardship and its support for the EMS. Communication means more than contributing a piece to the monthly company newsletter. More consequential is how the importance of the EMS is communicated in actions and daily decisions the company makes. Does management encourage research into alternative and substitute materials for the organization's products? Does management ask questions regarding the recycling, reuse, and disposal of new products during design reviews? Will management consider the use of new technologies to reduce the amount of emissions or wastes the organization generates? Does management actively encourage and recognize suggestions on how to improve the company's environmental performance and celebrate those that are implemented? Actions speak louder than words.

The ISO 14001 team leader and top management need to identify and communicate the drivers for change that resulted in the decision to implement an EMS. Research has shown that many individuals resist the change in practices, policies, and methods required to make meaningful improvements unless they can be shown why such changes are needed, or unless they are provided some input into the ways things will be done in the future. Getting the organization's employees to embrace the new system is important because many, if not most, of the more significant improvement opportunities come not from the senior management team or the management representative but rather from the frontline employees who know the processes the best. In this regard it is not unlike lean manufacturing, where the focus is on getting all employees involved in identifying and eliminating waste. For ISO 14001 the goal is to engage all employees in identifying environmental performance improvement opportunities.

The development of a comprehensive communication plan is discussed later in this section. This plan includes ideas and methods for obtaining organizational commitment to the ISO 14001 EMS. Assuming that you have your top management team's commitment, you are now ready to proceed.

APPOINT THE MANAGEMENT REPRESENTATIVE

As noted in Chapter 1, senior management must appoint the management representative. While this individual will not do all the work required to design, implement, and maintain the EMS, he or she will ultimately be responsible to see that it gets done. With that in mind, several considerations should be taken into account prior to making this appointment:

- Does the individual have an adequate level of authority to make things happen? The EMS will cross department boundaries. Will the management representative have the authority to get the support needed to drive action when necessary? If so, will this authority come from the individual's current positional authority (for example, the director of environmental affairs) or from formal reporting relationships to management? In either case, it is strongly recommended that the representative be a member of management, although not necessarily top management.

- Will this individual have the time needed to oversee the design, implementation, and maintenance of the system? Assigning the vice president of environmental, health, and safety as the management representative makes sense from an authoritative and positional point of view, but it may not be best from a time-available perspective. The representative will need to devote quite a bit of time to the EMS, especially during the initial design stage.

- Does the individual have the necessary knowledge? This consideration may be difficult to judge, especially in organizations without any environmental staff. The management representative does not have to be an expert in environmental engineering or regulations but should have the capability to learn about and understand environmental topics as needed. In addition, familiarity with management system principles helps. Often the organization's quality manager or facilities manager serves as the environmental management representative for these reasons.

- Finally, does this individual have the desire and motivation to be the management representative? Nothing can substitute for a belief in the job and a passionate desire to see the management system succeed. Far too many management representatives have been appointed against their will. Rarely do these systems produce meaningful results.

DETERMINE THE EMS SCOPE

The organization must also determine what the EMS will cover and what (if anything) it will not cover. As noted in Chapter 1, the organization can decide to include only certain facilities, processes, or products in the scope of the EMS. The organization may have good reasons for keeping certain activities outside the scope of the EMS, although this is not normally recommended. Keep in mind that the scope must be defined and documented. Normally this is accomplished through incorporation within the environmental policy manual.

CREATE THE CFT

The CFT can be assembled once the scope has been determined. The team should consist of members from various functions within the organization, but as a minimum it should include representatives from the following areas:

- Engineering
- Facilities/maintenance
- Production
- Human resources
- Logistics
- Environmental, health, and safety (if the organization has a dedicated representative)

In addition, representatives from the quality assurance department should be included if the organization already has an ISO 9001–based quality management system (QMS) in place to ensure compatibility with existing systems and procedures. The CFT is responsible for the initial environmental review, the development of system procedures and policies, and the deployment of operational controls. Team members often serve as internal auditors. Other employees may be brought into the team as needed, but the CFT will serve as the permanent core team while the EMS is developed. Criteria of selection of team members are similar to those set forth for the management representative, namely:

- Interest and enthusiasm

- Good knowledge of the operations and activities within their departments and functions

- Availability (a commitment of four hours per week will be required, along with a few eight-hour days for training and conducting the initial environmental review)

- Good reputation and standing within the organization

The last bullet is important, as the CFT will serve, along with the senior management staff, as the initial ambassador for the EMS. Team members should be opinion leaders capable of generating enthusiasm in their peers. The management representative normally serves as the team leader.

As a final consideration, it may be prudent to include one or more outside consultants to coach the team and provide expertise where lacking. As a minimum, it may be necessary to hire an environmental consultant to help with identifying and documenting regulatory requirements if this has not been previously developed, and to perform the environmental compliance reviews. These two tasks are discussed in more detail later in this chapter.

CREATE A PROJECT PLAN

As with any project, the team leader should consider developing a project plan to guide the implementation effort. The work breakdown structure normally includes the major phases of the project as discussed in this book, with tasks and deliverables outlined under each main phase. The project plan helps organize the project, assigns resources, and otherwise ensures that the project stays on track. A portion of a project plan for a typical rollout is shown in Figure 3.3.

In addition to the project plan, it is also often helpful to develop a project charter. This summary document outlines the scope of the project, the time and effort involved, and the goals of the project and documents the management team's approval to proceed. This is especially important for the team leader, as it represents management's commitment to provide the resources needed to support successful project completion. An example of a project charter for an ISO 14001 implementation is shown in Figure 3.4. A full example of a project plan and project charter is provided on the CD accompanying this book.

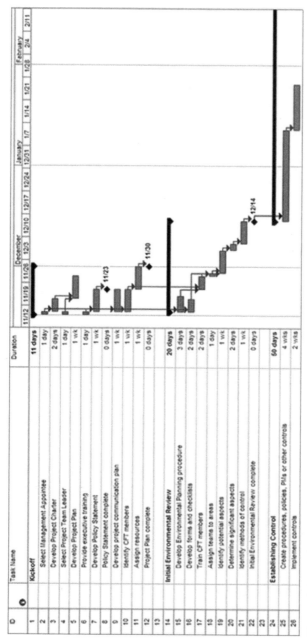

Figure 3.3   Project plan for ISO 14001 implementation.

Project Charter

October 20, 2006

Project: ISO 14001 EMS Implementation

Business need: ISO 14001 certification is now required by two of our major customers and by a potential large customer. Our two current customers have indicated an expectation that we will achieve such certification by the end of calendar year CY2006. Questions relating to our certification status and/or plans for certification have been received as part of the request for quotation from our potential customer. Certification to ISO 14001 is thus seen as a business requirement.

In addition, current energy costs have risen significantly over the last two years and are forecast to increase by another 25% by the end of CY 2006. Waste generation for both 2004 and 2005 increased by over 15% each year. Because of these rising costs, development of an integrated EMS that focuses on controlling and reducing the costs associated with these expenses is seen as an operational necessity impacting on our ability to execute our strategy of being the low-cost producer within our industry.

Finally, environmental stewardship is predicted to become a greater decision point in the general market as concerns with global warming and environmental degradation continue. ISO 14001 certification is thus seen as a useful marketing avenue to environmentally conscious consumers.

Expected project outcomes: Deployment and certification of an ISO 14001 EMS that contains and/or reduces our environmental costs.

Cost and schedule: The project must be completed by July 15, 2007. The budget authorized for this project is $120,000, not including internal personnel time.

Personnel and support: Chuck Bennet has been assigned as project manager and has been authorized to dedicate up to 25% of his time to this project through July, 2006. Each department will provide support as needed and will assign a department lead to work with Chuck on this project. The primary project sponsor is Bill Clark, president and CEO.

_____
President and CEO

_____
CFO

_____
VP, Engineering

_____
COO

_____
VP, Manufacturing

Figure 3.4   Example project charter for ISO 14001 implementation.

PROVIDE INITIAL TRAINING

Once the scope has been determined, the CFT assigned, and the project plan developed, it is time to initiate the team training. Training for ISO 14001 implementation is not extensive. A typical training series might include:

- One (or more) three-hour overview session(s) for the senior management team

- One two-day ISO 14001 training session for the CFT members and future EMS auditors

- One three-day training session in EMS internal auditing for the EMS auditors

- Several two-hour presentations to all employees, introducing the ISO 14001 model, the company's environmental policies, the roles of the employees, and other awareness training topics

At this point, only the three-hour executive overview sessions and the two-day CFT ISO 14001 training are needed. The internal auditing training should be deferred until the system is essentially deployed and audits are ready to begin. The two-hour all-hands presentations should wait until the system is ready to be deployed, so that essential information regarding key attributes of the system can be communicated.

Training for the executive team should focus on the importance of good environmental stewardship, the benefits expected from an effective EMS, the basic structure of the system, the overview of the project plan, and management's responsibilities for effective implementation, operation, and improvement of the system. A good idea is to follow up this training with a second two- to three-hour session a week later to develop the environmental policy statement (see next section).

Training for CFT members should include the topics provided during the executive overview plus a detailed review of the requirements in the ISO 14001 standard. I like to present the requirements in the order in which they will be implemented, but the flow and structure of the training is somewhat of a personal choice.

DRAFT THE ENVIRONMENTAL POLICY STATEMENT

The environmental policy statement truly forms the heart of the EMS, and the management representative and/or CFT team leader must ensure that an appropriate amount of thought and energy is put into its development. Remember that the policy statement is the responsibility of the senior management team. It should not be developed in isolation by the management representative or an outside consultant; rather, it should stem from a careful debate of what the organization feels is truly important from an environmental perspective. In essence, the environmental policy statement is both a mission statement and a vision statement rolled into one. The commitments made in this policy statement will shape the rest of the EMS and will go a long way toward determining whether your system achieves only certification or accomplishes significant good for the environment (and the organization's profitability).

The requirements relating to the policy statement are found in clause 4.2 of the standard and were previously discussed in Chapter 2. They are not repeated here. The art of developing an effective policy statement rests with its ability to provide a framework for setting environmental objectives and targets. As discussed in Chapter 2, this means going beyond the mandatory commitments of compliance, prevention of pollution, and continual improvement. It requires setting specific commitments that are meaningful to the organization. By "meaningful," we mean that the management team feels strongly enough about the commitments so as to provide the time, resources, and financial funding to drive their improvement. These specific commitments also serve as the basis for the development of criteria for significance determination for the environmental aspects identified during the initial environmental review.

As an example, compare the two environmental policy statements shown in Figure 3.5. Which one do you think will lead to meaningful environmental performance improvement? The policy statement on the left (which includes the minimum mandatory commitments required by the standard) could serve as a framework for setting environmental objectives and targets because the mandatory requirements are so broad and overarching as to include just about any improvement initiative launched. The problem is that it does not really focus the organization on anything. The policy statement on the right provides more focus for setting objectives by committing to the conservation of natural resources (water, land, materials), energy reduction (and therefore a reduction in greenhouse gases and other air pollutants), recycling and reuse methods (which gets into product design and development), total employee involvement, community involvement, and going beyond regulatory compliance. Many specific potential improvement projects come to mind when reviewing the statement on the right; few come to mind when viewing the one on the left. If you are serious about implementing an EMS that produces significant environmental per-

Worldwide Products (WPI) recognizes its responsibilities to the environment and to the community. In support of these responsibilities, WPI has established the following commitments: • Compliance to legal and other requirements • Prevention of pollution • Continual improvement	Worldwide Products (WPI) recognizes and accepts its responsibilities to be a good steward of the environment and to help achieve a state of sustainable development. In support of these responsibilities, WPI has established the following commitments: • Compliance to all applicable state, federal, and local legal requirements with the goal of beyond compliance wherever practical and possible • Conformance with the EPA Energy Star and Bright Lights programs • Prevention of pollution in all its forms • Conservation of natural resources, including energy, through reuse, recycling, and source reduction • Continual environmental performance improvement through the involvement of all WPI employees and partnership with the community

Figure 3.5   Two sample environmental policy statements.

formance gains, you should develop a policy statement that goes beyond the minimum commitments in ISO 14001.

DEVELOP A COMMUNICATION PLAN

Establishing an effective EMS that goes beyond compliance requires significant cultural and operational change for most organizations, and change is never easy. A simplified view of the steps needed to succeed in leading organizational change is shown in Figure 3.6.

The drivers for change were discussed in Chapter 1 in the section "The Case for ISO 14001." The evaluation of the current state and organizing and planning actions were discussed in the earlier sections of this chapter. At this point, our focus is on communicating the change to everyone in the organization. We also need to communicate with our suppliers, customers, and the local community. The communication plan is the tool we will use to target these communications to the various audiences. Some components of the communication plan are shown in Figure 3.7.

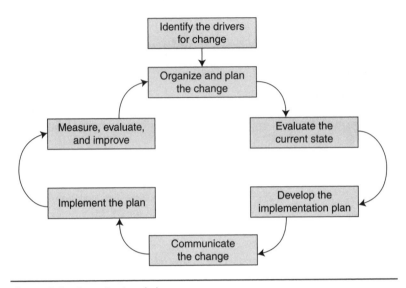

Figure 3.6 Organizational change process.

These components serve as the basis for the change management plan and do not address all the communication requirements in the standard. Some of these additional requirements can be addressed now; others will have to wait until later in the EMS development process. One of the communication requirements that can be addressed at this point is communication of the company's environmental policy statement. As noted in Chapter 2, everyone must be aware of the company's policy and should be able to relate it to his or her job activities. Methods to accomplish this awareness include the use of banners, plaques, inclusion of the policy statement in orientation training, and inclusion in some of the methods noted in Figure 3.7, such as company newsletters and the ISO 14001 communication boards. The policy must be made available to the public, and this is best accomplished on the company Web site and through external communications.

SUMMARY

At this point the decision to proceed has been confirmed, commitment obtained, a project plan developed, the management representative and CFT assigned, the initial training completed, an environmental policy statement defined, and a communication plan created. We are now ready to proceed to the EMS design phase.

Component	Audience	Purpose	
Initial announcements (top management team, CEO)	All employees	To generate awareness, involvement, enthusiasm, and support by defining drivers for change and explaining how ISO 14001 will benefit the environment, the company, and the employees.	All-ha supple compa formal ..., video, banners, and emails
Periodic updates (top management team, management representative)	All employees	To create momentum by showing the progress made and contributions by other employees.	Articles in company newsletter, creation of 14001 communication boards, inclusion in periodic communication meetings, and agenda topic in other management meetings.
Ongoing awareness (all management and supervisors with employee contributions)	All employees	To increase involvement by recognizing and celebrating success throughout the workplace.	Permanent section in company newsletter, updated and expanded 14001 communication boards, and award ceremonies. Consider implementing a company competition or award.
Customer notifications (sales, marketing, IT)	Customers and consumers, local community	To build market share and improve company reputation and image.	Formal letters, publication of the policy statement, inclusion on Web site and in stockholder reports, flying the ISO 14001 flag.
Supplier notifications (purchasing, engineering)	Suppliers, contractors, and vendors	To communicate the organization's commitment to the environment, policies, and procedures. To encourage improvement of environmental performance throughout supply chain.	Purchase orders, contracts, supplier briefing statements, Web site and formal letters.

Figure 3.7 Components of a communication plan.

4

The Design and Development Phase

The critical steps in the design and development phase include identifying the organization's legal and other requirements, planning for and identifying significant environmental aspects, identifying operational controls for the activities associated with these aspects, and developing the supporting systems and procedures needed to fully deploy the EMS. These actions are shown in Figure 4.1.

IDENTIFYING REGULATORY REQUIREMENTS

For those organizations without dedicated environmental specialists, identifying regulatory requirements may be the most difficult step in designing the EMS. It is not unusual to find that the organization has a general feel for those regulations that apply, but it does not know with certainty which of the laws (federal, state, or local) it must meet, why it must meet them, and what they require. Instead, the organization continues to operate to what it thinks it must meet pending a federal, state, or local agency review and identification of weaknesses in its environmental compliance. In many such cases the organization relies on an outside environmental firm to conduct a compliance review every two or three years, but even then no one within the organization really understands what is needed to remain in compliance.

The problem with this mode of operation is that environmental regulations change, as do the processes, facilities, materials, and methods used by the organization to produce its products or services. Without a solid knowledge of the regulations, the organization could find itself violating one or more of its regulatory obligations because of an increase in the amount of oil it stores on-site, the amount of hazardous waste it generates, or an increase in its emission of air pollutants. It is important to remember that the owner and operator of the facility, and not the outside consultant, bears the legal responsibility for compliance.

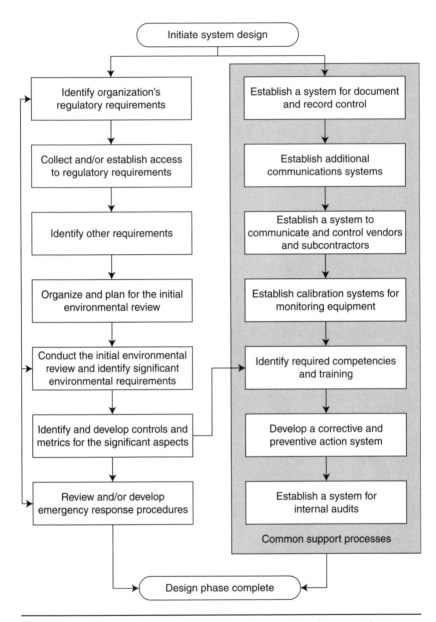

Figure 4.1 Process flowchart for the EMS design and development phase.

In order to meet the legal requirements of the ISO 14001 standard's, the organization must identify all of its regulatory obligations, ensure it has access to what the obligations say, and understand what it has to do to meet these requirements. Some of the federal environmental regulations that may apply include:

- Resource Conservation and Recovery Act

- Clean Water Act

- National Permit Discharge Elimination System Program

- Clean Air Act

- Superfund Amendments and Reauthorization Act

- Toxic Substances Control Act

- National Environmental Policy Act

- Pollution Prevention Act

- Safe Drinking Water Act

- Comprehensive Environmental Response, Compensation, and Liability Act

- Emergency Planning and Community Right-to-Know Act

These federal regulations appear in the Code of Federal Regulations, or CFR, and are available online through various government Web sites. They can also be purchased in hard-copy format (I prefer the online versions).

Each state has its own regulations covering the same topics as the federal laws. Many states have the authority to implement and administer the federal regulations. In these instances the state law must be at least as restrictive as the federal regulation, and often is more so; but if the organization complies with the state laws, it is also in compliance with the federal law. In cases where the state does not have the authority to administer the federal regulation, the organization must be aware of both the state and the federal regulations to ensure its compliance. In addition, most municipalities have their own local regulations regarding water usage, storm water and sewage, and runoff.

In order to keep all this information straight, the organization needs to develop a listing, or register as it is often called, of its regulatory obligations. This is easier said than done, however, because the environmental regulations themselves are complex and can be hard to use for those without specific training. For these reasons, it is recommended that an environmental regulatory expert create the register of regulations. If the organization has dedicated environmental specialists, they should be able to create the register in short order. If the organization does not have such personnel on site, but is a member of a larger corporation, it is often possible to get corporate specialists to develop the list. If neither of these two options is possible, it is best to hire an outside expert to create the list.

The most important thing is that the list must have all the information needed by the organization to understand its regulatory obligations and access them when needed. For this reason I recommend that a format similar to the one shown in Figure 4.2 be used, as a minimum, when creating the listing. If an outside consultant is used, show him or her the format you require before he or she conducts the review, to ensure it will meet your needs in satisfying the ISO 14001 standard's requirements and help you remain in compliance in between outside consultant reviews.

If a corporate or outside expert develops the register or regulations, it is often a good idea to have this individual review your environmental compliance at the same time. As mentioned in Chapter 2, the ISO 14001 standard requires that environmental compliance reviews be conducted, so now is a good time to get an initial review or to update an older evaluation.

Once the register is developed, establish hyperlinks to the online versions of the state and federal regulations. The CFR can be accessed at the Government Printing Office Web site, http://www.gpo.gov. Most states have their regulations similarly posted online. Establishing hyperlinks makes it easier to access the regulations that apply to you and simplifies document control because the government agency keeps these regulations up to date. One word of advice, however: look through the online documents after the hyperlinks are established. You will need to be familiar with the regulations and how to navigate through them. You don't have to be an expert, but you should have a general sense of the requirements and know what applies to you. As a minimum, you should be able to demonstrate your ability to verify the requirements when questions arise.

OTHER REQUIREMENTS

Other requirements include customer requirements relating to environmental management and control and voluntary participation in local, state, federal, and international programs that focus on sustainable development.

Examples of customer-specific requirements include those relating to ISO 14001 certification and restrictions or prohibitions on the use of certain types of hazardous or toxic materials. Examples of voluntary initiatives include the following EPA programs (resources for these programs are included on the CD-ROM accompanying this book):

REGISTER OF REGULATIONS FOR ADVANCED PRODUCTS, INC.

Item No.	Regulation	Applies?	Rationale	Status	Actions	Location of Regulation
1	**AIR QUALITY**	(Aspects: welding fumes and grinding dust)				
1.1	40 CFR 50 - 90: Clean Air Act and Part 55 of Michigan PA 451, as amended	Yes	Emission sources exist.	Substantially compliant	Maintain compliance with Part 55 per item 1.2 below.	http://www.access.gpo.gov/cgi-bin/cfrassemble.cgi?title=200540 http://www.michigan.gov/deq/0,1607,7-135-3307_4132-14902--,00.html
1.2	Part 55 of PA 451: Air pollution control	Yes	Air emission sources exist, however, exempt to permittingper item 1.2.1 below.	Substantially compliant	Evaluate new emission sources and changes in raw material usage for applicability to permitting requirements.	http://www.michigan.gov/deq/0,1607,7-135-3307_4132-14902--,00.html
1.3	R336.1201 of Part 55 of PA 451: Permit to Install	Yes	Company operates equipment that has the potential to emit air contaminants; however the dust collector in the grinding room and the welding equipment exhaust to the general room and are therefore exempt from permitting requirements per rule 285(1)(vi)(B)	Substantially compliant	Evaluate new emission sources and changes in raw material usage for applicability to permitting requirements.	http://www.state.mi.us/orr/emi/admincode.asp?AdminCode=Single&Admin_Num=33601201&Dpt=EQ&RngHigh=
2	**WASTE WATER**	(Aspects: Outside storage: tools, scrap containers, parts containers)				
2.1	40 CFR 122 and Part 31 of Michigan PA 451: National Pollutant Discharge Elimination System	Yes	Applicable based on SIC code 3465; company discharges storm water to the industrial park storm water retention pond which is hydraulically connected to a water of the state Bear Creek)	Company should evaluate storm water permit options and implement option most appropriate for API	Develop and implement a storm water pollution prevention plan (SWPPP), train personnel, obtain permit or submit a no exposure exemption.	http://www.access.gpo.gov/nara/cfr/waisidx_05/40cfr122_05.html http://www.michigan.gov/de135-3307_4132-14902--,00

Figure 4.2 Register of environmental regulations.

- WasteWise, which provides structure, assistance, and recognition for waste reduction activities. Solid waste reduction not only saves landfill space, it also conserves natural resources and lowers greenhouse gas emissions. It can also save money.

- GreenScapes, which focuses on the design and maintenance of environmental sustainable landscaping.

- Green Power, which provides information on how and where to purchase energy produced by sustainable and/or renewable means (for example, wind, solar, and biomass). Although renewable energy has a slight price premium, its costs are normally fixed for a period of time and can (and certainly have, at the time of this writing) fall below the cost of energy produced from other means.

- Climate Leaders, a program that obtains commitments for voluntary reduction in greenhouse gas emissions from industry partners. Many of the world's largest and most progressive companies are members, and total committed reductions amount to billions of pounds of greenhouse gas emissions. Participants receive technical assistance from the EPA and invaluable public recognition.

- Energy Star, which focuses on decreasing energy usage and lowering the resultant emission of greenhouse gases. Partners commit to reductions in their energy usage, develop plans to accomplish these reductions, measure their performance, and agree to educate their employees about energy efficiency and the Energy Star program (which also applies to homeowners). Extensive guidance on ways to reduce energy consumption is available from the EPA and other sources, and participants can save thousands, if not hundreds of thousands, of dollars in energy costs given today's market price, depending on facility size.

- Design for the Environment (DfE) program, which conducts life-cycle assessments and provides product and process design guidance for organizations in key industries such as printing, dry cleaning, and electronics.

In addition to these federal programs, similar programs are also operated at the state and international level. The International Chamber of Commerce's Business Charter for Sustainable Development, which provides general principles for industrial environmental stewardship, is an example of an international program. Many of the world's leading companies have signed on to these principles and use them to guide their design, manufacturing, and operating philosophies.

Each of these programs is voluntary, and participation is not a requirement for ISO 14001 certification. If an organization is serious about improving its environmental performance beyond compliance, however, these programs should be seriously considered. Remember that the purpose of ISO 14001 is to drive toward sustainable development, and these programs provide specific methods and structure to do just that.

Once an organization has made the commitment to participate in one or more voluntary programs, the ISO 14001 standard expects that the organization will establish methods, controls, and measures to ensure that environmental performance is achieved. Include these programs, or links to the Web sites that describe these programs, in your listing of requirements. More information on voluntary programs is provided in Chapter 8.

ORGANIZING AND PLANNING THE INITIAL ENVIRONMENTAL REVIEW

The major activity in designing your EMS is the initial environmental review. During this activity the organization evaluates its operations and facilities to identify its potentially significant aspects (those elements of its products, services, or activities that could impact the environment). Once the organization has identified these, it will conduct an assessment to determine those that actually have, or could have, a significant impact on the environment. The initial environmental review can be accomplished in a matter of days, but it requires careful planning and preparation. This section provides guidance on how to prepare for the review and develop the necessary tools for conducting the review.

One of the first steps in preparing for the initial environmental review is to select and train the CFT. The team should be multidisciplinary and include members from each functional department or operating area of the facility, such as the following:

- The environmental management representative, who will lead the planning and execution of the review

- A facilities/maintenance representative, who is knowledgeable in the tanks, auxiliaries, boilers, fluid transfer, and other supporting systems of the plant

- One or more production team members, who understand the processes, materials, and wastes used to manufacture the organization's products

- An engineering or administrative representative, who will lead the review of administrative operations

- A purchasing representative, who is familiar with and has access to records that show the different types of materials and substances bought and therefore consumed within the organization

- A shipping and receiving/logistics representative, who can lead the review in this area and who is familiar with the materials and wastes consumed in shipping and receiving and the processes used to receive materials and substances into the plant

- The plant safety representative, if one is available, who can rapidly cross-check material safety data sheets (MSDSs) for information on the use and toxicity of materials identified during the review

Naturally, if the company has dedicated environmental specialists on staff, they should also be included as key members of the team because they will be able to quickly answer questions that will arise during the assessment for significance. Many companies procure the services of an outside environmental specialist for the one- or two-day review to provide this knowledge if they lack this environmental expertise. Other potential team members include those involved in environmental management tasks, such as those who complete and maintain the hazardous waste manifests, the oil king responsible for the facility's oil management program, the janitorial staff responsible for the use and disposal of cleaning agents and solid waste, and a laboratory representative if chemicals are stored and used on-site.

In addition, some companies prefer to include their corporate attorney to provide some level of attorney-client privilege protection against what might be found during the review. I normally consider this to be unnecessary and a little paranoid. If you feel that you have environmental legacies of such magnitude to warrant such safeguards, you may want to focus first on removing those legacies and improving your compliance posture before embarking on a project to implement ISO 14001. For a moderate-sized facility, a team of 8 to 12 people provides an adequate number of personnel to conduct an efficient initial environmental review.

Once the team has been assembled, the next major step is to provide training. Prior to the training, I recommend that the management representative develop some of the tools that will be used to conduct the review so that these can be introduced during the training. As a minimum, the following tools are needed during the review:

- A checklist to guide the team in what to look for

- A facility layout to assist in making team assignments

- Process flowcharts, if available, for major production processes

Two examples of checklists for identifying environmental aspects are provided in Figures 4.3 and 4.4. Figure 4.3 shows a checklist suitable for evaluating a manufacturing process, where aspects are normally identified through the listing of all inputs (materials, chemicals, solvents, oils, energy, and so on) and outputs (wastes, sludge, air emissions, fumes, scrap metal, and so on) from the process. Figure 4.4 provides help in identifying aspects found in general areas such as administrative and engineering spaces, warehouses, facilities, and areas outside the plant. Both should be used during the review. Copies of the checklists are provided on the CD accompanying this book.

In addition to the checklists, the management representative should obtain a facility layout drawing that shows the general areas of the plant, if one is available. The drawing should include areas of importance surrounding the plant, such as raw material or waste storage areas, the location of all outfalls and storm drains, and storage buildings. This layout will be used to identify areas to be evaluated and to make team assignments. If such a drawing is not available, one can be generated. An example is provided in Figure 4.5.

Finally, if the company has developed process flowcharts of its major manufacturing processes (for example, as part of implementing a QMS), the teams can use these to help identify environmental aspects. When used with the checklist shown in Figure 4.3, such flowcharts help guide the team when evaluating complex manufacturing operations. An example of a process flowchart, annotated to include potentially significant environmental aspects using the inputs-outputs methodology, is provided in Figure 4.6.

Once the tools that will be used to help conduct the initial environmental review are prepared or collected, it is time to train the CFT.

For the process being evaluated, consider the inputs (materials and resources) and outputs (emissions and wastes) for the process. Look for:

Inputs	Outputs
Raw materials, parts	Air emissions, odor
Water	Solid nonhazardous waste (e.g., trash)
Energy	Hazardous wastes (liquid or solid)
Solvents	Industrial wastes (e.g., oils)
Chemicals	Waste heat, wastewater
Paper, wood, plastic, etc.	Sludge

Process:

Name:

Inputs into the Process	Outputs from the Process	Potentially Significant?* (Yes/No)	Comments (e.g., chemical name, amounts if known, functions involved in operation/handling)

*To determine if potentially significant, consider the amount consumed (materials, resources) or generated (wastes, emissions). For example, the water consumed in a process that uses 2 gallons of water per hour will probably not be significant, but consumption of 100 gallons per hour may be. If in doubt, indicate yes. Final determination of significance will be made during the assessment portion of the review.

Figure 4.3 Environmental aspects identification checklist (process).

Area review: _____   Date: _____

Perform a complete and thorough walk-through of the area assigned. Use the following questions to identify potentially significant environmental aspects. Some of these items may already be identified as part of the process reviews—in which case the focus should be on the common storage and collection points. The use of the word "significant" in the following questions is subjective and should be considered as a relative amount compared with other materials/wastes used or generated.

Are there any hazardous or industrial materials stored in this area (chemicals, paint, oils, solvents, etc.)?

Yes/No	Material	Amount	Comments

Are there any hazardous or industrial wastes stored in this area (waste chemicals, waste solvents, waste oils, etc.)?

Yes/No	Wastes	Amount	Comments

Are there any significant sources of energy consumption in this area (lighting, HVAC [heating, ventilation, and cooling], large pumps, auxiliaries, etc.)?

Yes/No	Energy Consumers	Amount	Comments

Figure 4.4   Environmental aspects identification checklist (area).   *(Continued)*

(Continued)

Are there any significant indoor air emissions in this area (e.g., oil mist, chemical vapors) that workers could be exposed to?

Yes/No	Indoor Air Emissions	Amount	Comments

Are there any air emissions from this area that are directed outside the plant?

Yes/No	Outdoor Air Emissions	Amount	Comments

Is there any storage, collection, or use of common raw materials such as cardboard, wood, or plastic in this area?

Yes/No	Common Raw Material	Amount	Comments

Is there any use or disposal of water in this area (e.g., floor cleaning—oily mop water)?

Yes/No	Water Disposal Source	Amount	Comments

Figure 4.4   (Continued)

(Continued)

Are there significant volumes of products or materials in this area that could be recycled (e.g., paper, cardboard, scrap wood, furniture, carpeting, old office equipment, aluminum cans, and toner cartridges).

Yes/No	Potential Recycled Material	Amount	Comments

For areas outside the plant, are there any sources of contaminated (i.e., oily, chemical contaminated) water runoff to storm drains or groundwater?

Yes/No	Contaminated Runoff Source	Amount	Comments

For areas outside the plant, are there any other sources of damage to wetlands, wildlife, or flora surrounding the plant (e.g., trash, pesticide runoff, deicing salt runoff, and transformers with polychlorinated biphenyls)?

Yes/No	Other Sources of Damage	Amount	Comments

Team: _____

Figure 4.4   (Continued)

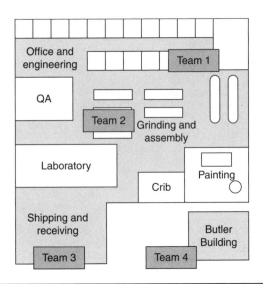

Figure 4.5 Example simple plant layout.

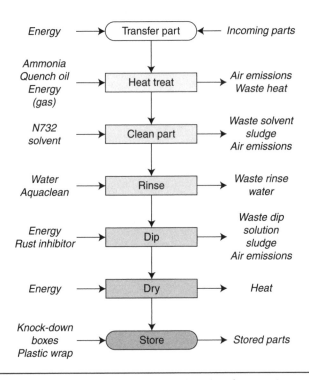

Figure 4.6 Use of process flowcharts to aid in identifying environmental aspects.

INITIAL TEAM TRAINING

Training is required for CFT members if they have not already received training in the ISO 14001 standard. Even if they have some background in the standard, additional training is warranted to prepare them for the initial environmental review. Team members should have a solid understanding of the definitions of environmental aspects and environmental impacts and know how they relate to each other. They should also be briefed on the organization's environmental policy statement, including the company's commitments made in the policy. They should understand the process that will be used to conduct the initial review and understand how the environmental aspects are evaluated for significance. Finally, options available for controlling the activities associated with these aspects should be discussed, as the team will also help identify operational controls for those aspects determined to be significant.

ESTABLISHING CRITERIA FOR DETERMINING SIGNIFICANCE

One of the most, if not the most, important actions required to complete the initial environmental review is to determine the criteria that will be used to establish which of the environmental aspects identified during the review are significant and which are not. Remember that significance is determined primarily with the potential or real impact, good or bad, that an aspect could have on the environment. Criteria for determining significance could include a material's toxicity, its hazardous or nonhazardous nature, its effect on air pollution or contribution to greenhouse gases, and its consumption/depletion of natural resources. Rather than simply pulling a half dozen or so criteria out of thin air, it is strongly recommended that the criteria stem from the commitments included in the policy statement. If the policy statement was crafted to provide a true framework for setting environmental objectives and targets, as discussed in Chapter 3, there should be ample opportunities to link your policy commitments to your criteria for determining significance. As an example, consider again the example policy statement presented in Chapter 3:

> *Worldwide Products (WPI) recognizes and accepts its responsibility to be a good steward of the environment and to help achieve a state of sustainable development. In support of these responsibilities WPI has established the following commitments:*
>
> * *Compliance to all applicable state, federal, and local legal requirements with the goal of beyond compliance wherever practical and possible*

- *Conformance with the EPA Energy Star and DfE programs*

- *Prevention of pollution in all its forms*

- *Conservation of natural resources, including energy, through source reduction, reuse, and recycling wherever practical*

- *Continual environmental performance improvement through the involvement of all WPI employees and partnership with the local community*

Let us now associate each policy commitment with some related criteria that could be used to establish environmental significance.

Commitment 1: *Compliance to all applicable state, federal, and local legal requirements with the goal of beyond compliance wherever practical and possible*

Possible criteria: Regulated nature of the material, waste, or emission

Commitment 2: *Conformance with the EPA Energy Star and DfE programs*

Possible criteria: Energy Star—Energy consumption of the activity

Possible criteria: DfE—Influence on the materials used, power consumed, amount and nature of wastes or emissions generated by, or ability to recycle or reuse our products

Commitment 3: *Prevention of pollution in all its forms*

Possible criteria: Too general, will be covered by the other criteria

Commitment 4: *Conservation of natural resources, including energy, through source reduction, reuse, and recycling wherever practical*

Possible criteria: Amount or volume of natural resources consumed, potential for reduction, recycling, or reuse

Commitment 5: *Continual environmental performance improvement through the involvement of all WPI employees and partnership with the local community*

Possible criteria: Significant community concern, significant employee concern

Using our policy commitments as our guide, we have come up with about a half dozen meaningful criteria for determining which environmental aspects are significant and must be controlled. In doing so, we have also ensured the alignment of our policy with our environmental aspects because the policy commitments directly influence what we consider to be significant. You may also recall that when we set our environmental objectives and targets, we were required to consider our significant environmental aspects and ensure consistency with the commitments we made in the policy statement. Because the objectives will stem from the policy commitments, and the policy commitments shaped the determination of what is a significant aspect, this alignment of the policy to the objectives to the significant aspects will be ensured.

The broad criteria we will use are restated in the following list, this time in the form of questions that we will direct at each potentially significant aspect we identify during the initial environmental review.

1. Is this aspect a hazardous or industrial material or waste? Is it in any other way regulated?

2. Does this activity influence the design of our products in regard to the materials used, power consumed, amount and nature of wastes or emissions generated by, or ability to recycle or reuse the product at its end of life?

3. Does this activity consume a significant amount of natural resources, including water, materials, or energy?

4. Does this aspect present a high potential for reduction, recycling, or reuse due to volume used or amount generated?

5. Is this aspect/activity a significant community or employee concern?

Once we have agreed on the broad criteria to be used to determine significance, we can then move to assign values and operational statements that define more precisely what each criterion represents and how the application of the criteria will be scored. A simple yes/no answer is not sufficient to determine significance, because it will result in far too many aspects being deemed significant. Instead, some type of rating scale is normally used to help separate the vital few from the more trivial many.

I normally recommend a 1-3-9 scale for ranking. This scale helps separate the clear winners from the others and makes it easier to identify what needs to be controlled. Figure 4.7 shows our operational definitions for the rankings.

These operational definitions can be developed by the team or by the management representative. The important point is that the criteria be developed before the initial environmental review in order to prevent the biasing of the criteria on the basis of what the team finds during the review. I usually transfer the criteria to the Environmental Planning Workbook spreadsheet (described in the next section) as a comment so that these criteria pop up when the mouse is placed over them. This facilitates the ranking of significance during the postreview assessment.

Is this aspect a hazardous or industrial material or waste? Is it in any other way regulated?	
1	Trace amounts of hazardous material (<1%) or is a hazardous material or waste, but only very small amounts (e.g., 1 liter) are generated or maintained on-site.
3	Not an RCRA hazardous waste, but regulated as an industrial waste by state, or small amounts of a hazardous material in mixture.
9	Material is a regulated hazardous waste under RCRA or contains a significant (>10% by volume) amount of a hazardous material by the Occupational Safety and Health Administration classification, as indicated on the MSDS.
Does this activity influence the design of our products in regard to the materials used, power consumed, amount and nature of wastes or emissions generated by, or ability to recycle or reuse the product at its end of life?	
1	Activity only indirectly influences in a small way the environmental design of our products.
3	Activity influences the environmental design of our products by limiting or expanding design options.
9	Activity directly impacts the environmental design of our products through selection of features that establish materials used, power consumed, radiation emitted, or disposal options and methods.
Does this activity consume a significant amount of natural resources, including water, materials, or energy?	
Note: Factor included to account for natural resource conservation opportunity. Subjective opinion by team. Takes into account relative amounts generated/used, from a conservation perspective.	
1	Activity or aspect consumes a relatively small amount of water, wood, plastic, oil, metal, or other natural resource.
3	Activity or aspect consumes a relatively moderate amount of water, wood, plastic, oil, metal, or other natural resource.
9	Activity or aspect consumes a relatively large amount of water, wood, plastic, oil, metal, or other natural resource.
Does this aspect present a high potential for reduction, recycling, or reuse due to volume used or amount generated?	
Note: Factor included to account for pollution prevention opportunity. Subjective opinion by team. Takes into account amounts generated/used, from a pollution prevention perspective.	

Figure 4.7 Operational definitions of criteria used to determine *(Continued)* environmental significance.

(Continued)

1	There is some minor potential to reduce, recycle, or reuse, but the volume or amount generated is relatively small, and there are no known secondary markets available for recycling.
3	There is a moderate potential to reduce, recycle, or reuse on the basis of the volume or amounts generated. Secondary markets are typically available for recycling.
9	There is a high potential to reduce, recycle, or reuse on the basis of the volume or amounts generated. Secondary markets are typically available for recycling.
Is this aspect/activity a significant community or employee concern?	
1	Activity or aspect has been cited once as a concern or issue by community or workforce. Examples include noise, dust, and odor.
3	Activity or aspect has been cited occasionally (two or three times) as a concern or issue by community or workforce. Examples include noise, dust, and odor.
9	Activity or aspect has been cited often as a concern or issue by community or workforce. Examples include noise, dust, and odor.

Figure 4.7   (Continued)

ENVIRONMENTAL PLANNING WORKBOOK

To speed the execution of the postreview assessment and to keep all the information relating to the EMS in one compact location, it is recommended that an electronic spreadsheet be developed. This spreadsheet, a copy of which is contained on the CD provided with this book, will form the centerpiece of all essential information relating to the organization's EMS. Several sheets in the workbook denote different design considerations for the system. Specifically, sheet 1 is used to document the results of the initial environmental review and the postreview determination of significance. Sheet 2 is used to document the operational controls used for each significant aspect. Sheet 3 is used to record the metrics used to monitor each significant aspect, along with the frequency of reporting of performance and submission of reports. Another sheet is used to document environmental objectives and targets and corresponding management programs, and additional sheets can be added to include training requirements for employees involved in activities that have or could have a significant environmental impact, documents that need to be controlled, and record retention requirements. The workbook maintains in one central file all important information needed to maintain and improve the EMS. Supporting the planning workbook are a series of procedures and instructions, maintenance requirements, and other tools used to ensure proper operation and control of the EMS.

The first sheet documents the results of the initial environmental review and facilitates the postreview assessment for significance. A portion of the worksheet is shown in Figure 4.8.

The top row in the worksheet lists the potentially significant aspects identified during the initial environmental review. The next six rows provide a place to record important information about the aspect. Rows 9 through 14 list the criteria used to determine the significance of each environmental aspect listed in the spreadsheet. The operational definition for each criterion is inserted in a comment so that the definition pops up when the mouse is placed over the criterion's cell. An example is shown in Figure 4.9.

Use your plant layout to help assign the teams to different areas of the plant. Teams of two or three work best. Plan to include on each team at least one member from the area being evaluated. In general, plan on using the following teams:

- *Production area team(s)*—Note that for large facilities it may be necessary to assign two or more subteams to the production area to ensure adequate coverage without overloading any one team. The production teams should evaluate each generic production process using the process checklist (Figure 4.3) and process flowcharts, if available. The team does not have to evaluate duplicate or similar lines if the same operations and types of materials are used on those lines. In addition, the production area teams should also complete the area checklist to ensure common areas and activities not associated with any one process are not overlooked. These might include common hazardous waste storage areas, lubricant and oil transfer stations, and battery-charging stations.

- *Administrative area team*—This team evaluates the engineering, administration, and other white-collar areas and activities. It evaluates the sources of solid wastes, energy consumption, inks, toners, cleaning solvents, excess furniture, recyclable materials, and activities that could impact on the environmental design of the company's products (assuming it is design responsible).

- *Facility team*—This team evaluates production support areas not assigned to the production team. Typical areas include the basement, where boilers, pumps, tank farms, and air compressors are located, maintenance areas, and tool rooms. In some cases this team might also be assigned to evaluate the area outside the plant, as described in the next bullet.

- *Outside plant team*—This team focuses on the review of the organization's outside property, including scrap and material storage

Environmental Aspects

Criteria weighting
9 - high correlation to criteria
3 - moderate correlation to criteria
1 - low correlation to criteria

Department or Area

Activity associated with aspect 1

Activity associated with aspect 2

Activity associated with aspect 3

Activity associated with aspect 4

Functions involved with aspect

Significance Criteria

Hazardous or regulated material or waste?

Influence the environmental design of our products?

Consumes significant natural resources (includes energy)?

Consumes a significant amount of natural resources, including energy?

Present a high opportunity for source reduction, reuse or recycling?

Significant community or employee concern?

Total Score

Significant?

Formally controlled, although not significant

Figure 4.8 Environmental Planning Workbook—significant environmental aspects.

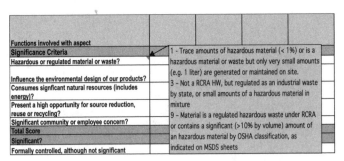

Figure 4.9   Using comments in the Environmental Planning Workbook.

areas, propane and other gaseous storage, fuel storage, the location of storm drains in relation to storage areas and runoff, pallet storage, empty drum or container storage, the parking area (including the use of any deicer in the winter), and the lawn (including the use of any pesticides). It should also evaluate whether any utility transformers located on the property are PCB free. A label stating this should be visible on the side of the transformer if it is PCB free.

- *Laboratory team*—If the organization has a research or testing laboratory, a team is usually assigned to evaluate this area, due to the concentration of chemicals, biologicals, or other nasty stuff.

- *Warehouse team*—If the organization has a warehouse facility, a team should be assigned to review this area. This team is primarily looking for the consumption of natural resources and opportunities to recycle items like wood pallets, cardboard, plastic, and shrink-wrap. In addition, this team may also find itself evaluating hazardous and industrial material storage and waste storage areas. The job of this team is not to list separately all materials stored in the warehouse; rather, it is looking for activities and areas that could present a significant risk to the environment.

The environmental specialist or consultant, if one is available, should be assigned to the production or facilities team. The safety team member, if available, should be assigned to one of the production teams. The purchasing team member can be placed on any team or can be assigned the task of retrieving a listing of all materials and chemicals purchased over the last six months while the rest of the team conducts the review. This list is used to cross-check what the team found on the floor against what was purchased for consumption to ensure that no potentially significant chemicals, materials, or solvents were overlooked during the review.

Each team should plan on spending at least three hours, and possibly up to six hours, in its assigned area. The production teams normally have the most to do because they will be conducting both process reviews and area reviews. Have the teams plan accordingly.

Now that the team has been trained, assignments made, tools and checklists provided, and criteria determined, the CFT should be ready to conduct the initial environmental review. The only thing left is to schedule one or two days for completion of the review. For a very small facility or a nonmanufacturing service organization, one day may be enough to complete the review. For a moderate-sized organization, two days work well. For very large or multiplant facilities, it is best to conduct the reviews in stages. The main consideration is once you initiate your review, keep at it until the assessment is complete. Do not break up the review over several weeks or months, because this is a surefire way to lose the momentum built up prior to the launch.

CONDUCTING THE INITIAL ENVIRONMENTAL REVIEW

If the CFT has prepared as described in the last section, conducting the initial environmental review is quite straightforward. Using its training and the checklists provided, each team should assess its assigned areas for potentially significant environmental aspects.

The team should not try to list every possible environmental aspect; rather, it should identify only those that are potentially significant. As noted in Chapter 2, an environmental aspect is any element of an organization's products, services, or activities that could interact with the environment. In essence, just about everything is an environmental aspect, and the number of aspects in a typical organization would number in the hundreds or thousands. Fortunately, the number of those that could have a significant environmental impact (which are those that we are seeking) is far less. An organization will typically identify between 40 and 100 that will need to be assessed for significance. The purpose of the checklists is to provide a calibration point for the team in what to look for. The checklists provide guidance on the types of aspects found in most organizations that could be significant. While the team should not feel constrained to list only those items on the checklist, it should be cautioned not to go overboard attempting to list everything it sees.

As an exercise, assume you are in an area where a chemical treatment is being applied to metal parts (see Figure 4.10). What might you identify as potentially significant aspects?

First, you would certainly list the chemicals (input) being used in the treatment process. You would probably also list the materials (input) being treated. You might also list the sludge (output waste) along with the waste

Figure 4.10   A chemical treatment process.

chemical solution (output waste) that must eventually be disposed of. You could also cite the water (natural resource input) used in the mixture to replenish the bath; the energy (input) used to power the pumps, process, ventilation, and lighting; and the residual rags and wipes used to clean up any spills or drips (waste output). During your review you may also note containers of certain additives used in the bath, empty 55-gallon drums, and several pallets of scrap cardboard sitting in a corner. In the office in the far corner you note the energy used to power the several personal computers and monitors and the electronics used to control the treatment process. Finally, although testing has consistently shown that there is no health concern with the indoor air quality, discussion with several operators in the area indicates they have frequently raised the issue of the light but still annoying fumes that permeate the area. Although you would undoubtedly find other potentially significant aspects, this simple virtual walk-through has already identified over a dozen items that should be assessed for their significance.

During this review the team should not only list the potentially significant aspects (chemicals, sludge, and so on), but it should also associate each aspect with its activities. *This is very important because, in general, we will not establish operational controls on the aspects themselves but rather on the activities or processes that use or generate them.* For example, if the chemicals are found to be a significant aspect, we may establish operational controls on the concentration of chemicals in the bath, the temperature of the bath, and the circulation rate of the chemical mixture. We would also

Figure 4.11   Typical administrative area.

control the storage and transfer of chemicals, which is another activity associated with this aspect. Team members must be disciplined to cite not only the aspect but also the activity or process in which it is being used or emitted from.

Let's try another one. Assume you are a member of the team evaluating the administrative areas. What you see is shown in Figure 4.11.

You would almost certainly list the stacks of paper (a recyclable) found on many of the desks in the area. You would probably also list the energy consumed by the computers, monitors, and other office equipment. Most likely you would list the energy used in the lighting, along with that used in heating and cooling. Some would probably also cite used toner cartridges, the cleaning agents found in the closet, and fluorescent bulbs (which contain trace amounts of mercury and are controlled as a special category of waste called universal waste) used in the overhead lighting. You may also find empty cardboard boxes, a trash can full of empty aluminum soda cans, a desk full of old catalogs, and a table piled with old newspapers. For many of these findings, the team will use its discretion on whether to list them. If the amounts are very small, the team may recognize that, relative to the organization's other environmental aspects, these are insignificant. On the other hand, just because an environmental aspect is not determined to be significant does not mean we will not establish some means to control its consumption or disposal through recycling and reuse. Obvious candidates for conservation or recycling should almost always be listed, although they may not be controlled as tightly as significant aspects, because conservation and recycling are relatively easy to set up and maintain. Listing them sends the right message, and every little bit helps. In the next section, we will discuss how to handle aspects that are not determined to be significant but that are still controlled.

Using these guidelines, the team may also want to list used office equipment, used furniture, and even used carpeting because each provides an opportunity to recycle or reuse. Used office equipment and furniture can be donated to local schools and charities and put to good use beyond taking up landfill space. Used carpeting can be recycled, and new environmentally friendly carpeting installed, assuming personnel are kept aware of this opportunity. Also, do not overlook the office plants, as they may be providing a positive environmental impact, both in terms of worker attitude and indoor air quality.

Finally, assume this administrative area is engineering. If your company also designs the products it sells, do not overlook the product's design and development process. Although you cannot physically see this activity, *the design phase has repeatedly been shown to have the greatest environmental impact of any phase in a product's life cycle.* Why? Simply because the design of a product establishes the way the product will be manufactured, used, and disposed of, as well as determining the materials (hazardous or nonhazardous, scarce or plentiful) used in its construction. A product designed with the environment in mind will have far fewer adverse environmental impacts during its manufacture, use, and disposal than will one that has not. There are many design techniques that can be applied during product design and development that can improve a product's overall environmental performance. If you design the products you sell, listing your design process as a potentially significant aspect should be automatic. Your purchasing process should be a close second.

Figure 4.12 provides a final example. This time you are with the team assessing the outdoor plant, and this is what you see. I will leave it up to you to make a list of potentially significant aspects.

Figure 4.12 Typical back lot.

During the review the team should list as much information as possible when it feels that it may have identified a significant environmental aspect. Besides listing the activity associated with the aspect, the team should also list the functions involved in the process, who has to handle or dispose of the aspect, who could be affected by the aspect (for example, bath technicians in the chemical treatment process), chemical names where available, approximate amounts, and any warnings on chemical barrels or containers. This information is useful when assessing significance or when developing operational controls. By getting the information now, you save yourself some time from having to go back on the floor later. An excerpt from the production team's checklist is shown in Figure 4.13. Note how the team

Process: Chemical treatment Name: Bill Barnett, Cindy Hanson			
Inputs into the Process	**Outputs from the Process**	**Potentially Significant?** (Yes/No)	**Comments** (e.g., chemical name, amounts if known, functions involved in operation/handling)
DynaClean 2000 used in chemical treating	(Bath technician)	Yes	Two 800-gallon tanks. Industrial but not hazardous chemical (label says strong irritant).
DynaFoam 350 used in chemical treatment	(Bath technician)	Yes	Three 55-gallon drums. Label says strong oxidizer.
Water used in chemical treatment	(Bath technician)	Yes	Operator says use about 5000 gallons per week.
(Maintenance)	Waste sludge in bottom of tanks generated during chemical cleaning	Yes	Pumped out about 1/month. Will need to review manifest for amount and characterization.
(Bath technician)	Indoor air fumes from chemical treatment	Yes	Operators say air is frequently tested— safe, but annoying. Many complaints.
(Production supervisor)	Two used and obsolete computers in production office	No	Still work, could be donated or recycled.

Figure 4.13 Partially completed checklist.

members provided additional information in the comments section. They used the open column next to each aspect to list the functions involved.

The team has now completed its review for potentially significant aspects and has returned to the conference room. The next section presents one process for determining the significance of the aspects the teams identified.

DETERMINING SIGNIFICANT ENVIRONMENTAL ASPECTS

The teams are back. Depending on the number of environmental aspects identified during the review, the management representative now has two choices. If the team found a moderate number of aspects, say between 50 and 100, the management representative can group the aspects into common categories and enter them in the Environmental Planning Workbook to prepare for the significance determination. This will probably take two or three hours, so it is best to release the team while this is done and reconvene the next morning to conduct the assessment. If the team found a large number of aspects, say 200 to 300, then it is best to have the team go through an affinity process first to help organize the findings. This will take about an hour.

Organizing a Large Number of Aspects

In order to get through the significance determination in a reasonable amount of time, the team needs to consolidate its aspects from 200 to 300 to no more than 30 to 50 common aspects. This is easier to do than it may at first appear. The first step is to ask each team to write its aspects on 3 × 5 cards or sticky notes, one aspect per card. (I like to use 3 × 5 sticky notes. If you are using sticky notes, make sure you use the kind that will not fall off the wall during the affinity process.) Not all information from the checklist needs to be placed on the card; instead, only the aspect and its associated activity or process need to be identified, along with the location if this is not apparent from the activity cited. This will take perhaps 10 or 15 minutes. Once this is complete, an affinity process is used to organize the aspects into common groupings and to eliminate duplicates found by all the teams.

The affinity process is a quality-related tool that works for any situation where it is necessary to organize a large number of ideas or to bring order out of chaos. The cards or sticky notes are randomly laid out on a large table or stuck to the wall in a random fashion. The initial step may look something like Figure 4.14, multiplied by 10.

The next step is for the team to move the cards into columns of natural groupings. The items in the groupings should be related in one or more

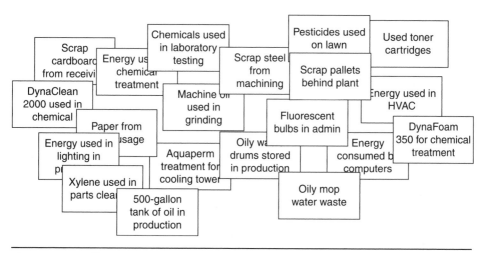

Figure 4.14 Affinity process—initial steps.

ways. The affinity process is a way to use the synergy of the team to recognize these groupings. If the CFT has more than seven people, it's best to use subteams of four or five, with each team getting five minutes to rearrange the cards. The key is to do this silently—no talking during the organization of the cards. During the process, duplicate cards are stacked together (or stuck over each other if using sticky notes) to further reduce the number of aspects. For example, all the teams probably cited "energy used in lighting"; these all make up one aspect, so these cards would be stacked together. The team can also set aside cards that members feel are obviously not significant, such as "electricity for floor fan."

Once all the team members are satisfied with the groupings, talking is allowed. The team then comes up with header cards that best describe the items in each grouping. Depending on the number of cards, groupings, and the strength of the relationships between items in the groupings, the team can choose to assess individual aspects (as represented by the cards) or entire groupings (as represented by the header card) for significance. An example of the result of an affinity process might appear as shown in Figure 4.15.

The goal is to reduce the large number of identified aspects, which might be as many as 300 to 400, down to a more manageable number of 30 to 50 for significance determination. The largest number of aspects I have initially worked with was about 300. By eliminating duplicates and by using the affinity process, the CFT was able to reduce this large number of aspects to approximately 40 in about an hour. Aspects can be evaluated as a group if their environmental impacts are similar and, most importantly, if

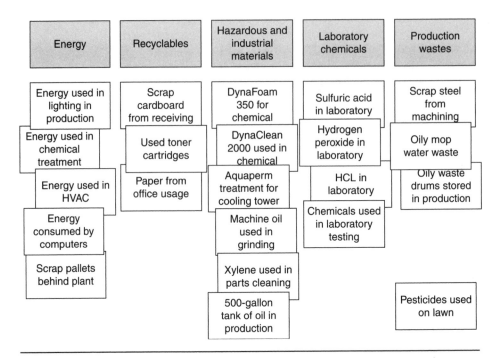

Figure 4.15   Results of the affinity process for potentially significant environmental aspects.

they would be controlled as a group were they to be deemed significant. As an example, consider the energy grouping in Figure 4.15, which includes energy used in lighting, for computers, for production equipment, and for heating, ventilation, and cooling (HVAC). Taken separately, these items may not appear especially significant unless the company is in an industry that consumes very large amounts of power. Taken together, however, their overall impact on the environment can be and is significant. Just as important, these items will probably all be controlled through the development of a set of energy conservation guidelines that will include practices for each of the listed sources of energy consumption. It makes sense to assess these items for significance as a group. Similar arguments could be made for the items under the recyclables (recycling program guidelines) and laboratory chemicals (chemical management program) groupings.

Generally, it is best to assess production-related hazardous materials and wastes individually because the volumes, toxicity, and methods of control can vary widely. Any items that do not naturally fit into any one grouping, such as the pesticides, should be kept separate and assessed individually.

PERFORMING THE ASSESSMENT

The next step is to transfer the aspects to the spreadsheet to allow for assessment. Each item to be assessed should be entered into its own column on the spreadsheet. The results should look something like Figure 4.16. A blank template has been provided on the CD accompanying this book. Open up the file titled "Environmental Planning Workbook" and select the first tab. It may take about an hour to transfer the aspects to the spreadsheet, so the management representative may want to give the CFT a break or schedule the assessment for the first thing the next morning. During this time the purchasing department representative can cross-check the items identified against the materials and chemicals purchased to ensure nothing significant was overlooked during the review.

Note that information relating to the area(s) where the aspect is found, the activities associated with each aspect, and the functions involved in handling or controlling the aspect (or activity) have also been identified on the worksheet. This information will help in the determination of significance, but even more importantly, it will provide the context for establishing operational controls if the aspect is determined to be significant. Some aspects will be common to all areas, such as energy consumption, while others will be restricted to specific activities or areas. Also keep in mind that you can insert notes for any cell in Microsoft Excel, so you can expand on the information shown in the spreadsheet. As an example, the management representative may want to add important information about the DynaFoam 350 found on the label or in the MSDS for the chemical, such as "categorized as a hazardous material for toxicity by OSHA (Occupational Safety and Health Administration)."

Once the spreadsheet has been populated with the results of the initial environmental review, the CFT can assess the aspects for significance. The criteria established earlier will form the basis for this review. A note detailing the operational definition of each criterion should be inserted into each criterion's cell, as shown in Figure 4.9, to facilitate the review. As an alternative, the criteria can be printed out and a copy provided to each team member to use as the aspects are evaluated.

I recommend setting up for the assessment by obtaining a projector and a laptop and displaying the spreadsheet on a screen so that all team members can see the progress being made as the worksheet is completed. The management representative or other team member can enter the rankings as they are being developed. You should also have the last 12 months of waste manifests and the organization's MSDS book available for the assessment. These documents will come in handy when questions come up during the

Environmental Aspects	Energy	Recyclables	DynaFoam 350	DynaClean 2000	Xylene	Laboratory Chemicals	Product Design and Development
Criteria weighting 9 - high correlation to criteria 3 - moderate correlation to criteria 1 - low correlation to criteria							
Department or Area	All areas	All areas	Production	Production	Production	Testing Laboratory	Engineering
Activity associated with aspect 1	Lighting	Scrap cardboard	Chemical Treatment	Chemical Treatment	Parts cleaning	Material testing	Product Design
Activity associated with aspect 2	HVAC	Used toner cartridges	Material storage and handling	Material storage and handling	Material storage and handling	Chemical storage and handling	
Activity associated with aspect 3	Computers, Production equip.	Scrap paper	Disposal	Disposal	Disposal	Chemical disposal	
Activity associated with aspect 4		Aluminum cans					
Functions involved with aspect	All employees	All employees	Bath Techs & Material Handlers	Bath Techs & Material Handlers	Prod. Operators & Material Handlers	Lab. Techs	Design Engineers
Significance Criteria							
Hazardous or regulated material or waste?							
Influence the environmental design of our products?							
Consumes significant natural resources (includes energy)?							
Present a high opportunity for source reduction, reuse or recycling?							
Significant community or employee concern?							
Total Score							
Significant?							
Formally controlled, although not significant							

Figure 4.16   Entering aspect information into the Environmental Planning Workbook.

review. If the organization has an environmental specialist or a consultant, it will be very helpful to have this individual attend so that he or she can answer some of the questions the team may have during the assessment.

To conduct the significance determination, the management representative should guide the team through the assessment of each listed aspect using the criteria developed prior to the review. If the team was successful in the affinity process, no more than about 40 items should have to be assessed. Each aspect is evaluated against each criterion and given a numerical ranking relative to the correlation between the aspect and the criterion being discussed. I recommend using the 1-3-9 scale to provide more separation between the vital few and the trivial many. An assignment of 1 indicates a minor correlation with the criteria, a 3 indicates a moderate correlation to the criteria, and a 9 indicates a high correlation to the criteria. More specific guidance is provided by the operational definitions previously developed. An assignment of 0 indicates no correlation.

During the assessment the team will struggle a little bit with some of the criteria that are by their very nature somewhat subjective. As an example, the criteria that evaluate the aspects' consumption of natural resources are a relative ranking; it is not typically possible to assign absolute amounts or volumes to be used when assigning numerical rankings. The team must keep in mind that these are relative rankings, where "relative" means relative to the other resources that the organization consumes (does this aspect represent a small, moderate, or large usage of natural resources?). The same considerations apply to the criteria for opportunity for source reduction, reuse or recycling, and to a lesser extent, the influence on environmental design of the organization's products. Assuming that opportunity is allowed for discussion, the team can normally come up with a basis for the numerical rankings. An example of a team's assessment of some of the aspects identified during the initial environmental review is shown in Figure 4.17.

As an example, the CFT would assign a 0 ranking to energy for its correlation to the first criterion because it is not a material or a waste. Similarly, the CFT would probably assign a 0 for energy's influence on product design because the organization's energy consumption will not be a major consideration in the design of its own products. For the consumption of natural resources (including energy) criterion, the team would obviously assign a 9 (high correlation). Similarly the team may also consider that the organization has quite a bit of room to reduce the amount of energy it consumes, because it has never followed any kind of energy conservation program in the past. Therefore, the team also gives energy a ranking of 9 for this criterion. Finally, the team notes that many employees have questioned the energy efficiency of the building (especially the drafty doors and windows in the winter), and the local utility has been pushing energy efficiency in the

Criteria weighting
9 - high correlation to criteria
3 - moderate correlation to criteria
1 - low correlation to criteria

Environmental Aspects	Energy	Recyclables	DynaFoam 350	DynaClean 2000	Xylene	Laboratory Chemicals	Product Design and Development
Department or Area	All areas	All areas	Production	Production	Production	Testing Laboratory	Engineering / Product Design
Activity associated with aspect 1	Lighting	Scrap cardboard	Chemical Treatment	Chemical Treatment	Parts cleaning	Material testing	Product Design
Activity associated with aspect 2	HVAC	Used toner cartridges	Material storage and handling	Material storage and handling	Material storage and handling	Chemical storage and handling	
Activity associated with aspect 3	Computers	Scrap paper	Disposal	Disposal	Disposal	Chemical disposal	
Activity associated with aspect 4	Production equip.	Aluminum cans					
Functions involved with aspect	All employees	All employees	Bath Techs & Material Handlers	Bath Techs & Material Handlers	Prod. Operators & Material Handlers	Lab. Techs	Design Engineers
Significance Criteria							
Hazardous or regulated material or waste?	0	1	9	1	9	9	9
Influence the environmental design of our products?	0	0	0	0	0	0	9
Consumes significant natural resources (includes energy)?	9	3	0	0	0	0	3
Present a high opportunity for source reduction, reuse or recycling?	9	9	3	3	9	3	3
Significant community or employee concern?	3	1	3	0	3	1	0
Total Score	21	14	15	4	21	13	25
Significant?	Y	Y	Y	N	Y	N	Y
Formally controlled, although not significant	Y	Y	Y	Y	Y	Y	Y

Figure 4.17   Example of significance determination results.

community in an effort to keep energy commodity expenses down. Therefore, the team assigns energy a ranking of 3 in the last criterion. The same kind of analysis is repeated for each aspect on the list.

The greatest difficulty during the review comes from the analysis of materials and wastes, especially when the team ranks them for the first criterion (is it a hazardous or industrial waste or otherwise regulated?). Quite simply, the team may not know. This is where an environmental specialist can really help. If one is present during the assessment, he or she can quickly provide the answer. If one is not available, a review of the MSDS data (for materials) or waste manifests (for wastes) can provide insight into the regulated nature of the material or waste. This is why these tools should be available to the team during the review.

Another important consideration is that the review and significance determination should be repeatable. In other words, if a different team were to rank the same aspects using the same criteria, would they come to roughly the same conclusions? Consistency is important because the environmental aspects must be kept up to date, and you cannot be constantly changing the rules. Because some of the rankings are subjective and are the result of discussion among the team members, how do you obtain such consistency? I recommend inserting comments into the cell for any ranking where the value assigned is not intuitively obvious. By inserting the note, the team can explain its rationale for giving the aspect the ranking that it did. When done in this manner, the spreadsheet becomes a complete record of not only the review but also the assessment for significance. An example of such a comment is shown in Figure 4.18.

On occasion it may appear that some aspects are getting the benefit of double weightings on some criteria. For example, refer back to Figure 4.17 and the ranking for product design and development. This aspect received a ranking of 9 for the first criterion because the team felt that the product design greatly influenced the nature and amounts of hazardous materials needed to manufacture the product, and the team also gave the aspect a 9 for the second criterion because it highly influences (and in fact controls) the environmental design of the product. Is this unfair? Not really. The overall high ranking that this aspect receives is simply recognition that product design significantly influences several of our significance criteria, which in turn were developed from our policy commitments. In essence, controlling our product design activities helps us achieve several of our environmental policy commitments, so the high ranking is warranted.

Once the rankings are complete, the total points given to each aspect are summed and entered into the total score row. These totals provide guidance as to what should be considered significant and therefore subject to special controls and monitoring. In our example, the team decided to use a

Environmental Aspects	Energy	Recyclables	DynaFoam 350	DynaClean 2000
Criteria weighting 9 - high correlation to criteria 3 - moderate correlation to criteria 1 - low correlation to criteria				
Department or Area	All areas	All areas	Production	Production
Activity associated with aspect 1	Lighting	Scrap cardboard	Chemical Treatment	Chemical Treatment
Activity associated with aspect 2	HVAC	Used toner cartridges		
Activity associated with aspect 3	Computers	Scrap paper		
Activity associated with aspect 4	Production equip.	Aluminum cans		
Functions involved with aspect	All employees	All employees	Bath Techs & Material Handlers	Bath Techs & Material Handlers
Significance Criteria				
Hazardous or regulated material or waste?	0	1	9	1
Influence the environmental design of our products?	0	0		0
Consumes significant natural resources (includes energy)?	9		9	0
Present a high opportunity for source reduction, reuse or recycling?	9			3
Significant community or employee concern?	3			0
Total Score	21	14	15	4
Significant?	Y	Y	Y	N

Note: The team feels that there is great opportunity to reduce the amount of energy used in the facility through conservation.

Figure 4.18 Using notes to explain significance rankings.

threshold ranking of 15 or greater to determine what is significant and what is not. Note that these are guidelines only, and some aspects that do not add up to 15 may still be considered significant by the team, while some that are slightly above 15 may not. The note, shown in Figures 4.19 and 4.20, explains this and simply requires the team to insert a comment into the cell of any aspect classified differently than the guidelines suggest.

There is also a row where the team can identify aspects that are formally controlled, even though they are not considered significant environmental aspects. Examples may include laboratory chemicals, if the company has such small volumes that they are not a significant threat to the environment. Even so, the company will still want to have a chemical management plan, if for no other reason than to protect its laboratory workers. In this example, a Y would be inserted in this cell for laboratory chemicals. Another example may be recyclables such as waste paper and aluminum cans, where these did not meet the criteria for significant, but the company still feels that it is important to establish a formal recycling program to send the right message on environmental stewardship. The difference between designating an aspect as significant as opposed to calling it insignificant but still formally controlled lies in the setting of objectives and targets and in environmental performance monitoring. Significant environmental aspects are subject to performance monitoring and measurement, and they will be favored during the setting of environmental objectives and targets. Insignificant but still formally controlled aspects need not be so tightly monitored, and they may not be subject to focused improvement projects to the same level as significant aspects.

Once all the rankings are complete, significance is determined, and comments are inserted, the team has completed the initial assessment portion of the EMS. I say "initial" because the information must be maintained as the organization's processes, facilities, and methods change. For this reason I recommend inserting a field in the spreadsheet to show the date of the last update. Later we will discuss keeping the information updated. I also like to bold the environmental aspects determined to be significant in order to make them stand out.

Present a high opportunity for source reduction, reuse, or recycling?	9	9	3
Significant community or employee concern?	3	1	3
Total score	In general, any aspect totaling more than 15 is considered significant. Exceptions can be made, but the rationale for the exception should be explained by inserting a comment into the Significant cell for the aspect.		15
Significant?			Y
Formally controlled, although not significant			
Date last reviewed and updated			

Figure 4.19   Determination of significance.

Department or Area	All areas	All areas	Production	Production	Production	Testing Laboratory	Engineering
Activity associated with aspect 1	Lighting	Scrap cardboard	Chemical Treatment	Chemical Treatment	Parts cleaning	Material testing	Product Design
Activity associated with aspect 2	HVAC	Used toner cartridges					
Activity associated with aspect 3	Computers	Scrap paper					
Activity associated with aspect 4	Production equip.	Aluminum cans					
Functions involved with aspect	All employees	All employees	Bath Techs & Material Handlers	Bath Techs & Material Handlers	Prod. Operators & Material Handlers	Lab. Techs	Design Engineers
Significance Criteria							
Hazardous or regulated material or waste?	0	1	9	1	9	9	9
Influence the environmental design of our products?	0	0					9
Consumes significant natural resources (includes energy)?	9	3	0	0	0	0	3
Present a high opportunity for source reduction, reuse or recycling?	9	9					3
Significant community or employee concern?	3	1					0
Total Score	21	14					25
Significant?	Y	Y					Y
Formally controlled, although not significant							
Date last reviewed and updated							

Comment box (pointing to a Production aspect's Significant? cell): Although < 15, the team considered that this aspect should be catergorized as significant because of the organization's commitment to source reduction and the need to get everyone involved in environmental improvement. It was also noted that recycling and reuse concepts learned at work will also be transferred to employees residence in some cases, leveraging this aspect's importance.

Figure 4.20   Commenting on an exception to the guidelines for determining significance.

The time needed to complete this assessment varies, but generally it can be completed in three to four hours if the team was organized and was able to condense the number of items to be evaluated to no more than about 40. Before moving to the next step of assigning operational controls, we will briefly review some other methods used to determine significance.

OTHER METHODS FOR DETERMINING SIGNIFICANCE

Methods other than the one described in this book can be used to determine significance of environmental aspects. We will discuss two of the more common ones.

Severity × Likelihood of Occurrence

The severity × likelihood of occurrence approach, derived from the failure mode and effects analysis (FMEA) and favored by organizations that have experience in FMEA, assigns numerical rankings to each aspect on the basis of the severity of its potential environmental impacts and the likelihood that a release, emission, or incident will occur that would result in the impact. The combined score of severity × occurrence provides a numerical sum that is compared against a target level for significance, similar to the approach presented in this book.

Although I am well versed in FMEA and highly endorse its use in other applications, I do not recommend this method for several reasons. First, the severity criteria must be broken down into numerous subcategories to be useful because the very term "severity" is subjective. Severity means one thing when you are considering natural resource consumption, and something very different when you are considering chemical toxicity, persistence, or reactivity. These subclassifications can become very complicated and make the significance determination more difficult and time consuming. Second, obtaining data on the likelihood of occurrence can be very difficult and often turns out to be wildly speculative. The third reason is that it is more difficult to relate the severity criteria directly to the environmental policy commitments. While it can be done through the subclassifications, the linkage is not as transparent as the way demonstrated in this book.

Simple Yes/No

In the simple yes/no method, the criteria are rephrased to require a simple yes or no response. For example, instead of ranking correlation to the criteria on a 1-3-9 scale, the question, is the aspect a hazardous material or regulated material or waste? is answered by a simple yes or no. In most such systems any aspect that had a yes response to any of the criteria would be considered significant. The problem with this method is that, quite simply, almost everything will be classified as significant. An upper limit for most EMSs, in terms of the number of significant aspects that can be reasonably controlled, is about 20. Many end up with between 10 and 15. Using the yes/no approach would probably result in over 30, which for most organizations would simply be too many to effectively control. Remember, it is better to more aggressively control and improve the vital few than to attempt less aggressive control of the trivial many.

Other variations are also possible, such as substituting low, moderate, and high for the 1-3-9 rankings used in this book's examples. There are many approaches; the key is to find one that makes sense, doesn't require an overwhelming amount of analysis, and provides a reasonable and consistent rationale for determining significance. A section of our completed workbook is shown in Figure 4.21.

IDENTIFYING OPERATIONAL CONTROLS

The next step after identifying the significant aspects is to assign or develop operational controls. In many, if not most, cases, controls already exist. In others, controls will need to be improved or developed to provide safeguards against any adverse environmental impact. *It is important to note that, in general, the operational controls are applied to the activities that generate, consume, or use the aspect, and not to the aspect itself.* For example, we cannot control energy, but we can control our energy consumption by establishing guidelines and criteria (that is, controls) on the types of lighting used, on the use of advanced power management features in computers and thermostat settings, and on the proper securing of equipment and lighting when they are not in use. Similarly, we will not control the DynaFoam 350; rather, we will control its storage, handling, use, and disposal. This is why the CFT was directed to record the activity associated with the aspect during the initial environmental review.

As a first step in establishing operational controls, the management representative should populate the second worksheet in the Environmental Planning Workbook with the aspects determined to be significant from the first sheet. This can be accomplished by a simple copy-and-paste operation and should not take more than a few minutes. In addition, the real or potential impacts of these aspects should also be shown. Once this is done, the team is ready to define current methods used to control the activities or to identify new controls that will need to be developed. An example of the worksheet and these initial steps is shown in Figure 4.22.

Environmental Aspects

Criteria weighting
9 - high correlation to criteria
3 - moderate correlation to criteria
1 - low correlation to criteria

	Energy	Recyclables	DynaFoam 350	DynaClean 2000	Xylene	Testing Laboratory Chemicals	Product Design and Development
Department or Area	All areas	All areas	Production	Production	Production	Production	Engineering
Activity associated with aspect 1	Lighting	Scrap cardboard	Chemical Treatment	Chemical Treatment	Parts cleaning	Material testing	Product Design
Activity associated with aspect 2	HVAC	Used toner cartridges	Material storage and handling	Material storage and handling	Material storage and handling	Chemical storage and handling	
Activity associated with aspect 3	Computers	Scrap paper	Disposal	Disposal	Disposal	Chemical disposal	
Activity associated with aspect 4	Production equip.	Aluminum cans					
Functions involved with aspect	All employees	All employees	Bath Techs & Material Handlers	Bath Techs & Material Handlers	Prod. Operators & Material Handlers	Lab. Techs	Design Engineers
Significance Criteria							
Hazardous or regulated material or waste?	0	1	9	1	9	9	9
Influence the environmental design of our products?	0	0	0	0	0	0	9
Consumes significant natural resources (includes energy)?	9	3	0	0	0	0	3
Present a high opportunity for source reduction, reuse or recycling?	9	9	3	3	9	3	3
Significant community or employee concern?	3	1	3	0	3	1	1
Total Score	21	14	15	4	21	13	25
Significant?	Y	Y	Y	N	Y	N	Y
Formally controlled, although not significant				Y		Y	
Date last reviewed and updated	4/19/2006						

Figure 4.21   Documentation of the environmental review and significance determination.

Significant Aspect	Environmental Impact	Procedural Controls	Mechanical and system controls	Subcontractor	Maintenance
Energy	Natural resource depletion, greenhouse gas emissions, acid rain				
Recyclables	Natural resource depletion, landfill usage				
DynaFoam 350	Groundwater contamination, harm to wildlife				
Xylene	Groundwater contamination, harm to wildlife, human health effects				
Product Design and Development	Natural resource depletion, greenhouse gas emissions, groundwater contamination, landfill usage				

Method of Control

X = Primary method of addressing aspect
O = Secondary method of addressing aspect

Figure 4.22 Environmental planning worksheet for identifying operational controls.

The next step is to list the controls used to manage the activities associated with the significant environmental aspects in the categories established in the workbook. In general, the following types of controls are normally used to establish operational control:

- *Procedural controls*—Procedures and policies such as material and waste handling procedures, permits, energy conservation guidelines, recycling program guidelines, chemical management plans, and the identification of designated storage locations and controls all fall into this category. This is the primary type of control for many of the activities associated with significant environmental aspects. Nondocumented but well understood procedures could also be cited, but only if there is confidence in operator compliance to the policies.

- *Mechanical and system controls*—These include things like secondary containment, stack monitoring and alarm systems, treatment facilities, and other forms of engineered safeguards. These types of systems are normally superior to procedural controls in that they do not rely exclusively on human intervention.

- *Subcontractor controls*—The organization may rely on outside vendors or service providers for some of its controls. Examples include the use of an environmental waste disposal firm to characterize and dispose of the firm's hazardous and industrial wastes and the reliance on an HVAC subcontractor to properly capture and reclaim the refrigerant in the organization's HVAC system.

- *Maintenance*—This is another form of control for some significant aspects. Periodic inspections of tank, piping, and system integrity may be an important element of the organization's control of its liquid hazardous and industrial wastes. Similarly, periodic energy surveys of the organization's facilities using thermography would be equivalent to a maintenance check that would form part of the control of the company's energy consumption.

An example of some of the operational controls planned for our sample company is shown in Figure 4.23. A control may be used to address multiple environmental aspects, and any given aspect may have several controls associated with it. This provides defense in depth and helps ensure that adverse environmental impacts are avoided. In the figure, an *X* indicates that the method is the primary method of control for the aspect, while an *O* means it is a secondary form of control.

Every significant environmental aspect should have at least one primary means of control. In many cases the organization already has some of the procedures or plans. In these cases, carefully review the content of the

X = Primary method of addressing aspect
O = Secondary method of addressing aspect

Significant Aspect	Environmental Impact	Energy Conservation Guidelines	Recycling Procedure and Program	Material and Waste Handling Procedure	Quality Planning Checklists	D/E Training Program	Chemical Management Plan	SWPPP and Permit	Secondary containment	Designated storage	Motion detectors	Automatic thermostats	Interlocked filtered hood ventilation	Safety/Source Disposal Inc.	Annual tank integrity inspection	Semi-annual facility thermography inspection
	Method of Control	**Procedural Controls**							**Mechanical and system controls**					**Subcontractor**	**Maintenance**	
Energy	Natural resource depletion, greenhouse gas emissions, acid rain	X									O	O				O
Recyclables	Natural resource depletion, landfill usage		X													
DynaFoam 350	Groundwater contamination, harm to wildlife			X				O	O	O				O	O	
Xylene	Groundwater contamination, harm to wildlife, human health effects			X				O	O	O			O	O		
Product Design and Development	Natural resource depletion, greenhouse gas emissions, groundwater contamination, landfill usage				O	X										
Storm Water Runoff	Groundwater and surface water contamination, harm to wildlife			O				X								
Chemical Handling and Disposal	Groundwater and surface water contamination, harmful health effects			O			X			O				O	O	

Figure 4.23   Example environmental planning worksheet for identifying operational controls.

existing document. Does it adequately address the environmental aspects of concern? Could it be modified to include them if it does not? Are the procedures properly structured and organized considering the users of the document? For example, if the primary function of the material handlers is associated with hazardous or industrial materials and wastes, it makes sense to combine the controls for both materials and wastes into one procedure. This way the material handlers have one procedure to train on and one procedure to reference, rather than multiple separate instructions. Of course, if you have just one procedure, that procedure must be properly structured, and information must be easy to find. If, on the other hand, material handlers handled all the materials while the maintenance department handled and controlled all wastes, it may make more sense to develop separate procedures for the control of materials and wastes.

Once these controls are identified, the next step is to verify existing controls or to commence development of new ones where needed. The development of these controls will probably represent the longest block of time required to deploy the ISO 14001 system. Even so, all the procedures should be drafted, reviewed, and issued within one or two months of completion of the initial environmental review. The electronic spreadsheet on the CD has a column that allows the team to indicate the status of developing operational controls using a familiar red-yellow-green format. The team can use this to monitor its progress in developing these controls.

IDENTIFYING ENVIRONMENTAL METRICS

The team also needs to define the measurements that will be used to monitor the organization's performance in controlling its significant environmental aspects. Each significant aspect should have at least one measure to monitor whether the controls are working. Developing these metrics is one of the most challenging elements of putting together an effective EMS. While it is easy to come up with a metric for just about any aspect, identifying measurements that will be meaningful, comparable, and reasonable to obtain is not.

For example, most organizations cite energy consumption as a significant environmental aspect. But how do you measure your performance in limiting or reducing your energy consumption? Easy, you say—simply measure the number of kilowatt-hours (kWh) consumed each month. But what happens if you have to add a third shift to keep up with rising customer demand for your product? Despite solid action to conserve and reduce your energy consumption, you will probably still see a rise in your energy usage due to the increased production.

Okay, you think, we'll simply adjust our usage by dividing by the production hours that we worked. You might instead use the amount of product manufactured, or the sales figure for the month. This is an example of normalizing, or adjusting the measurement of interest by some unit of activity, in this case production volume. Normalizing is often required in order to compare month-to-month or year-to-year trends, which is critical for monitoring environmental performance improvement. Even if we find a suitable unit to normalize to (that is, production activity, volume, or sales), we still have the complicating factor of seasonal and monthly variations in temperature, which will increase or decrease the demand for energy required to heat or cool the facilities. If we use monthly sales as our normalizing factor, we would also have the added complexity of price fluctuations for our product. Although monitoring our gross energy usage based on our utility bill and normalized for activity provides a useful picture of our efforts to conserve, it is not a complete picture, because it can be affected by so many things. At best, it should be used for long-term performance monitoring (trends) and not short-term operational monitoring.

Another strategy is to supplement the monitoring of overall energy usage with behavioral measurements. By "behavioral measurements," we mean monitoring of the behaviors we seek to instill in the workforce. To conserve energy, we would like our employees to turn off the lights when they are not in their office, turn off their computers at the end of the day, utilize the advanced power management features on their computers and monitors (the settings that power down monitors and hard drives after a certain period of inactivity), and keep office thermostats to a reasonable range that provides comfort without wasting a significant amount of energy. These controls would be defined in our energy conservation guidelines that all employees are trained in. We would also like production employees to turn off equipment that is not in use and when it is safe to do so. These are behaviors, and the extent to which our employees exhibit these behaviors will directly affect the amount of energy we consume.

The question is, can we monitor how well these behaviors are exhibited in the workplace? If the organization has a security guard, it may be possible to have the guard note any instances when lights or computers were left on after hours. The management representative may instead assign an individual to do this check once a week on a random basis. This responsibility could be rotated around the office so that employees remain aware of the need to save energy. Random sampling of advanced power management settings on computers and monitors could be added to checklists used for internal audits. Exceptions (instances where lights were left on, thermostats were set too high, and so on) would be reported and tracked to indicate the need to provide additional awareness training or the opportunity to celebrate improvements in behaviors that led to improved environmental performance.

In addition, we might also monitor our performance in replacing energy-wasting lighting with high-efficiency lamps and our efforts to install motion sensors that turn lights on and off in areas like restrooms and conference rooms. In essence, we have developed a portfolio of metrics that includes both the operational (or tactical) metrics that drive performance and the strategic indicators (overall energy usage) that provide long-term evidence of results.

The third tab on the Environmental Planning Workbook provides a methodology for the team to develop these metrics and to summarize other important information that will be useful for the control of the EMS. An excerpt from the workbook is shown in Figure 4.24.

The columns for measurement type assist the team in developing the system of metrics. The categories and their application are:

- *Amount generated, used, or emitted:* Appropriate for most types of materials, wastes, or resources. Most commonly used type of environmental performance metric, focuses on results versus actions and behaviors that drive results. It may be a very important metric for conditionally exempt small-quantity generators and small-quantity generators who need to carefully monitor the amount of waste disposed of to ensure they do not move up into the next category of waste generator with all of its additional controls, training, and monitoring.

- *Amount in inventory or storage:* This metric is used primarily for hazardous and industrial materials where the focus is on minimizing the amount of such material stored and consumed. This can be especially important for materials with shelf lives, where maintaining a large inventory of material inevitably results in the need to discard expired material. It can also be important for materials that are highly flammable, reactive, or could otherwise create serious problems in an emergency such as a flood or fire.

- *Number of occurrences:* Appropriate when performance is driven by behaviors. Examples include energy conservation, recycling, and reuse. Also necessary for those aspects with regulatory reporting requirements (spills, incidents, and so on). In an effective EMS, monitoring for occurrences of incidents will show zero.

- *Level or concentration:* This metric may be appropriate when the control of the aspect involves reuse, such as maximizing the use of a chemical solution (and thereby reducing the amount of waste

Significant Aspects	Amount generated/used/emitted	Amount in inventory/storage	Number of Occurrences	Level or concentration	Condition or Integrity	Metric	Specific metric	Frequency of Monitoring	Frequency of Reporting	Regulatory Report	Report Due	Limit or trigger point
Energy	X						Kw-Hr/Production Hours	Monthly	Quarterly	No		
			X				Weekly environmental patrol	Weekly	Monthly	No		
Recyclables	X						Volume recycled-paper, cardboard	Quarterly	Quarterly	No		
			X				Weekly environmental patrol	Weekly	Monthly	No		
	X						Volume consumed/Prod. Hours	Monthly	Quarterly	No		
		X					Amount in inventory	Monthly	Quarterly	Yes	March	10,000 lbs
DynaFoam 350					X		Preventive Maint. completion	Internal Audit	Annually	Yes	March	
	X						Volume disposed of/Prod. Hours	Quarterly	Quarterly	No	March	100 kg
					X		Preventive Maint. completion	Internal Audit	Annually	Yes		
Xylene		X					Amount in inventory	Monthly	Quarterly	Yes	March	
	X						Percent recyclable, end-of-life	Each launch	Annually	No		
Product Design and Development	X						Percent hazardous materials	Each launch	Annually	No		
Storm Water Runoff			X				Number of incidents	Annually	Annually	Yes	Each Occur.	
			X				No. of occurrences improper outdoor storage	Monthly	Monthly	No		
Chemical Handling and Disposal		X					Amount in inventory	Monthly	Quarterly	No		

Figure 4.24 Environmental performance metrics.

generated) by filtration and monitoring of chemical concentration as opposed to automatic disposal after a certain number of hours. It is also commonly used for monitoring air emissions for certain types of pollutants.

- *Condition or integrity:* When the operational control involves the use of tanks, alarms, piping systems, and the like, monitoring to ensure the condition or integrity of these safeguards is warranted. This is normally accomplished through the preventive maintenance system.

The specific metric is shown in the next column. Note that each metric gets its own row. The final columns provide space to record how often the monitoring is performed, how frequently the results are reported to top management, whether there are any regulatory reports associated with the monitoring, and if so, when the reports are due. These last two columns, along with the final column, "Limit or trigger point," can help the management representative stay in compliance with regulatory requirements.

It is very important that the planned monitoring be initiated as soon as possible. Inevitably the team will find that some of the metrics are just too hard to capture or do not really provide meaningful information for one reason or another. The team should expect that some changes will be needed to the system of metrics. The key is to identify these changes early so that a consistent basis for evaluating long-term environmental performance can be established as soon as possible. I've seen some companies change the basis for their environmental metrics every few months and never establish the ability to evaluate long-term performance. Don't let this happen to you.

REVIEWING AND DEVELOPING EMERGENCY PREPAREDNESS AND RESPONSE PROCEDURES

Another action that should be taken during the EMS design phase is to review and, where necessary, modify (or develop) emergency preparedness and response procedures. The following plans should be included:

- Fire and general emergency plan

- Evacuation plan

- Storm water pollution prevention plan

- Spill prevention, countermeasures, and controls plan

- Spill response procedures

- Any other site-specific plans unique to the company, industry, or state in which the company operates

In most Western countries, including the United States, there are regulatory requirements associated with these plans and procedures. For the most part, these procedures already exist. At this point the team should review these procedures and plans to verify their currentness, their content, and their utility in addressing any new significant environmental aspects that may not have been recognized when the plans were developed.

As an example, one company I worked with identified the existence of a number of mercury switches in its production machinery during its initial environmental review. The company planned to replace these switches but knew it would take some time to do so. It already had a general spill procedure, but that procedure only addressed spills of solvents and oil. It subsequently modified this procedure to include actions in the event of breakage of one of these mercury switches. The information on how to appropriately respond to this type of event was available on the state department of environmental quality Web site, but it required some searching to find it. Subsequently, a mercury switch was in fact broken, resulting in a spill of solid mercury. Because the company had already recognized the potential for such an event and modified its spill procedure to include the appropriate response, the spill was handled quickly and safely and without the need for outside resources.

Keep in mind the title of this clause in ISO 14001—environmental *preparedness* and response. In my experience most procedures and plans are heavy on the response and light on the preparedness. The design of your EMS provides you with an opportunity to review and possibly improve the prevention/preparedness portion of your plans and procedures.

Finally, make sure your procedures and plans reflect current contacts, responsibilities, and phone numbers. It is almost a given that most such procedures will be out of date. I've audited many a company in which the individual listed as the emergency response coordinator no longer worked there. These plans must be regularly reviewed and updated.

DEVELOPING COMMON SUPPORT PROCESSES

The remainder of this chapter focuses on the design and development of the common supporting processes needed to maintain and improve the EMS. Those with existing QMSs already in place will find that many of these processes have already been developed and can be used either as a template for their environmental procedures or as a place to put the expanded controls needed to manage the EMS common elements. I recommend developing integrated processes for common elements wherever possible because it normally results in less confusion, better systems, and less effort to maintain, compared with separate processes for the quality, environmental, or health and safety management systems.

Document and Record Control Process

Chapter 2 presented the requirements relating to document and record control. It was noted that the ISO 14001 standard requires only minimal documentation, and a discussion was presented to help guide the organization in its determination of where and when written procedures should be developed. It is important that documented environmental procedures, where developed, be adequately controlled. Usually, the first step in establishing control is to develop a master listing of the procedures, instructions, forms, and other documents that form the basis for the EMS. This is usually called the master list. An example of a simple master list is shown in Figure 4.25.

The example shows the different categories of documents and the information on how each is controlled. The numbering system shown is very simple and can be used with systems that do not have many procedures. In this format, ESP stands for environmental system procedure, ESI for environmental system instructions, and ESF for environmental system form. Documents are numbered sequentially starting with 001. External documents use a control number as assigned by the agency that issued them (for example, the permit numbers in this example). Many other formats are possible, but the important thing is for each document to have a unique identifier, typically by both name and number but sometimes by name only, to ensure documents are not confused.

The second column includes the current revision date of the document. This is probably the most important piece of information on the master list, as it can be used to ensure that the most current (and therefore correct) revision is being used. In addition, the list shows where the documents are located, in both electronic and hard-copy form. This allows for updating the documents and removing the obsolete versions when documents are revised. Retention periods are also shown, although these generally apply more to records than documents. Finally, all records and any documents that are retained after they are obsolete have their storage locations identified so they can be retrieved if needed.

The example shows only a few of the documents and records needed for a typical EMS. For larger companies or those with more complex environmental operations, it is often best to create a separate workbook or database to use as the master list. Figure 4.26 shows the typical structure of most formal document management systems, with a level 1 policy manual,

Document Name	Number	Current Revision	Locations	Retention Period	Record Storage
Procedures					
Environmental Policy Manual	ESP-001	4/16/2006	PI/EMS/Procedures	Until Superceeded	NA
Environmental Planning Procedure	ESP-002	5/2/2006	PI/EMS/Procedures	Until Superceeded	NA
Energy Conservation Guidelines	ESP-003	5/10/2006	PI/EMS/Procedures	Until Superceeded	NA
Recycling Guidelines	ESP-004	5/10/2006	PI/EMS/Procedures	Until Superceeded	NA
Material and Waste Handling	ESP-005	6/14/2006	PI/EMS/Procedures Shipping office Maintenance	Until Superceeded	NA
Storm Water Pollution Prevention Plan	NA	11/5/2005	PI/EMS/Procedures Storm Water Operator	7 years	PI/EMS/Obsolete
Instructions					
Waste Characterization Instruction	ESI-001	12/15/2005	PI/EMS/Instructions Mgmt. Representative	Until Superceeded	NA
Bulk Liquid Unloading	ESI-002	7/1/2006	PI/EMS/Instructions Maintenance	Until Superceeded	NA
Cooling Tower Water Treatment	ESI-003	7/21/2004	PI/EMS/Instructions Maintenance	Until Superceeded	NA
External Documents					
General Storm Water Permit	PA-000003-01	9/3/2004	Mgmt. Representative	7 years	Mgmt. Rep. Office
City of Oakly Fire Safety Code	NA	5/23/2005	Mgmt. Representative	Until Superceeded	NA
Consolidated Air Permit	PA-000041-01	1/6/2005	Mgmt. Representative	7 years	Mgmt. Rep. Office
Forms and Records					
Environmental Communication Log	ESF-001	5/19/2006	Mgmt. Representative	3 years	Mgmt. Rep. Office
Management Review Report	ESF-002	5/19/2006	Mgmt. Representative	3 years	Mgmt. Rep. Office
Weekly Environmental Patrol Report	ESF-003	5/10/2006	Mgmt. Representative	1 year	Mgmt. Rep. Office
Waste Manifests	PA-00341-A	NA	Shipping office	3 years	Shipping office
Land Disposal Restriction Reports	PA-00346-C	NA	Shipping office	3 years	Shipping office

Figure 4.25   Simple master list of documents and records.

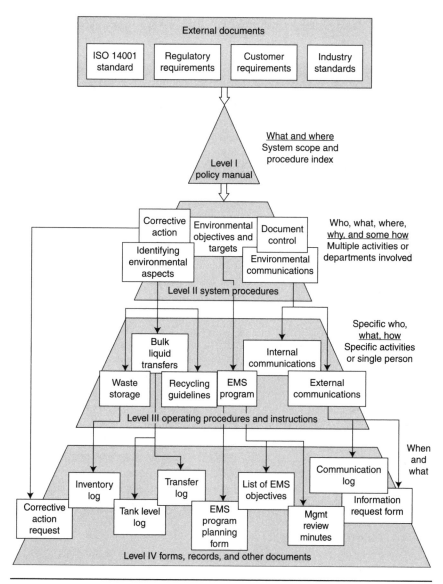

Figure 4.26   Typical document management structure.

level 2 procedures, level 3 instructions, and level 4 forms, records, and other documentation.

The policy manual serves primarily as a road map, outlining the basic structure of the EMS and guiding the reader to other more specific documents for more details on how or when. An example of an environmental policy manual is provided on the CD. Keep in mind that the exact format of the policy manual, or even whether it is one document or a compilation of many, is up to you. As a minimum it must provide a general description of the elements that make up the EMS and how they interact, and it must reference other related documents. It also serves as a good place to put information on certain activities that need to be described but do not warrant their own stand-alone procedure or instruction. The timing, attendance, and reporting of the management review is one such example.

Procedures (also called level 2 documents) describe core processes that span multiple departments or that are made up of several distinct activities. They provide a description of what and details on who and when, and they serve to integrate the various departments or activities. Not every clause in the standard requires a separate procedure. As previously noted, some do not require a documented procedure at all. I recommend combining clause activities when it makes sense. For example, I often address clauses 4.3.1, 4.3.2, and 4.3.3 in a single environmental planning procedure because in many companies these activities are related. Likewise, document and record control can usually be combined, as can internal audits and evaluations of compliance. Examples of common procedures are provided on the CD.

Instructions, also called level 3 documents, provide very detailed information on how to complete a specific task. A company may have a general waste handling procedure that provides common rules for all types of wastes, and it may have many waste handling instructions that provide details on the steps needed to properly package, contain, and control specific types of wastes. Whether to use one large procedure or many smaller and more focused instructions is a decision the organization must make. The best advice is to get the opinion of the users of the document. What would be most convenient for them?

Finally, level 4 includes all those forms (which will become records), lists, and other types of documents that need to be controlled. The structure implies that, in general, there are more documents of each type as you move down the pyramid, and the level of detail provided in each type of document increases as you move toward the base.

Although the structure just described is the most common, keep in mind that the structure of your document control system is up to you. You could put everything in one big procedure if you wanted, although such a structure would be cumbersome to use and I certainly would not recommend it. The bottom line is that the system you elect to establish must work, as evidenced by employees' familiarity with, access to, and use of the documentation.

The exact format of your documentation is likewise up to you. Many companies favor flowcharts, some prefer text, and still others prefer a combination of flowcharts and text. A recommended format that has worked well for me is shown in Figure 4.27. In this format there is a cover page that includes a standard boilerplate, a flowchart that shows the major steps in the process, and a textual portion that provides a place to expand on any details that cannot be put into a flowchart. This hybrid approach is probably the most flexible.

Note that the boilerplate includes sections that detail key inputs, key outputs, and metrics. I recommend including this key information for all your core environmental processes. Generally, your core processes will be the ones you develop level 2 procedures for. I do not include this information on instructions and forms. This format borrows from the process approach used in quality management and recognizes that for the process to deliver results, it is not enough to simply follow the steps of the procedure. Instead, the key inputs into the process must also be available and controlled or the old adage "garbage in, garbage out" will prove true. Likewise, the key outputs from the process must be known and determined to be acceptable because these outputs will, in fact, be inputs into other processes. The metrics section details the methods used to ensure that the process is producing good outputs and achieving planned results.

Record forms are one type of document. After they are filled out, they become records and must be controlled as such. Control of records is especially important in an EMS because many of the records have a regulatory retention period of three years or longer. You must check the regulation to confirm the mandatory retention period. Nonregulatory records should be kept on the basis of their potential need. Typically, records for management reviews, internal audits, and corrective actions are kept for three years to give the company a solid history of problems and improvements. Remember that the primary use of a record, beyond demonstration of compliance, is in its analysis for improvement. Records provide the information needed to establish trends and patterns and should be used for the same.

The ISO 14001 standard requires that you establish retention periods for records. The retention period may be listed as a minimum retention period, which allows you to keep them forever, if you so choose. Most experts caution against this, however, as there is a cost associated with keeping records forever, in terms of money, effort, and space. It is best to dispose of records, typically through some type of annual review and disposal program, after they have exceeded their specified retention periods.

1.0 Purpose
This procedure defines the process used to determine significant environmental aspects, methods for controlling and monitoring these aspects, and the process used to determine and achieve environmental objectives and targets.

2.0 Scope
This procedure covers all areas and operations within the Michigan facility.

3.0 Definitions
Environmental aspect: element of an organization's activities, products, or services that could interact with the environment.

Environmental objective: overall environmental goal, arising from the environmental policy, that an organization sets for itself and that is quantified where practicable.

Environmental target: detailed performance requirement, quantified where practicable, applicable to the organization or parts thereof, that arises from the environmental objectives and that needs to be set and met in order to achieve those objectives.

Environmental management program: the means, time frames, and personnel responsible for achieving an objective and target.

4.0 Responsibility
The EMS management representative is responsible for ensuring that the annual environmental aspects review is performed and that the aspects, objectives, targets, and programs are up to date. The CFT is responsible for conducting the environmental aspects review and determining significance.

5.0 Key Inputs
- Environmental policy commitments and criteria for significance determination
- Environmental regulations and other voluntary requirements
- List of significant environmental aspects
- Information on facility, process, and process changes and modifications

6.0 Primary Outputs
- Identification of the environmental aspects that need to be controlled
- Identification of methods to control these aspects and their related activities
- Identification of methods for monitoring these aspects and controls
- Identification of environmental objectives and targets, and the achievement of these objectives

7.0 Metrics
- Monitoring of the effectiveness of this process will be through the monthly management reviews, external audit surveillances, and by the success in achieving defined environmental objectives and targets

Figure 4.27 Example procedure format—environmental planning.

You must also ensure that you have indicated where the records are stored, to permit easy identification and retrieval. A clear and consistent indexing method to quickly locate the specific record needed should also be established. By "indexing method," we mean by date, by activity, by part number, or some combination of these. It is especially important to clearly label the boxes or file folders (for electronic storage) with their contents. You must also ensure that the locations used to store records safeguards them from damage, deterioration, and loss (or inadvertent deletion).

What records must you keep? Certainly all legal records required by environmental regulations. These include hazardous waste manifests, land disposal restrictions, records to show waste characterizations, records of effluent point discharges, and certain training records, to name but a few. Also, all records mandated by the ISO 14001 standard must be retained. Examples of these include audit results and records of management reviews and environmental compliance reviews. Beyond that, you must keep records that demonstrate you are complying with your EMS. As a general rule, you should keep records of all formal reviews and approvals, along with records of all ongoing environmental monitoring.

An example of a document and record control procedure is included on the CD provided with the book.

COMMUNICATIONS PROCESS

There are two elements of the communications process that must be addressed. The first is a system of internal communications to convey important information about the EMS to the workforce. The second is a system for receiving and responding to outside inquiries. We will look at this system first.

To establish a system for dealing with outside communications, you need to do two things. First, decide how such inquiries and other communications will be routed. Who will handle a request for information about your EMS or environmental performance? Because environmental management does occur within a framework of regulatory control, most companies designate one individual as the focal point for all questions or issues dealing with the EMS, including questions dealing with the company's environmental activities and performance. For most companies that individual is the management representative. In large companies it might be a more senior officer. In some companies the responsibility for responding to such inquiries is distributed. The public affairs officer might respond to general questions from the media or local governments, the corporate attorney to any questions relating to regulatory compliance, and the management representative to other requests for information. Even if the responsibilities are distributed, there still needs to be a focal point to log in the communication and assign it to the right person. This leads us to the second element of the external communication program: the communication log.

In essence, a *communication log* is a simple form used to document the nature of the communication, who it was from, the date, who it was assigned to, and the response provided. The ISO 14001 standard requires that external communications (that is, communication from interested parties) be documented and responded to. You will need to show evidence of compliance, so some form of log is needed. An example log is shown in Figure 4.28.

The log is maintained by the individual designated as the focal point for external environmental communications. You also need to make sure your receptionist knows who this person is so that he or she can route the calls to this individual.

You are required to make your environmental policy statement available to the general public. Note that the EMS management representative provided a copy of the policy statement as part of the response to the first inquiry shown in the communication log in the figure. You are not required to make information about your significant environmental aspects public, but you do have to decide whether to document your decision. Providing this information tells a lot about what you do that could harm the environment if not properly controlled. Arguments for making this information public include:

- The voluntary disclosure demonstrates an openness that can substantially improve a company's image with the community.

- Providing this information establishes a high degree of accountability for the senior management team. If the general public is knowledgeable about your significant environmental aspects, it is reasonable to expect that they will want to know about your performance in minimizing their impacts. The management team will thus be under more pressure to truly improve the organization's environmental performance in critical areas.

Arguments commonly cited against making this information public include the risk of damaging the company's image, especially if it does not substantially improve its environmental performance, and possibly attracting more interest from local environmental activist groups. In the United States, most companies elect not to make information on their significant environmental aspects public. As previously noted, the decision must be documented. The company can document this decision within its environmental policy manual.

The second element of the communication involves internal communications. The company first needs to consider what information should be communicated. Then, methods to provide (or collect) this information can be developed. I normally recommend that the company walk through the ISO 14001 standard, picking out information that must be communicated, and then assign communication methods for each item. An example of a table created to accomplish this is shown in Figure 4.29.

External Communication Log						
Date	Name	Contact Info.	Communication	Assigned to	Response	Date
1/15/2006	C. Tomlins	734-944-9834	Requested information about our ISO 14001 status.	T. Baker - EMS MR	Faxed copy of our ISO 14001 certificate and EMS policy	1/15/2006
1/25/2006	MIDEQ - T. Bennet	763-934-0583	Called to provide information regarding the final report from December on-site visit.	S. Grendeen - corporate attorney	Forwarded the information to our corporate attorney and plant manager.	1/25/2006
3/20/2006	Cindy Smith	734-944-3789	Called to complain about the odor from the plant that occurs when we are evaporated our oily mop water	T. Baker - EMS MR	Explained source of odor to Ms. Smith, indicated we would look into options for minimizing odor.	3/28/2006
4/12/2006	WDXV TV - Sheryl Weis	964-837-8976	Indicated wanted to do a local segment on our ISO 14001 EMS and how it has helped us improve our environmental performance.	K. Pierce - President	Pending	
4/19/2006	Bob Woodruff	734-984-0989	Complained about odor from plant. Could not give specific days but pretty upset. Sounds like the oily mop water evaporation odor.	T. Baker - EMS MR	Explained source of odor to Mr. Woodruff, indicated we would look into options for minimizing odor.	4/20/2006

Figure 4.28 EMS communication log.

Clause	Communication Item	Methods for Communication
4.2	Environmental policy statement—internal communication of	Banners, newsletter, orientation training, local posting in each work area
	Environmental policy statement—external communication to public	Posting in lobby and on company Web site
4.3.1 4.4.2	Significant environmental aspects—awareness of	Environmental bulletin postings in each work area, orientation training, on-the-job training
4.3.2	Regulatory requirements affecting normal operations	Embedding requirements in local procedures and instructions
4.3.3	Environmental objectives and targets and associated management programs	Business plan, posting of environmental objectives on environmental communication board, company newsletter
	Environmental objectives and targets—obtaining the views of interested parties	Internal—gather concerns, issues, and suggestions from the employee suggestion program External—communication log
4.4.1	Roles, responsibilities, and authorities	Job descriptions, organization chart, embed in procedures and instructions
4.4.2	Competence and training	Training requirements matrix, training plans, on-the-job training
	Awareness training—importance of conformity with policies and procedures, consequences of not following procedures	Orientation training, on-the-job training, company newsletter, environmental bulletin posting in each area
4.4.4	Documentation and document control—location of and revision status	Master list available on the P drive (orientation training will demonstrate how to access and use the master list)
4.4.6	Operational controls and criteria	Environmental bulletin posting in each area, on-the-job training, embed in operating procedures and controls
	Environmental aspects of purchased goods and materials	MSDSs maintained in shipping and receiving and production supervisor's office
	Environmental aspects of service providers and contractors	Obtain information through use of the contractor briefing form, provided to each prospective contractor
	Your company's relevant environmental policies and procedures—communication to suppliers and contractors	Incorporated into Supplier Quality and Environmental Manual, provided to each supplier and contractor

Figure 4.29 Examples of communication methods for EMS information. *(Continued)*

(Continued)

Clause	Communication Item	Methods for Communication
4.4.7	Emergency preparedness and response procedures and actions	Orientation training, drills
4.5.1	Environmental monitoring requirements	Environmental bulletin posting in each area, embed in local procedures and instructions
4.5.3	Nonconformities identified by employees	Corrective action requests, which can be initiated by any employee

Figure 4.29   (Continued)

The table shows some of the information items that need to be communicated. Undoubtedly, you will uncover others as you develop your EMS. The point of the table is to systematically analyze your communication needs and then design programs for communicating relevant information throughout the workforce. Some of the methods in the table have already been discussed; others will be discussed in the sections that follow.

Remember that communication is more than a requirement; it is also your main tool for building employee support and involvement. And as noted in Chapter 2, significant, sustained environmental improvement is not possible without everyone's active support and involvement. Spend the time and effort to build effective two-way communication systems.

VENDOR AND SUBCONTRACTOR CONTROL

Suppliers are an important part of your EMS. We will discuss two categories of suppliers and two primary requirements. The two categories are suppliers of materials or products and suppliers of services. The two requirements are related to obtaining information about the environmental aspects of materials and services from the supplier, and communicating relevant information about your EMS and policies to these same suppliers.

For providers of materials and parts, information regarding the environmental aspects and potential impacts of their products is normally obtained through receipt of MSDSs. The MSDS provides information on the hazards associated with the product, along with any precautions necessary for its safe use or disposal. It will also normally note any environmental regulations that apply, which can help categorize the material as to its hazardous or nonhazardous nature. The biggest problem with the MSDS is that the format may vary. Some provide very detailed information; others do not. Learning how to read the MSDS is an important skill for the EMS management representative. The MSDS must be available to the organization's employees as part of the employee right-to-know laws. It is a good idea to establish a policy whereby the management representative is given an opportunity to review the MSDS for any new chemicals or products purchased by the organization, so that the materials can be assessed for significance, if appropriate, and so that operational controls can be established to minimize any adverse impacts, including those that impact the organization's employees.

Environmental requirements are normally communicated to material providers as part of the contracting process. These requirements include prohibited or restricted materials and any requirements for certification.

Service providers are a little more complicated because the nature of the service may vary considerably. Examples of service providers who need to be considered include:

- Waste disposal services

- Facility maintenance providers

- Lawn care services, snow removal

- Bulk material providers (oil, ammonia, and so on)

- Construction firms (expansion, renovation, demolition)

- Laboratory services (for environmental monitoring equipment calibration)

- Professional services firms (for example, environmental consultants)

Your company has an obligation first to understand how the contractor's work could impact the environment, and second to ensure that it is properly controlled while the firm is working on your behalf. You must also communicate relevant information relating to your EMS that these firms need to be aware of during their work. This may include your policies for waste handling and disposal and bulk liquid unloading and transfer and/or recycling. The most common way to both obtain information from and communicate information to the supplier/contractor is through the use of a contractor briefing form, a portion of which is provided in Figure 4.30.

Other sections in the briefing form list the organization's policies and procedures that the contractor will need to comply with during the work, a listing of licenses and/or certifications held by the contractor, key names and contact data, and information relating to emergency response. A copy of the contractor briefing statement is provided on the CD.

The contractor briefing statement should provide you with the information you will need to evaluate and control the contractor's work from an environmental perspective. Some areas of consideration for specific categories of suppliers are:

Environmental Briefing Packet and Contractor Method Statement Template

Section V. Contractor Method Statement

Respond to the following questions: (use additional space where required)

This method statement must be completed, signed, and returned to the facility's environmental management representative before contracted work commences.

(a) Work description:

Briefly describe the work to be performed while on-site, including the activities of subcontractors.

_____

_____

_____

(b) Air emissions

Will the work you perform produce or cause the release of any air emissions?

YES ___ NO ___

If yes, list air emissions and method for preventing impact to the environment.

_____

_____

_____

(c) Water discharges

Will the work you perform produce or cause the release of any wastewater?

YES ___ NO ___

If yes, how will the wastewater be handled?

_____

_____

_____

(d) Materials

What materials (chemicals, oils, etc.) and/or equipment will you be handling or bringing on-site to perform the contracted work?

_____

_____

_____

Figure 4.30   Contractor briefing form.

- Waste disposal services—are they licensed? Where do they dispose of their wastes? Is the waste disposal facility licensed for the types of waste you will be sending there?

- Facility maintenance providers—are their technicians trained and certified to handle solvents, refrigerants, and so on?

- Lawn care services and snow removal—are organic pesticides used or can they be used? Do they use salt for snow removal or a more environmentally benign substance?

- Bulk material providers (oil, ammonia, and so on)—what kinds of safeguards do they take to prevent spills during liquid transfer? Is their equipment in good working order? Also, consider safeguards you should take during the transfer (for example, cover or dike nearby storm drains and check operation of storm drain shutoff valves if installed).

- Construction firms (expansion, renovation, demolition)—how will they dispose of their solid and liquid wastes? If asbestos is involved, are they certified to handle it?

- Laboratory services (for environmental monitoring equipment calibration)—are they accredited to calibrate your instruments? What information do they provide on their calibration reports?

- Professional services firms (for example, environmental consultants)—for regulatory specialists, are their consultants licensed? What training have they had? For other consultants, what is their training and experience?

Although it is not required by ISO 14001, it is not a bad idea to set up vendor history files for your key environmental contractors/suppliers. These files provide a place where you can store the contracts, contractor briefing forms, and details of any problems you may have had with the contractor or incidents they may have caused. This history should be reviewed before extending a contract or offering a new contract to the supplier. Careful evaluation and selection of service providers is the first step toward improving your environmental performance for activities that involve contractors or suppliers.

CALIBRATION SYSTEMS

Environmental monitoring equipment includes items such as pH meters used to monitor liquid wastes prior to discharge, stack emission monitoring equipment, and alarm systems associated with storage tanks. This equipment serves as operational controls to ensure that the environment is not harmed as a result of your activities or services. If your company has any such equipment, and many companies do not, you must ensure that the equipment is reliable and accurate. Periodic calibration and maintenance of these devices are required to provide confidence in the data these instruments provide.

If you already have a QMS in place, it is a simple matter to include these measurement devices in your existing calibration program. Most manufacturers, even without a formal QMS, recognize the need for calibration of measurement devices and will therefore have some type of program in place. If not, you will have to develop a program. In many cases it will be easier to outsource the calibration of your environmental monitoring equipment rather than go to the expense of buying standards, obtaining calibration protocols, and training your employees in how to properly perform the calibrations. If you outsource, consider the questions posed in the last section for laboratory services providers when you choose a calibration supplier.

As a minimum, you will need a list of all the measurement and monitoring devices that require calibration, their serial numbers or other unique identifiers, their calibration frequency, the date last calibrated, and the date they are next due. For a simple system, this information could be included as a sheet in the Environmental Planning Workbook. An example is shown in Figure 4.31. For a more complex system with many devices, a dedicated calibration database is normally used. You may also want to list any periodic maintenance or checks performed on monitoring and alarm systems. Finally, you will need to set up a system to store the records of calibration. Make sure someone reviews the results of the calibration as marked on the record if you outsource.

An entire book could be devoted to establishing and maintaining a calibration program. I have provided the basic information here to get you started. Again, the best option is to fold your environmental monitoring equipment into an existing calibration program if you can.

Device	Serial No.	Location	Frequency	Date Calibrated	Date Due	Maintenance
						Daily reference check
Orion pH Meter	A3482	Laboratory	Annual	5/12/2006	5/12/2007	Weekly probe check
	T174	Plating tank 1	Annual	3/15/2006	3/15/2007	
	T175	Plating tank 2	Annual	3/15/2006	3/15/2007	
Temperature Sensor	T176	Plating tank 3	Annual	3/15/2006	3/15/2007	None

Figure 4.31   Simple calibration list.

TRAINING, COMPETENCY, AND AWARENESS SYSTEM

There are two requirements your training program must meet to satisfy ISO 14001. The first is competency. All personnel whose work could impact the environment must be competent. Competency is more than just providing training. Competency attainment means that the individual has mastered the essential skills needed to safely perform the task. Competency may be attained through training, formal education, and experience, or more commonly through a combination of these.

There are three primary steps involved in establishing competency. The first is identifying who needs to be trained and the knowledge and skills that these employees must have. Competency identification should have already started as part of the initial environmental review. The CFT performing the review was asked to note the functions involved in the activities associated with potentially significant environmental aspects. This information was recorded in the Environmental Planning Workbook, as shown in Figure 4.32. This information provides a good starting point for identifying the competencies that will need to be achieved or verified during EMS training program development.

Figure 4.32 shows that energy is a significant aspect that must be controlled. It also shows that all employees are involved in energy consumption, and therefore all employees should receive training in energy conservation. The same goes for recycling, which was also determined to be significant. The proper control of the DynaFoam 350, however, primarily involves the bath technicians and the material handlers. They will need competency in proper handling, storage, and disposal of the solution as well as proper operation of the bath itself. Note that the DynaClean 2000 was not deemed significant, but the CFT still determined that it should be formally controlled. Therefore, competencies should be established for this chemical as well. The team will continue to identify the functions involved in environmental activities and the competencies needed by reviewing the rest of the items in the Environmental Planning Workbook.

The focus of the training should be on the controls established for each significant (or formally controlled) environmental aspect. These items will be shown on the second worksheet of the Environmental Planning Workbook, a section of which is shown in Figure 4.33.

Combining the information in Figures 4.32 and 4.33 gives us the basis for developing our training program. For energy, everyone should receive training on the energy conservation guidelines. Everyone should also receive training on the company's recycling program procedure. Bath technicians and material handlers should also be trained on the material handling and

Environmental Aspects

Criteria weighting
9 - high correlation to criteria
3 - moderate correlation to criteria
1 - low correlation to criteria

	Energy	Recyclables	DynaFoam 350	DynaClean 2000	Xylene	Testing Laboratory / Chemicals	Product Design and Development
Department or Area	All areas	All areas	Production	Production	Production	Testing Laboratory	Engineering
Activity associated with aspect 1	Lighting	Scrap cardboard	Chemical Treatment	Chemical Treatment	Parts cleaning	Material testing	Product Design
Activity associated with aspect 2	HVAC	Used toner cartridges	Material storage and handling	Material storage and handling	Material storage and handling	Chemical storage and handling	
Activity associated with aspect 3	Computers	Scrap paper	Disposal	Disposal	Disposal	Chemical disposal	
Activity associated with aspect 4	Production equip.	Aluminum caps					
Functions involved with aspect	All employees	All employees	Bath Techs & Material Handlers	Bath Techs & Material Handlers	Prod. Operators & Material Handlers	Lab. Techs	Design Engineers
Significance Criteria							
Hazardous or regulated material or waste?	0	1	9	1	9	9	9
Influence the environmental design of our products?	0	0	0	0	0	0	9
Consumes significant natural resources (includes energy)?	9	3	0	0	0	0	3
Present a high opportunity for source reduction, reuse or recycling?	9	9	3	3	9	3	3
Significant community or employee concern?	3	1	3	0	3	1	0
Total Score	21	14	15	4	21	13	25
Significant?	Y	Y	Y	N	Y	Y	Y
Formally controlled, although not significant							

Figure 4.32 Identifying who needs to be trained.

X = Primary method of addressing aspect
O = Secondary method of addressing aspect

Significant Aspect	Environmental Impact	Method of Control → Procedural Controls									Mechanical and system controls		
	Champion/Process Owner	Energy Conservation Guidelines — Hendricks	Recycling Program Procedure — Blazek	Material Handling Procedure — Dillon	Waste Handling and Disposal Procedure — Dillon	Storm Water Pollution Prevention Plan — B. Smith	Spill Prevention, Countermeasure and Control Plan — B. Smith	Parts Cleaning Instruction — Nyung	Chemical Cleaning Instruction — Nyung	Advanced Quality Planning Procedure — O'Leary	Cleaning Tank Hood Exhaust System — Cory	Chemical Treatment Transfer System — Cory	Tank Liquid Level Alarm System — Cory
Energy	Natural resource depletion, greenhouse gas emissions, acid rain	X											
Recyclables	Natural resource depletion, landfill usage		X										
DynaFoam 350	Groundwater contamination, harm to wildlife			X	X	O	O		O			O	O
Xylene	Groundwater contamination, harm to wildlife, human health effects			X	X	O	O	O			O	O	
Product Design and Development	Natural resource depletion, greenhouse gas emissions, groundwater contamination, landfill usage									X			

Figure 4.33   Identifying training topics.

waste handling and disposal procedures. In addition, they should also be familiar with the spill prevention and reaction controls contained in the storm water pollution prevention plan (SWPPP) and the spill prevention, countermeasure, and controls (SPCC) plan. Finally, bath technicians should be familiar with the local instruction for chemical cleaning. Figure 4.33 also shows that there are mechanical and system controls (not specifically identified in Figure 4.32) associated with the DynaFoam 350 and Xylene aspects, and the maintenance and/or facilities personnel must be competent in the operation, maintenance, and control of these systems.

Once these basic competencies have been identified, the second step is to develop plans for achieving these competencies. Options include formal classroom training, on-the-job training, self-study and testing, apprentice programs, drills and walk-throughs, and certification programs, to name but a few. It would be helpful to set up a series of training matrices, one for each department, to formalize the competency requirements and status in achieving competency. An example of a training requirements matrix for the material handlers is shown in Figure 4.34.

In this matrix the competencies are listed by row. These are separated into two components: the job-specific competencies and the general competencies required for all employees. The training elements focus on the procedures used to control the activities and in some cases demonstrations of the competencies by performance. Each employee in the department is listed across the top, and the function the employee fills is shown beneath his or her name. The required competencies are shown with an X in the cell formed by the competency row and the individual's column. An X indicates that the competency has been assigned but not yet attained. An actual date replaces the X when the competency is achieved and/or verified. The *PE* in the last column for the manager indicates that this individual was grandfathered in because of previous experience. A simple spreadsheet calculation, not shown in the figure but included on the template on the CD, calculates the percentage of competencies achieved, which can be useful for training performance tracking.

ISO 14001 also requires awareness training. Competency involves knowing *what* to do and *how* to do it, while awareness implies an understanding

Department/Function: Material Handling

Functions Filled	Personnel	Robertson	Lindel	Tomy	Sizemore	B. Smith	Dillon
	Manager						X
	Supervisor					X	
	Material Handler	X	X	X	X		

Job Specific Competencies

Aspects	Competencies	Training Elements	Competency Requirements					
			Robertson	Lindel	Tomy	Sizemore	B. Smith	Dillon
DynaFoam	Handling, storage and disposal	Material Handling Procedure	6/1/2006	X	6/8/2006	6/8/2006	5/10/2006	PE
DynaClean 2000		Waste Handling and Disposal Procedure	6/1/2006	X	6/8/2006	6/8/2006	5/10/2006	PE
HiLo Batteries		Bulk Liquid Transfer Procedure	5/11/2006		X		5/2/2006	PE
		Perform bulk liquid transfer	5/15/2006		X		5/7/2006	
HiLo Batteries	Battery Charging	Battery Charging Instruction	6/1/2006	X	6/8/2006	6/8/2006	5/10/2006	PE

General Competencies

Aspects	Competencies	Training Elements	Robertson	Lindel	Tomy	Sizemore	B. Smith	Dillon
Recyclables	Accumulation and storage		1 5/20/2006		5/20/2006	5/20/2006	5/20/2006	5/20/2006
Energy	Energy conservation	Energy Conservation Guidelines	5/20/2006		5/20/2006	5/20/2006	5/20/2006	5/20/2006

Figure 4.34   Training requirements matrix example.

of *why* it is important. Win the heart and you will win the mind. The standard requires that all employees have an awareness of the following:

* The importance of complying with policies, procedures, and the requirements of the EMS

* The significant environmental aspects and their potential impacts and the environmental benefits of improved personal performance

* Their individual roles and responsibilities

* The potential consequences of failing to follow specified operating procedures

This awareness can be provided through orientation training, on-the-job training, the company newsletter, all-hands meetings, or a combination of these. One of the best tools to help in maintaining a high level of awareness is the environmental bulletin. This one-page form summarizes the significant environmental activities performed in a specific area, their controls, and the potential environmental impacts if these controls are not followed. One bulletin should be prepared for each major area, and it should be posted in a prominent location visible to employees in the area. Figure 4.35 shows an example of an environmental bulletin.

The final step in establishing an effective training program is to verify the effectiveness of the training or other actions taken to establish the competencies and awareness needed. Methods of training verification include interviews, tests, personal observation of the employee performing the task, and a review of the data relating to how well the activity is being performed. In addition, internal audits can and should be used to verify competency and awareness. Internal auditing is discussed in the final section of this chapter.

Finally, keep in mind that the organization must retain records of its training activities. Some of these records are required by law; others are needed to provide evidence that your EMS is operating as it should. Records may be in the form of certificates of successful completion of a training course, sign-in sheets providing evidence of attendance, and supervisory signoff for on-the-job training activities. While keeping a formal record of all training that occurs on a daily basis is impractical, ensure that you have records for all regulatory required training, all formal training, and all initial training. One innovative and simple way to show evidence of training in organizational procedures is to have the employee sign the back of the procedure when training is completed. The procedure, which should be available at its point of use, then provides an easy way to verify who has and who has not been trained. When a procedure is revised and the new procedure replaces the superseded one, this method ensures that all team members are trained in the new procedure.

Environmental Bulletin	Rev. 4/23/06

Area: Shipping and receiving

Worldwide Product's Environmental Policy Statement

Worldwide Products (WPI) recognizes and accepts its responsibilities to be a good steward of the environment and to help achieve a state of sustainable development. In support of these responsibilities, WPI has established the following commitments:

- Compliance to all applicable state, federal and local legal requirements with the goal of beyond compliance wherever practical
- Conformance with the principles set forth in the EPA Energy Star and Bright Lights programs
- Prevention of pollution in all its forms
- Conservation of natural resources, including energy, through reuse, recycling, and source reduction
- Continual environmental performance improvement through the involvement of all WPI employees and partnership with the community

Environmentally Sensitive Activities	Environmental Impact if Not Properly Controlled	Method of Control
Energy consumption	Natural resource depletion, greenhouse gas emissions, acid rain	Energy conservation guidelines
Recycling of cardboard, wood pallets, scrap metal	Natural resource depletion, landfill usage	Recycling program procedure
DynaFoam 350 and DynaClean 2000 handling, storage, and disposal	Groundwater contamination, harm to wildlife	Parts cleaning instruction Chemical cleaning instruction Material handling procedure Waste handling and disposal procedure
Xylene storage and disposal	Groundwater contamination, harm to wildlife, human health effects	

Please note that failure to follow these procedures and controls may result in adverse impacts to the environment as shown.

Your environmental management representative is Brenda Smith. Please contact Brenda at extension 4593 if you have any questions, concerns, or suggestions regarding our environmental performance or EMS. You may also use the employee suggestion program to make recommendations on how we can improve our environmental performance. Thank you for your participation.

EMS management representative:	*Brenda Smith*
Production control manager:	*Arlie Henry*
President:	*Susan Tomlins*

Figure 4.35 Environmental bulletin.

NONCONFORMANCE, CORRECTIVE AND PREVENTIVE ACTION SYSTEM

Systems must be in place to properly respond to deficiencies in operations and to weaknesses in the EMS. Before reviewing the steps necessary to develop such a system, it is worthwhile to discuss corrective action, preventive action, and continual improvement.

Corrective action is action to address an actual violation to requirements. Requirements in this sense include violations of regulatory requirements as well as violations of what we say we do in our procedures and policies that make up the EMS. These occurrences represent nonconformities. Preventive action is action to address a potential violation to requirements before one actually occurs. Both corrective and preventive action seek to identify the root cause of such violations and to put in place effective countermeasures to eliminate the cause and prevent the occurrence (preventive action) or recurrence (corrective action) of the nonconformity. An example of a corrective action would be the steps taken to identify the root cause of an oil spill in a production area. An example of a preventive action would be the recognition of the potential for such a spill before one happens and taking steps to correct the practices that could lead to the incident.

Continual improvement, on the other hand, is action taken to improve a situation or performance that is not directly tied into a requirement. Continual improvement is best accomplished through the development of environmental objectives and targets. Actions to reduce emissions, to recycle, and to reduce the amount of hazardous wastes generated go beyond regulatory requirements. Actions taken to build a roof over the outdoor area where you store your oily scrap steel containers in order to prevent contaminated storm water runoff is more of an example of preventive action, although you could possibly take credit for it as an environmental improvement objective.

To establish a system for identifying, documenting, evaluating, and tracking nonconformities and resultant actions, you will need to take the following steps:

1. Develop a form for documenting the nonconformities and any resultant corrective or preventive action

2. Develop a process for determining root cause

3. Develop a system for tracking the actions taken to identify and eliminate the cause

4. Develop a system process for verifying the effectiveness of the actions taken (did they eliminate the cause?)

Forms used to document nonconformities and actions come in all shapes, sizes, and names. Common names include the corrective action request (CAR), preventive action request (PAR), action request, and nonconformance report (NCR), but it really does not matter what you call it. If you have an existing QMS, you may want to borrow the same form used for quality issues. In this case, some companies add an *E* prefix to the form name—for example, ECAR, EPAR, or EAR. The choice is up to you—what is in the report is more important than its name. Figure 4.36 shows an example of an action request form.

The form shown in Figure 4.36 could be used for any type of system deficiency, audit finding, or other event requiring root cause analysis and

Action Request			Source		Type	
Problem ID: 12-06	**Team Contact:**	Gyuna	Audit	☐	Repeat	☑
Date: 6/14/2006	**Champion:**	B. Smith	OH&S	☐	Corrective	☑
Area: Production	**Activity/Process**	Machining	EMS	☑	Preventive	☐

Problem Description	**Problem Impact:**		**Response Due Date:** 6/20/2006
30 gallons of machine oil was spilled during sump filling. Note that this is the second such error this month.			

Immediate Containment Action	**Who**	**Date**
The oil was immediately contained and cleaned up	B. Smith	6/14/2006
Waste oil and all cleaning material was properly disposed of	B. Smith	6/14/2006
An evaluation confirmed that no oil reached any discharge path out of the plant	B. Smith	6/14/2006

Problem Root Cause Analysis

5 Why Analysis
1 Why: The sump drain valve was left open

2 Why: The valve was left open after the last sump cleaning operation
3 Why: No one verified the valve lineup after draining or prior to filling
4 Why: There is no requirement to verify the valve lineup in the instruction
5 Why

Root Cause: there is no requirement to verify valve lineup after sump draining or prior to refilling.

Cause and Effect Analysis
Methods   Human   Environmental

Procedure

Inattention to detail

Valve Lineup

Materials   Equipment/Tooling

Error Proofing Was error proofing a part of the long-term actions? Yes ☐ No ☑

Long-Term Actions and Verification		**Date**	**Indicator**	**Before**	**After**
Action	B. Smith - Develop valve lineup check sheets for all oil transfer				
Who	operations	6/19/2006	Valve CS	None	Issued
Action	B. Smith - Modify instructions to include reference to valve lineup			No	Ref. in
Who	check sheets	6/19/2006	Ref. to CS	reference	instruct.
Action	Gyuna - Train all maintenance and facility operators on the proper		Lineup		
Who	use of the new valve lineup check sheets	6/20/2006	errors	2/mo.	0/year
Acton	Tomlins - Complete internal incident critique		Transfer		
Who		6/15/2006	spills	2/mo.	0/year
Action	Tomlins - Review spill response procedure for modifications based				Review
Who	on this event	6/15/2006	Review	No review	complete
Action					
Who					

Systematic Prevention and Horizontal Application
Valve lineup checksheets were developed for all oil transfer operations, not just draining and filling.

Estimated Cost/Environment Impact of Problem and/or Dollars Saved/Pollution Prevented through Elimination
$1200 per incident based on cleanup, lost productivity, disposal costs and cost of replacement oil.

System Updates (Check those updated)		**ECI/ECR Submitted?**	Ye ☐	No ☑	No.
Mgmt Program ☐	MCCS/PM Instructions ☑	Standard Work ☑	Environmental Bulletin ☑		
Objectives ☐	Inspection Sheets ☐	Training Plans ☑	Aspects Worksheet ☐		

Figure 4.36   Action request form.

permanent corrective action. It shows the immediate containment action, root cause analysis using 5 why analysis and cause-and-effect analysis, permanent corrective action, verification of action, and horizontal application (what other activities would benefit from the permanent actions). It also shows the estimated cost of the problem, which would be eliminated if future problems are prevented. Finally, checkboxes to show document updates have been added to ensure that no supporting actions are overlooked. This format, which goes well beyond that required by ISO 14001, is borrowed from the QMS and is common to the automotive industry.

In order to ensure that the problem does not recur, some method of root cause analysis is needed. Some of the more common tools are discussed in the following sections. Note that these are summary descriptions only. Skillful application of these techniques takes practice and maybe some training.

Brainstorming

In brainstorming, team members are asked to come up with as many ideas on potential causes as they can. A team of five to seven individuals works best. Instructions should include:

- No criticism of ideas is allowed

- The goal is quantity of ideas, not necessarily quality of ideas at this point

- "Outside the box" ideas are welcomed

- Team members may pass on a round if necessary

- Team members should build off each other's ideas

All ideas should be recorded on flip charts. Assign one or two team members to collect ideas. Continue until the team runs out of ideas. Allow humor—it will result in team members feeling more comfortable and contributing more ideas. A typical brainstorming session will generate between 50 and 100 ideas, and up to 200 ideas is not uncommon.

5 Why Analysis

The 5 why analysis drills down to the root cause by continually asking the question *why* after each answer. You are essentially looking for two types of root cause: the technical or behavioral root cause (for example, no one verified the valve lineup) and the system root cause (for example, there is no requirement to perform a valve lineup after sump draining or prior to refilling). Sometimes it takes only four "whys" to get to the root cause, sometimes six. When you get down to the management system–related cause, you have probably come to the root cause.

Cause and Effect (Fishbone Diagrams)

The cause-and-effect technique is essentially guided brainstorming. It is guided because the team will systematically consider each main category shown on the "fishbone" and ask the question, is there any way that this category could have caused the problem? In our example the categories are methods, human, environmental, materials, and equipment and tooling, which are the typical default categories. We show the main results on our fishbone diagram, embedded in the action request. In practice the analysis would be done on a white board or flip chart with the team, and there would be many more potential causes. The drawback is that the root cause is not as readily evident as it is with the 5 why analysis.

Nominal Group Technique

If brainstorming or cause-and-effect analysis is used to generate possible causes, the team will have too many causes to act on. To reduce the causes to a reasonable number, say 5 to 10 for action assignment, or to identify what the team feels is the root cause, some technique must be used to narrow down the list. The nominal group technique, a very structured tool for ensuring that all participants have an equal voice in the decision-making process, is one such method. A facilitator displays on the flip chart the causes to be ranked. Each participant picks 5 items from the list and ranks each using a scale of 1 to 5. If there is a very large number of items, the facilitator may instead have each member pick 10 items and rank them on a scale of 1 to 10. Typically the number ranked should be about one-third of the number of items on the list. The votes from each team member are recorded on the flip chart next to the listed items, and the summed score for each item is tabulated and the top items selected.

These are just a few of the tools that can be applied to help identify the root cause. The important point is that the organization should pick one or more of these techniques to use, master the technique, and then skillfully and consistently apply it to nonconformities as they are identified.

The next step is to develop some method of tracking the actions taken to correct nonconformities. Although you could simply track them using the long-term action and verification section of the action request form, this would be cumbersome if more than a few were outstanding, and some actions would probably fall through the cracks. A simple spreadsheet or table can be used to provide more comprehensive, yet simple tracking of actions and follow-up. An example of a simple tracking log is shown in Figure 4.37 and is included in the Environmental Planning Workbook provided on the CD.

Action Request Tracking Log

AR Number	Date	Description	Repeat?	Action Assignee	Due Date	Action Complete Date	Verification Date	Comments
008-06	4/14/2006	Internal audit found that several material handlers had not been trained on proper material and waste handling techniques	No	Harris	5/1/2006	4/27/2006	5/1/2006	Verified training records available, interviewed the 3 operators.
009-06	4/14/2006	Internal audit noted that Feb and March monthly PMs on the parts cleaning hood filtration system had not been performed	No	Kuhn	5/1/2006			Awaiting replacement switch
010-06	4/14/2006	Audit finding - No evidence of the completion of the Supplier Briefing Form for the new HVAC contractor could be provided.	No	Bennet	5/15/2006			Form has been sent out, no response yet. Bennet said she will follow-up 5/20/06.
011-06	5/3/2006	The recycling of scrap steel cannot be performed as indicated in the Recycling Program Procedure. The locations for scrap steel containers is incorrect.	No	Harris	5/18/2006	5/16/2006	5/16/2006	Verified procedure was corrected.
012-06	6/14/2006	30 gallons of machine oil was spilled during sump filling.	Yes	B. Smith	6/20/2006			2nd occurrence this month.

Figure 4.37 Action request tracking log.

The log, normally maintained by the management representative, allows quick and easy tracking of the status of all action requests issued. Comments can be added to show the status of outstanding corrective actions. The management representative should follow up on outstanding and overdue corrective actions and should also verify that the actions were completed. The worksheet also has a section for summary statistics (not shown in Figure 4.37) to tabulate performance in completing corrective action.

The last step is to follow up on the actions to ensure that they were taken and were effective in eliminating the cause and preventing recurrence. Verification of actions taken can be performed by confirming the changes made in procedures and policies, interviewing employees, or otherwise personally checking the results of the actions. Verification may also be performed as part of EMS internal audits by having the auditors confirm that corrective actions are in place when they next evaluate the area. Long-term verification of the effectiveness of the actions must normally wait some period of time to ensure the problem does not recur. The comments section of the action request log provides a convenient place to document verification actions. Also note that the long-term actions and verifications section of the action request form also has a section to document verification. The TBD (to be determined) in the "After" columns of the example indicate that the verification of long-term effectiveness will have to wait until several months have passed with no lineup errors of transfer spills before the organization can have confidence that the actions have solved the problem.

INTERNAL AUDIT PROCESS

The last core design element that we will discuss is the internal audit process. The company needs to have the capability to critically assess its EMS. In simple terms, the objectives of any management system audit are threefold:

- To identify any weaknesses that may exist in the management system

- To identify opportunities for improvement

- To identify best practices that should be communicated throughout the organization

The extent to which these objectives can be met will depend on the maturity of the EMS itself, the skill and training of the internal auditors, and the level of support provided by the management team for the realization of these objectives. A detailed discussion of the strategies and techniques for conducting internal EMS audits is presented in Chapter 7.

A fundamental purpose of any audit is to verify that the organization is conforming to the ISO 14001 standard and to its own internal policies and procedures. A management system cannot produce results if it is not followed. Noncompliance is a weakness that leads to inferior performance of the EMS, and such instances must be identified during the audit.

Conformance means that the organization is adhering to the requirements set forth in its internal procedures, policies, and guidelines and to the external requirements set forth by the standard, regulatory agencies, and/or adopted industry practices. Basically, it verifies that the organization is doing what it says it does. Auditors generate *nonconformance* findings, or NCs, to document areas where deviations to the requirements are noted.

Opportunities for improvement (OFIs) are any areas where improvements in a process, typically associated with results, are obviously possible. An example might be an instance where an auditor notes significant drafts or a high level of heat loss in an area during an EMS audit. In this case the auditor cannot generate an NC, because there is no definitive requirement relating to the observed practice and/or results. In the example, the auditor notes that there is no requirement to insulate all areas of the facility, but he or she understands that energy conservation is an important aspect that directly affects environmental performance and thus notes the energy loss as an OFI. An OFI does not require action on the part of the auditee, because there are not any defined requirements that must be met.

Because there is no clear requirement related to the practice being observed, the auditor must use judgment and perspective when generating OFIs. This is why the generation of OFIs is more difficult than conformance verification. It takes experience and some level of familiarity with a process to generate meaningful OFIs. Auditor training should provide clear guidelines for generating OFIs and meaningful examples.

Identifying *best practices* is a valid objective of an audit but one that requires significant perspective and objectiveness. Experienced internal auditors in particular are in a very favorable position to identify best practices during audits so that they can be communicated and implemented throughout other portions of the organization as appropriate. Citing a best practice is appropriate when the auditor finds performance to be significantly better than average and well beyond the minimum required to comply with the standard or the organization's basic requirements. The systematic identification of best practices, however, looks beyond the performance numbers and seeks to identify the enablers of performance so that others within the organization can judge whether the practice should be adopted by his or her team, department, or business unit. This type of "deeper dive" is primarily within the realm of internal auditors.

Verifying *effectiveness* is one of the most important objectives of any management system audit. This objective goes beyond basic correction of identified weaknesses and evidence of some improvement and focuses on the primary purpose of the process and the extent to which the process is accomplishing that purpose. In today's lean organization, all tasks must add value—they must provide results. While management may see broad, overall metrics relating to strategic objectives, auditors are in a unique position to identify waste and inefficiencies at the process or subprocess level. Furthermore, when auditors identify areas where expected results are not being achieved, they must then be able to thoroughly investigate those areas to help identify the reasons why. In most organizations these reasons are associated with poorly designed and poorly validated processes, poor quality inputs from or alignment with other processes, or nonconformance to established policies and procedures.

For the long term, the goal is to establish a mindset where the auditor is always looking for evidence that actions are effective, not just on an overall process basis, but also for each activity within the process. In effect, the auditor also performs an informal value analysis of the process, looking for opportunities to improve the effectiveness and efficiency of the process by identifying instances where the resources and inputs are not providing the expected outputs or results. Once this is achieved, attitudes relating to the value of the audit itself will start to change. Of course, this is a lot easier to say than to actually do, and it requires strong management commitment and support.

The basic elements of an internal audit program include the selection and training of the auditors, the development of checklists to guide the auditors in what to look for, the development of an audit schedule, and the design of a system to track audit findings.

To be effective, internal auditors need to be trained both in the audit process and in the standard to which they will be auditing. Details of this training are beyond the scope of this book. Readers are referred to *The Management System Auditor's Handbook* (ASQ Quality Press) for a comprehensive discussion of auditor training, techniques, and audit program design and management.

Checklists are not required for the internal audit, but they do help ensure a comprehensive review and consistency in audit performance. New auditors in particular will benefit from a detailed checklist. A set of audit checklists for ISO 14001 is included on the CD. Note that these checklists combine related clauses together to form natural audit processes. A complete discussion on how to properly use the checklists to full advantage is provided in *The Management System Auditor's Handbook*. Note that these checklists address requirements contained only in the ISO 14001 standard, however. You must also ensure that you are complying with your local policies and procedures.

The audit schedule shows the areas or topics that will be evaluated and when they will be conducted. A typical audit schedule covers one year. The schedule should be responsive to the needs of the organization. By "responsive," we mean that the schedule should evaluate more important elements more often, along with any areas where problems or issues have repeatedly occurred. For most systems this will mean that the deployment of the operational controls will be evaluated more often than will common system elements such as document and record control. An example of a typical audit schedule is shown in Figure 4.38. A template for this schedule has also been included in the Environmental Planning Workbook on the CD.

The schedule shows the areas to be audited. A pop-up comment in each topic's cell provides details on the scope of each audit. As in the other worksheets, a formula has been built in to calculate the performance statistics for audit completion.

Note that this audit schedule identifies the current environmental objectives and what the organization believes are its most significant environmental activities. This provides guidance when scheduling the different audit topics. Those areas that are more important or that are key to achieving the organization's environmental objectives should be evaluated more frequently than other areas. The schedule also shows when the environmental compliance reviews and drills are scheduled to be performed.

Environmental compliance reviews are similar to an audit, but they are performed at a more detailed level and are normally done by those having specific knowledge of the regulatory requirements that the organization must adhere to. While internal management system auditors will check to ensure that the compliance reviews are being completed, environmental specialists normally conduct the compliance reviews. The compliance review will evaluate conformance to the detailed regulatory requirements that apply to the organization.

Many companies hire an outside environmental consulting firm or use a corporate environmental specialist to perform the review(s). In this case it is important that the management representative receive a detailed report of the compliance review. You should be able to demonstrate that all regulatory requirements listed on your register of regulations have been examined and actions taken to correct any deficiencies.

Audit tracking systems usually mirror the system to track nonconformities and related corrective and preventive action. I normally recommend that the same system be used. Any nonconformities resulting from the audit should be written up on an action request form and tracked using the action request log. The same requirements for root cause identification, long-term

Internal Audit Schedule - CY 2006
Initiated - 12/16/05
Last Revised - 4/16/06

Audit Area/Process/Month	Jan	Feb	Mar	Apr	May	Jun	Jul	Aug	Sep
Environmental Planning									
Completed				X 4/12/2006		X			
Status (R-Y-G)				G					
Environmental Improvement									
Completed				X 4/12/2006		X			
Status (R-Y-G)				Y					
Document and Record Control									
Completed				X 4/12/2006			X		
Status (R-Y-G)				Y					
Training, Purchasing, and Communication									
Completed				X 4/13/2006			X		
Status (R-Y-G)				G					
Management Support									
Completed				X 4/13/2006		X			
Status (R-Y-G)				G					
Operational Control - Materials Management									
Completed				X 4/13/2006					X
Status (R-Y-G)				Y					
Operational Control - Waste Management									
Completed				X 4/14/2006			X		
Status (R-Y-G)				Y					
Operational Control - Conservation									
Completed				X 4/14/2006			X		
Status (R-Y-G)				G					
Environmental Compliance Review - Waste Mgmt									
Completed			X 3/9/2006						
Status (R-Y-G)			G						
Environmental Compliance Review - Air and water									
Completed			X 3/9/2006						
Status (R-Y-G)			G						
Spill Drill									
Completed					X				
Status (R-Y-G)									

Most Important Environmental Aspects
- Oil Management and Disposal
- Scrap Steel Management
- Energy Conservation

Current Environmental Objectives
- Reduce energy consumption
- Reduce the amount of scrap steel generated

Figure 4.38   Example EMS audit schedule.

action to prevent recurrence, and action verification should apply to audit nonconformances. Using one system to track all deficiencies is usually easier than maintaining separate systems.

Finally, note that records of the audits must be maintained. As a minimum, you should maintain copies of the completed audit checklists, the audit action requests, and the cover sheet that summarizes the results of the audit. Most organizations keep these records for a minimum of three years to correspond to the typical certification cycle, which is also three years.

SUMMARY

This chapter started with the identification of the organization's legal and other requirements and significant environmental aspects. Together with the policy statement, these actions form the core of the EMS. Because of their importance, significant detail was provided in how to identify environmental aspects and determine which ones are significant and must be controlled. The chapter then moved into the selection of appropriate controls for the significant aspects, including the use of procedures, mechanical and system controls, subcontractors, and maintenance requirements. Monitoring of the control of significant aspects was then discussed, followed by the design of common supporting systems such as document and record control, training, communication, corrective and preventive action systems, and the internal audit program. Throughout this chapter, tools and techniques were provided to facilitate the design of these systems. Especially useful is the Environmental Planning Workbook, which provides a central file that can be used to manage almost all elements of the EMS. The workbook and the tools, along with the example procedures, are also on the CD provided with this book.

Although it has been noted in several sections, it is worth repeating that the organization should capitalize on any systems already in place as a result of prior implementation of a quality or OH&S management system. This is especially true for the common support elements like document and record control, training, corrective and preventive action, and internal audits. While you can maintain completely independent systems if you wish, it will take longer to implement and will probably result in some redundancy and possibly a little confusion if you do.

At this point the basic EMS foundation has been designed. The next chapter examines issues involving the deployment of the system.

5

EMS Deployment

In this chapter we will focus on the steps needed to successfully roll out your EMS. Successful deployment doesn't just happen—it must be carefully planned and skillfully executed. Remember that the overall success of your EMS depends on obtaining the support and involvement of your entire workforce. If only five or six individuals "own" the EMS, it will not provide the environmental performance improvements that result in significant benefit to the environment or increases in your bottom line.

The major steps involved in deploying the EMS include:

- Reviewing, approving, and issuing the system's policies and procedures

- Deploying any other operational controls associated with your significant environmental aspects

- Providing initial all-hands awareness training, if not already completed

- Providing activity-specific training on the procedures, policies, and other operational controls implemented

- Initiating the monitoring defined in the design phase and trending the results

- Conducting the first round of internal management system audits

Each of these steps will now be covered in detail.

REVIEWING, APPROVING, AND ISSUING SYSTEM POLICIES AND PROCEDURES

Many of the company's operational controls will be in the form of policies and procedures. Identification of the procedures needed will have been accomplished during the design phase, and some procedures may have already been drafted. In this section we will discuss some of the most common procedures needed to support a typical company's EMS. We will also discuss the steps necessary to ensure the accuracy of these documents and to get them issued to locations where needed.

- *Material and waste handling procedure* (see Figure 5.1): this procedure provides a central repository for controls needed to properly manage a company's hazardous and industrial materials and wastes. Sometimes organizations will develop separate procedures for material handling and for waste handling. This is recommended if the primary functional responsibilities for materials and wastes differ. An example might be a situation where the logistics function (for example, material handlers) has the primary responsibility for material handling, storage, and control, while the facilities function has the primary responsibility for the management of all waste streams. The recommended structure for the procedure(s) is as follows:

  - *General section:* provides general requirements that apply to all materials and/or wastes. Examples might include labeling and identification, upright storage, container integrity verification and covering, and other common requirements.

  - *Specific precautions and controls:* these sections include requirements unique to each specific material or waste that needs to be controlled. Separate sections may be developed for oils, gases, solvents, paints, universal wastes (for example, batteries and fluorescent bulbs), oily scrap steel, and/or chemicals. Because the general section provides common requirements applicable to all materials and/or wastes, these sections are normally fairly short. If there are more detailed instructions for the handling of any of these materials or wastes, these instructions are also referenced in the appropriate section. Required personal protective equipment should also be listed here.

  - *Spill response:* this section may contain general instructions for responding to spills or other minor incidents. Reference to more detailed emergency response procedures should be included.

−Inspections, verifications, and records: this section outlines the various inspections of materials in storage, container verifications, and other checks needed to ensure proper maintenance of materials and wastes. A short discussion of the completion, collection, and retention of records relating to these inspections should also be included, along with a reference to the document and record control procedure.

- *Recycling program procedure* (see Figure 5.2): this procedure provides a convenient place to list the system controls used to manage the organization's recycling program. Within the body of the procedure, separate sections call out the methods and locations for each type of recyclable, such as paper, cardboard, scrap wood, aluminum cans, bottles, plastics, and metal. Each section identifies the types of materials and wastes recycled within that category and where to deliver them for recycling. A separate section could also be added to address used office furniture, carpeting, and other such items that can frequently be donated or recycled, along with the name of the company coordinator to contact.

- *Energy conservation guidelines* (see Figure 5.3): this procedure contains recommended practices for minimizing energy consumption. The procedure is typically made up of separate sections for environmental aspects, such as lighting, HVAC, office equipment (including computers and monitors), production equipment, building maintenance, and purchasing. Within each section are the recommended controls for each aspect. Examples would include a recommended range for setting thermostats in the winter and summer, settings for the advanced power management features on computers and monitors, and requirements to turn off the lights when the office or conference room is not in use. Notice these are called guidelines because they may not be appropriate in all situations (for example, you should not shut down the company's Internet server at the end of the day). Even though these are stated as guidelines, internal auditors and inspectors can still evaluate compliance to the recommended practices during assessments, and trends can be developed showing adherence to these practices so that actions can be taken if they are ignored. The purchasing section would alert any potential requisitioner to consider energy efficiency as a criterion for selection of new equipment.

- *Chemical management plan* (see Figure 5.4): this formal plan is typically used when the company has an on-site laboratory where reagents or laboratory/testing chemicals are used. It is not used to address bulk chemicals used in the production process, which would be found in the material and waste handling procedure. The chemical management plan covers general precautions for the safe storage, handling, and disposal of laboratory chemicals, along with any unique instructions for specific chemicals. It also typically addresses the organization's chemical inventory system, including minimum and maximum amounts for each chemical, periodic inventories, and shelf-life controls.

• *Bulk liquid transfer procedure* (see Figure 5.5): this plan is used in organizations that receive bulk liquids or gases. The procedure covers safeguards used to prevent spills and incidents that may occur during the transfer of liquids from the carrier to the organization's storage tanks. Examples of some of the safeguards would potentially include staging of spill materials, covering or diking of storm water drains (or closing of shutoff valves), integrity checks of hoses and fittings prior to transfer, and monitoring of tank levels during filling operations.

Each of these procedures, plus any others developed as part of the EMS, should be thoroughly reviewed and approved by those having in-depth knowledge of the activity prior to issuance. Once approved, each procedure (or instruction) should be placed on the master list and then distributed to the locations where it will be needed, or could be needed in the event of an incident. Where electronic document control is used, folders should be set up that provide a clear pathway to the document that any user can understand. Training of personnel will be required in the procedures and is addressed in a later section.

DEPLOYING OTHER OPERATIONAL CONTROLS

The organization probably identified other operational controls beyond procedures and instructions. Several examples were provided in the previous chapter and could include *engineered safeguards* such as filtered ventilation systems, wastewater treatment systems, and alarm systems. Each of these systems should be examined for proper operation, for maintenance, and for documentation detailing how to properly operate and maintain the system. If needed, separate instructions should be developed for each engineered system. Personnel competencies required to properly operate these systems should also be added to the training requirements matrix, developed during the design phase.

You may also have to set up specific areas for collecting recyclable wastes, batteries, and other such materials. Obtaining and staging collection containers may also be needed.

Preventive maintenance may also be used as an element of operational control. Maintenance should be conducted on tanks, piping systems and valves, pumps, and engineered safeguards noted earlier. In addition, keeping production equipment free of leaks and operating at a high efficiency reduces manufacturing's environmental impact. Buildings also need to be maintained, with special consideration given to the condition of production floors (for example, no cracks or other effluent pathways to the soil or groundwater), sumps, and weatherproofing. Also consider the building's HVAC and other energy management systems. Verifying that maintenance requirements are in place and are being conducted as scheduled is an important part of establishing operational controls.

Finally, it was noted in Chapter 4 that *subcontractors* form an element in your operational controls. Most important are the environmental services firms such as waste disposal companies and suppliers of maintenance on HVAC and other building systems. Bulk material providers may also be listed in this group. For each subcontractor listed, verify that this individual is properly carrying out his or her responsibilities as expected. For example, verify that your HVAC contractor uses only certified technicians trained in the capture and reclamation of refrigerants. Verify that your calibration provider is ISO 17025 certified and that you have a copy of his or her certification and laboratory scope on file. If your environmental waste disposal supplier also characterizes your waste streams for you, verify that you have copies of the analysis performed.

At this initial stage the implementation of operational controls will primarily be focused on developing some new procedures and verifying other existing controls. Major expenditures for new systems will not normally be needed at this stage; rather, they would be considered as part of your potential environmental objectives, discussed in the next chapter.

PROVIDING INITIAL AWARENESS TRAINING

At this point in the project some initial awareness training may have already been provided. That session would have focused on the decision to implement an EMS and would have included a discussion on the need for environmental performance improvement and how such a system could benefit the organization. If the organization had already developed an environmental policy statement, this would also have been discussed. Not known at the time, however, and therefore not yet communicated would have been the results of the initial environmental review. Most importantly, everyone should be made aware of some of the more important significant environmental aspects and how their associated activities will be controlled to minimize any adverse environmental aspects and to drive performance improvement. This training session will focus on communicating this information along with employees' responsibilities for following procedures and participating in environmental improvement projects. Topics that should be discussed include the following:

- The organization's environmental policy statement and how it relates to the company's activities, products, and services.

- The organization's major environmental aspects and how employees can help to reduce their environmental impacts. While some significant environmental aspects affect only a few employees and may not warrant discussion at an all-hands briefing, more global aspects such as energy conservation, recycling, natural resource conservation, and material and waste handling (in general, not specific) can and should be briefly discussed so that each employee can see his or her role in environmental performance improvement.

- The procedures and instructions that have been developed to control the significant environmental aspects discussed earlier. Each employee should be aware of the organization's energy conservation guidelines, material and waste handling procedure, and recycling program.

- The systems that have been established to allow communication and involvement of the workforce in environmental performance improvement. As noted earlier, sustained performance improvement will not occur without the participation of the organization's rank-and-file employees. They need to be instructed as to how they can become involved and participate.

This orientation will typically run between 30 minutes and 1 hour. It should be reinforced by articles in the company newsletter, staff meetings, and postings on area communication boards as the system is deployed and matures. Lack of such communication will seriously impact the effectiveness of the management system.

PROVIDING ACTIVITY-SPECIFIC TRAINING

Although the orientation training provided a brief discussion on some of the organization's significant environmental aspects, it did not go into any detail on either the aspects or their associated controls. Because each area will have unique environmental aspects associated with its activities, there will be a need for activity-specific orientation and training. This is best carried out by the area supervisor or team leader. Environmental bulletins, if prepared, can assist the supervisor in presenting this orientation.

Remember also that the standard requires competency in tasks that could impact the environment, so detailed training on procedures and/or systems should also be conducted where needed to ensure that employees are aware of the activities they do that could impact the environment, the harm that could be done if not done correctly, and most importantly how to do them correctly. This will typically involve training in the procedures and instructions developed for operational control that are applicable to that area. This activity-specific training should be recorded and shown on the training requirements matrix or other system used for tracking competency attainment.

INITIATING ENVIRONMENTAL MONITORING

One of the final steps in designing the EMS was to assign metrics to monitor and measure performance in controlling significant environmental aspects and/or environmental improvement. Implementation of this monitoring requires developing records to keep track of data, training appropriate functions on the collection of data (frequencies, where to record, where to keep the records, and so on), and initiating monitoring and analysis of the data. Do not put this off. You will need some kind of history to show that your system is working, and you should have some data on your performance prior to setting environmental objectives and targets. Because it will take some time to generate this information, get an early start.

Keep in mind that many metrics sound good when you are sitting in a conference room and brainstorming how one might measure environmental performance as part of the initial environmental review. Often a different perspective arises when the data must actually be collected and analyzed. What once appeared to be a good metric may suddenly become not very useful because of production volume changes or an inability to correlate the amount of waste produced or energy used to a level of performance due to inherent fluctuations in activity. Expect to modify your metrics somewhat from your initial attempts to implement your environmental monitoring. If the information provided by the metrics is not providing the insight needed to establish performance, come up with a more useful metric.

Once the metrics have been gathered, communication of the organization's performance in key areas should begin. If area communication boards were established, the posting of indicators of performance important to that area should be made on the board. Especially important will be efforts to highlight areas where improvement is evident. Show that the system is working.

CONDUCTING THE FIRST ROUND OF INTERNAL MANAGEMENT SYSTEM AUDITS

With operational controls in place, workforce training completed, and environmental monitoring initiated, the core EMS is now in place, and the first round of internal management system audits should be performed. Plan on conducting at least two rounds of internal audits prior to any certification assessments. The first round will verify proper implementation along with training and general awareness of the new policies and procedures. Expect to find quite a few weaknesses. Despite your best efforts, pockets will be found where individuals or groups will be slow to implement the new controls and practices. This may be due to incomplete implementation (for example, procedures are not available in these areas) or normal resistance to change. Identified weaknesses will be documented so that they can be addressed.

If not already completed, training should be provided for the organization's internal auditors. It is often best to schedule this training just before the first round of audits. Auditing is a skill, and skills are forgotten unless they are applied. This initial audit needs to be a complete system audit and should be accomplished in a short period of time to permit timely reaction to implementation issues. The first round of audits should take no longer than one week and could be accomplished in one or two days if multiple audit teams are used.

Actions resulting from the first complete system audit should be aggressively tracked by the management representative and/or the audit program manager. There is often a natural letdown after passing a major milestone. Some employees may let their guard down and slip into old habits. Do not let this happen. This is the most critical stage in the life cycle of the new program. Fix any weaknesses in the program and continue the push to get results. The greatest gains in environmental performance improvement are often accomplished during the first six months to a year after implementation, as there will be a lot of low-hanging fruit to pick. Take advantage of the momentum that such victories can provide to solidify the EMS.

1.0 Handling and Storage of Hazardous Materials

    1.1 General Precautions for Handling of Hazardous Materials

        1.1.1 All containers shall be properly labeled to identify their contents. Identification must be retained when transfer is made to other containers (including pails and buckets for sampling) unless the material stays at all times within the direct control of the operator. Incoming hazardous materials can normally be identified by the National Fire Protection Association rating on the material label or by review of the material's MSDSs.

        1.1.2 All operators shall adhere to proper safety instructions, including the wearing of appropriate personal protective equipment while handling hazardous materials. Any spills of hazardous materials shall be immediately contained and addressed using the *Spill Containment and Cleanup of Liquid Spill Instruction.* Notify the management representative of any such events as soon as possible after initial containment actions are complete.

        1.1.3 All hazardous materials will be stored in designated storage locations. Hazardous materials must be properly identified and the identification retained as described in section 2.2. Hazardous materials must be stored in their upright position with all closures, caps, etc. intact except during active transfer operations. Refer to the material storage requirements for more information on hazardous material storage.

    1.2 Propane Tanks

        1.2.1 *Add specific instructions and precautions for handling this material.*

    1.3 Welding Gases

        1.3.1 *Add specific instructions and precautions for handling this material.*

    1.4 Welding Flux, Rods, and Other Materials

        1.4.1 *Add specific instructions and precautions for handling this material.*

    1.5 Oils, Lubricants, and Greases

        1.5.1 *Add specific instructions and precautions for handling this material.*

    1.7 Other Solvents and Chemicals

        1.7.1 *Add specific instructions and precautions for handling this material.*

2.0 Handling and Disposal of Hazardous and Industrial Wastes

    2.1 General Precautions for Handling of Hazardous and Industrial Wastes

        2.1.1 All industrial waste streams must be properly characterized to indicate their content nature of the wastes. Wastes may be characterized based on knowledge of the materials and process or by analysis. Industrial wastes shall be stored in a manner that prevents adverse impact on the environment. These practices include storage of all containers in their proper upright position to minimize the potential for leakage. Oil drums must be provided with secondary containment when in use and all caps, lids, or other closures except when actively transferring to or from containers.

Figure 5.1   Material and waste handling procedure example.   *(Continued)*

(Continued)

2.1.4   The conduct of monthly inspections to ensure the integrity and condition of waste containers. Monthly inspections should also verify proper labeling of wastes. These inspections are performed as part of the monthly safety walk-through.

2.1.5   If any hazardous or industrial waste is spilled, follow the guidance provided in the *Spill Containment and Cleanup of Liquid Spill Instruction* to recover from the incident. Notify the management representative of any such events as soon as possible after initial containment actions are complete.

2.1.6   All hazardous and industrial wastes must be manifested. Manifesting is performed by the maintenance department in accordance with the Michigan Department of Environmental Quality regulations.

2.2   Waste Oils, Sludge, and Byproducts (rags, filters, etc.)

2.2.1   *Add specific instructions and precautions for handling this waste.*

2.3   Waste Chemicals

2.3.1   *Add specific instructions and precautions for handling this waste.*

2.4   Used Fluorescent Bulbs and Batteries

2.4.1   *Add specific instructions and precautions for handling this waste.*

Figure 5.1   (Continued)

1.0   General Recycling and Reuse Requirements

1.1   Recycling is recognized as a preferred approach for minimizing the depletion of natural resources and landfill usage. All employees have a responsibility to recycle or reuse whenever possible.

1.2   Recycling will be pursued only when appropriate markets exist for the products to be recycled. Reuse will be pursued only when it does not impact the quality or efficiency of the product or process.

1.3   Questions regarding recycling and reuse should be directed to the environmental management representative.

2.0   Specific Requirements

2.1   Paper, Magazines, Newspapers, and Catalogs

2.1.1   Dedicated containers have been established for the recycling of paper, magazines, newspapers, and catalogs. Collection areas have been set up in engineering, shipping, and administration areas. Recycled material should be placed in its designated, labeled container.

2.1.2   All paper, magazines, newspapers, and catalogs should be free of paper clips, rubber bands, or other materials before being placed in the containers.

Figure 5.2   Recycling procedure example.   *(Continued)*

(Continued)

2.2 Bottles and Aluminum Cans

    2.2.1 Dedicated containers have been established in engineering, shipping, the cafeteria, and the two break rooms for the recycling of bottles and aluminum cans. All bottles and aluminum cans should be disposed of in the appropriate containers.

2.3 Computers, Monitors, and Other Office Equipment

    2.3.1 Computers, monitors, and other office equipment should be recycled or reused. The individual responsible for disposing of any such equipment shall indicate with a tag or other label whether the equipment is functioning or not functioning. A list of any functioning equipment slated for disposal shall be provided to the environmental management representative at least one week prior to the scheduled disposal date.

    2.3.2 The environmental management representative maintains a clearinghouse of potential internal and external users for used office equipment. Preference is given to internal users with a need. If no internal user for the used equipment can be found, the management representative will attempt to locate an external user (e.g., a school or community program) with a need for the equipment. If no internal or external user can be found, the management representative will provide instructions for the disposition of the equipment. Note that some obsolete office equipment may contain hazardous materials and may require controlled disposal.

2.4 Cardboard, Packaging Material, and Wooden Pallets

    2.4.1 Dedicated containers or storage areas have been established in receiving for the recycling of cardboard, packaging materials, and scrap wooden pallets. Recycled material should be placed in its designated container or storage area.

    2.4.2 All cardboard, packaging materials, and scrap wooden pallets should be free of nails, metal bands, or tie-wraps before being placed in the containers.

    2.4.3 Cardboard will be bailed by qualified material handlers as needed. All cardboard should be bailed prior to the scheduled pickup day. The production control coordinator schedules and arranges for pickup of cardboard, packaging materials, and scrap wooden pallets.

2.5 Office Furniture and Carpeting

    2.5.1 Used office furniture, shelving, carts, and carpeting will be recycled and/or reused whenever practical. The individual responsible for disposing of any such items should notify the environmental management representative at least one week prior to the scheduled disposal date.

Figure 5.2 (Continued)

(Continued)

2.5.2 The environmental management representative maintains a clearinghouse of potential internal and external users for these items. Preference is given to internal users with a need. If no internal user for the used equipment can be found, the management representative will attempt to locate an external user (e.g., a school or community program) with a need for the equipment. The management representative will notify the individual responsible for disposing of these items within one week if another user has been located. If no response is provided within one week, the material may be disposed of normally.

Figure 5.2 (Continued)

1.0 General

1.1 These guidelines are meant to be observed by Advanced Product employees whenever feasible. Because of the generic nature of these recommendations, it is understood that exceptions may occur from time to time. In general, however, these recommendations can and should be followed by all employees.

2.0 Office Equipment

2.1 Turn off unneeded computers, monitors, printers, copiers, and other office equipment at night.

2.2 Procure Energy Star–rated equipment whenever possible.

2.3 Activate power management features on computers, monitors, copiers, and printers to save energy during the workday. Monitors should be set to power down after 30 minutes of inactivity, and hard drives should power down after approximately 1 hour.

3.0 Lighting

3.1 Lighting in individual offices and common areas should be turned off at the end of the day and whenever these spaces will be unoccupied for more than 1 hour.

3.2 Reduce work-area lighting in areas that are near windows and adequately lighted by natural daylight.

3.3 When replacing lighting, consideration should be given to energy-efficient lamping wherever possible. Contact the environmental management representative for options involving alternate lighting sources.

4.0 Personal Comfort

4.1 Set thermostats at 68°–70° for heating and 74°–76° for cooling. If programmable thermostats are an option, the thermostat can be set for 55°–50° for heating and 80° for cooling during unoccupied hours.

4.2 Turn off electric space heaters at the end of the day and whenever the heated space is unoccupied for more than 1 hour.

4.3 Use window blinds to block direct sunlight during the day and prevent the overheating of spaces. During cold months, fully close blinds at night to reduce heat loss.

Figure 5.3 Energy conservation guidelines example. *(Continued)*

(Continued)

5.0 Production and Laboratory Equipment

    5.1 Turn off processing equipment during off shifts or when not in use.

6.0 Maintenance

    6.1 Regularly clean and inspect HVAC systems.

    6.2 Regularly check, clean, and/or change other filtering mechanisms throughout the facility.

    6.3 Keep light fixtures clean.

    6.4 Keep doors and windows tightly shut when not in use. Report drafts from doors, windows, or other areas to the environmental management representative.

    6.5 The production spaces are maintained by the facility HVAC system. Keep rollup doors shut except when necessary to receive or ship products.

7.0 Home Energy Conservation

    7.1 Significant energy and expense can be saved through home energy conservation. The environmental management representative maintains a library of energy conservation tips that can be used to make any home more energy efficient. These tips are available to all employees free of charge. All employees are encouraged to obtain these materials through the environmental management representative.

Figure 5.3 (Continued)

1.0 General Principles for Work with Laboratory Chemicals

In addition to the more detailed recommendations listed, "Prudent Practices" expresses certain general principles, including the following:

1. Minimize all chemical exposures.

2. Avoid underestimation of risk.

3. Provide adequate ventilation.

4. Observe the PELs and the TLVs. The permissible exposure limits (PELs) of OSHA and the threshold limit values (TLVs) of the American Conference of Governmental Industrial Hygienists should not be exceeded.

2.0 Ventilation

    2.1 General Laboratory Ventilation. This system should provide a source of air for breathing and for input to local ventilation devices; it should not be relied on for protection from toxic substances released into the laboratory; ensure that laboratory air is continually replaced, preventing an increase of air concentrations of toxic substances during the working day; direct air flow into the laboratory from nonlaboratory areas and out to the exterior of the building.

    2.2 Modifications. Any alteration of the ventilation system should be made only if thorough testing indicates that worker protection from airborne toxic substances will continue to be adequate.

Figure 5.4 Chemical management plan example.   *(Continued)*

(Continued)

2.3 Performance. Rate: 4–12 room air changes/hour is normally adequate general ventilation if local exhaust systems such as hoods are used as the primary method of control.

2.4 Evaluation. Quality and quantity of ventilation should be evaluated on installation, regularly monitored, and reevaluated whenever a change in local ventilation devices is made.

3.0 Chemical Procurement, Distribution, Storage, and Handling

3.1 Procurement. Only the amount of each chemical needed for the near-term future should be procured to minimize disposal due to expired shelf lives and the risk of breakage or accidents. Minimum and maximum levels of inventory have been established for each chemical used. Chemicals should be ordered when the minimum level of chemicals on hand has been reached, and only the amount needed to the maximum amount should be ordered. Chemical inventories shall be performed each month.

3.2 Distribution and Storage. All chemicals shall be stored in designated storage cabinets or lockers when not in use. Each designated storage areas shall contain a listing of the chemicals stored within on the outside of the cabinet or locker. Only the chemicals indicated on the list may be stored in the cabinet or locker to prevent mixing of incompatible materials.

3.3 Chemical Labeling. All chemical shall be stored in their original containers when not in use. Any secondary containers shall be visibly labeled with the name of the chemical except when the secondary container is under the direct control of the chemist (e.g., when storing chemicals in a 250 ml beaker while awaiting analysis). Chemicals shall never be stored in aluminum cans or bottles that could be mistaken for beverage containers.

3.4 Chemical Handling

3.4.1 When chemicals are hand carried, the container should be placed in an outside container or bucket.

3.4.2 Chemicals shall be handled only by those trained and qualified to do so. Training must include the use of appropriate personal protective equipment. Face shields and/or other approved eye protection is required during the mixing, analysis, and/or transfer of any chemical; other safeguards may also be required (e.g., gloves and apron).

3.4.3 All chemical containers must be capped when not in use and should be stored in a safe location to prevent inadvertent collision or breakage.

4.0 Chemical Disposal

Minor amounts of residual chemical wastes (e.g., analysis waste and rinse water) may be disposed of down the laboratory drain in accordance with local municipality regulations. Exceptions include all wastes associated with silver nitrate analysis, which must be collected in designated containers. All silver nitrate waste and larger amounts of expired or obsolete chemicals must be disposed of as hazardous wastes.

Figure 5.4 (Continued)

Procedure

When the bulk material transporter arrives at the facility, an area or department representative will direct the transporter to the appropriate tank. The transporter and the area or department representative will follow this transfer procedure:

- The transporter is responsible for ensuring that the truck has appropriate Department of Transportation placarding prior to entering the facility.

- The transporter is instructed by the area or department representative regarding the facility's bulk material transfer protocol.

- The area or department representative indicates proper tanker spotting.

- The area or department representative verifies that the volume available in the bulk storage tank is greater than the volume of product to be transferred from the delivery tank. The transporter is responsible for ensuring capacity of the tank truck is not exceeded.

- The area or department representative will remove pipeline caps or blanker flanges and will ensure connection to the correct delivery transfer lines.

- The area or department representative inspects facility transfer connections for damage or material leaks.

- The transporter will make all connections necessary for material transfer.

- The area or department representative will stay alert and have a clear, unobstructed view of the operation at all times during the transfer.

- The area or department representative will verify the transporter is in attendance, monitoring the transfer operation.

- The area or department representative is authorized to order the transporter to terminate the transfer and have the driver move to the tanker during an emergency.

- The transporter will remove transfer lines such that excess material will flow back toward the receiving tank or catchment basin.

- The area or department representative will monitor the termination process.

Inspections

The bulk material storage area is inspected weekly by the appropriate area or department, and an inspection log is completed.

Records

Copies of shipping manifests are retained by the appropriate area or department. Waste manifests and the inspection log are retained by the environmental management representative or designee.

Figure 5.5   Bulk liquid transfer procedure.

SUMMARY

This relatively short chapter focused on the initial deployment of your EMS. It was short because most of the real effort occurred during the planning and design phases. Remember that deployment involves more than simply issuing procedures. It involves verification, training, initial monitoring, auditing, and communication. Communication also involves visible management support for the system, not just by actions but by words. Leaders who take the time to talk with employees, ask the right questions, demand accountability, and demonstrate the right behaviors accomplish more than any specified set of actions in creating the culture for the EMS to succeed. This leadership will be especially critical during the early stages of the system deployment, pending success at getting everyone involved in environmental performance improvement.

Part III

EMS Improvement

P art III focuses on the steps needed to improve the EMS and the organization's environmental performance. Chapter 6 describes the actions needed to address ISO 14001's requirements for environmental objectives and targets and management reviews. Chapter 7 discusses the internal audit process in more detail, and Chapter 8 gives ideas and examples for moving beyond compliance to sustainable development.

6

The Improvement Phase

The improvement phase completes the implementation of your ISO 14001 EMS. During this phase the organization uses the results of its internal audits and environmental performance metrics to assess how well the system is working and where environmental improvement objectives are warranted. Although many organizations identify their environmental objectives and targets much earlier, I recommend waiting until a firm baseline of the organization's environmental performance has been established. That way, meaningful objectives can be established that focus on continual improvements in areas that will significantly benefit the environment.

The improvement phase also completes the first Plan-Do-Study-Act circle of improvement, as indicated by the inner ring of actions shown in Figure 6.1. It also initiates the second round of improvements based on the results of the management review and the setting of environmental objectives and targets, as shown by the solid dark arrow and outer ring of Figure 6.1. The process will continue as the organization continually looks for ways to improve both its management system and its environmental performance.

PREPARING FOR THE MANAGEMENT REVIEW

The management review is a major event in the life cycle of your EMS. This may be the only time senior management is available for a focused review of both the EMS and the organization's environmental performance. Obviously, careful planning for this meeting is essential to ensure the greatest benefits are obtained.

There are several considerations relating to scheduling the management review. First, the review should be scheduled during a day when most, if

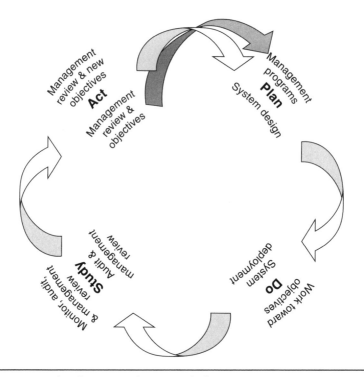

Figure 6.1 The Plan-Do-Study-Act spiral of improvement.

not all, of the senior management team can attend. As a minimum, the management representative, the president (or plant manager, if a manufacturing facility), the senior production manager, the chief engineer, and the facilities/maintenance manager should be present. If any of these key executives are not available, rescheduling should be considered. As many other top managers as possible should also be available, although it is probably acceptable for them to send alternates if they have schedule conflicts and cannot attend.

Second, plan on spending at least three hours, and possibly up to a full day, to conduct the review. For companies that hold monthly, quarterly, or semiannual management reviews, the review might be accomplished in two or three hours. Most companies hold annual reviews, and in this case it will take some time to review and discuss all the information required. Even when the organization holds several reviews during the year, it is best to have a comprehensive end-of-year review to ensure long-term trends and patterns can be analyzed. It also serves as a great platform for evaluating performance in achieving annual environmental objectives and to set new objectives for the coming year.

Third, schedule the annual review to occur shortly before the organization's strategic planning and budgeting process. One of the goals of the management review should be to identify environmental objectives and targets for the coming year. It doesn't do any good to identify meaningful objectives if there is no money left to fund them because the budget has already been set.

Once the schedule has been set, it is time to develop the agenda. I strongly recommend creating a formal agenda and communicating it well in advance of the review. The agenda should list not only the topics to be discussed but also who will lead the discussion of each topic and how much time each topic will be allocated. During the meeting the agenda should be used to focus the meeting and keep it on track.

A listing of topics that should be discussed during the review includes:

• Internal audit results and the results of reviews of compliance to regulatory and other requirements

• External communications (including complaints)

• Environmental performance (monitoring and measurement results)

• Performance in achieving objectives and targets

• Status of corrective and preventive actions

• Follow-up from previous reviews

• Changes in regulatory and other requirements

• Needed changes to the environmental policy

• Needed adjustments to environmental objectives and targets

• Any other changes to the EMS needed to meet the organization's commitment to continual improvement

These topics, when discussed in full, should provide ample information to evaluate the management system's overall suitability, adequacy, and effectiveness. The purpose of the review, however, is not to simply note the status of the EMS but rather to prompt action. The management review provides a unique forum, when those having the responsibility and the authority to commit to action are all present and focused on the EMS. A format for a management review agenda is provided in Figure 6.2.

Once the agenda has been set, the management representative should begin gathering and summarizing the data that will be presented during the review. In order to cover the topics on the agenda in the allocated time (about four hours in the example), the presentations will need to be organized. Not every topic will be discussed in detail. For example, the discussion on audit

Annual Management Review Agenda and Report Form

Date of review: 3/02/06

Time: 11:00 AM–3:00 PM

A management review of the EMS will be conducted on the date and time indicated above. The review will include the items checked below. Please come prepared to discuss the checked items that you are assigned as Champion. Please contact the environmental management representative if you are unable to attend.

Review Item	Champion	Time
❑ Follow-up actions from previous management reviews	EMS management rep	20 min.
❑ Results of EMS audits (internal and external)	Audit program manager	20 min.
❑ Results of EMS compliance reviews	EMS management rep	20 min.
❑ Summary of EMS communications		
❑ From external parties	EMS management rep	10 min.
❑ From employees	EMS management rep	10 min.
❑ Environmental process performance including trends		30 min.
❑ Natural gas and propane	Facilities manager	
❑ Welding gases	Production manager	
❑ Gas flux	Production manager	
❑ Energy	Facilities manager	
❑ Ethylene glycol	Facilities manager	
❑ Lubricating oils	Production manager	
❑ Wastewater oils	Production manager	
❑ Cardboard, pallets, and shrink-wrap	Production control manager	
❑ Status of significant preventive and corrective actions	EMS management rep	15 min.
❑ Status of any new or pending EMS regulations	EMS management rep	10 min.
❑ Changes that could affect the EMS	All	5 min.
❑ Status in achieving EMS objectives and goals	EMS management rep	30 min.
❑ Recommendations for improvement	All	15 min.
❑ New EMS objectives and targets	All	30 min.
❑ Other (list)	All	30 min.

Figure 6.2 Management review agenda. *(Continued)*

(Continued)

Summary of Actions and Agreements Reached			
Action	**Who**	**By When**	**Date Completed**

Note: Include any carryover items from the previous review that were not completed (assign new estimated completion date).

Distribution:

President

EMS management representative

Figure 6.2   (Continued)

results should not examine every finding from every audit performed during the previous 12 months, but it should instead focus on trends and patterns in the findings and repeat findings and on those that had special significance. The same could be said for the review of corrective and preventive action, with the primary focus being on any that remain outstanding and on indicators that the actions were effective in eliminating the problems. Summaries are best presented using graphs, charts, and tables. The management representative should assemble these prior to the review.

The management representative will also need to prepare the environmental performance monitoring data for presentation. Although many of these metrics may have been reviewed monthly, this review should focus on long-term trends and comparisons with previous periods. The management representative should develop a standard format for data presentation that shows current performance, performance over the last 12 months, and perhaps annual comparisons over the last 3 years. Once the format has been prepared, it can be provided to others responsible for presenting their data during the review. An example is shown in Figure 6.3.

The format shown in the figure allows the management team to quickly assess current and long-term performance in reducing the amount of oily wastewater generated and subsequently disposed of. Notice that the graph also shows the goal for oily wastewater disposal set for current year (CY) 2006 and how much money was saved by the reduction efforts. The

Waste Water Oil Disposal	Jan	Feb	Mar	Apr	May	Jun	Jul	Aug	Sep	Oct	Nov	Dec	Total
Waste quantity	850	900	1,200	900	780	700	650	700	620	600	580	550	9,030

Annual quantity	2004	2005	2006	Cost savings 2006	$900
	12,080	12,040	9,030	($0.30/gallon disposal costs)	

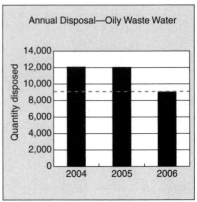

Figure 6.3   Format for displaying performance data.

management team may question the spike in March 2006, and it may ask about actions to further decrease the amount of oily wastewater generated. The management team may learn that most of the current costs of disposal are associated with transportation costs and that plans are to reduce the frequency of disposal to once every two months now that the monthly volume has been reduced below 600 gallons (the plant has one 1300-gallon holding tank). This should result in additional savings of $1200 in CY 2007. This discussion will also serve as a backdrop, along with the discussions on the other metrics, for identifying environmental objectives and targets for the next year.

To prepare for the discussion on pending regulatory changes that could impact the EMS, the management representative should talk with the company's environmental attorney (if it has one) or outside consultant, or he or she can visit the federal or state Web sites where new and upcoming regulatory changes are normally posted. Planned facility modifications, expansions, new products, and process lines should be considered to help plan for the discussion on changes that could impact the EMS.

The summary of internal and external communications should be sourced from the organization's communication log or other system for collecting the views of outside interested parties and employees. Complaints, concerns, and suggestions for improvement should all be considered during the review.

Once the material for the review has been assembled, the management representative should consider providing a copy of the presentation and its charts, graphs, and summaries to attendees a week or so before the review if possible. This will give the management team a chance to scan the information and identify areas of concern or question prior to conducting the review. This will lead to a more focused and timely management review. This pre-review review of the data cannot be allowed to become a surrogate for the actual review, however. If the management representative has indications or experience that some senior managers will not attend the review if given a chance to see the data beforehand, he or she should not distribute the data prior to the review. Remember that the purpose of the review is to promote discussion and action, not simply to conduct a status review. This cannot happen unless the senior management team actually meets. Always provide a copy of the agenda at least two and preferably four weeks prior to the review to all attendees. This allows them time to prepare their assigned areas and to clear their schedule.

CONDUCTING THE MANAGEMENT REVIEW

The agenda should serve as the template for conducting the actual review. Follow the agenda, and use basic meeting management skills to keep the review focused and on track. Because all attendees have received the agenda and know what topics they are responsible for and how much time they have to summarize that topic, the meeting should flow smoothly. Allow additional time for serious discussions as long as they are focused on actions. Note that there is an additional 30 minutes for other items at the end of the example agenda.

Check off each item as it is discussed. You will also need to generate meeting minutes, or records of the review. These records need not document the details of each topic discussed, but rather they should summarize the overall discussion. Together with the presentation package (graphs, charts, and so on) used for the review and the action matrix on the form, this summary will provide adequate documentation of what was discussed, the results of the discussion, and the details of any actions, decisions, or agreements reached. I prefer to use an electronic copy of the agenda to keep my meeting minutes. A short summary of each topic can be inserted underneath each review item. This can be done by hand by inserting five or six spaces between each topic in the form and then printing it out before the meeting for use in taking notes. An individual may be assigned to enter the notes directly using a laptop during the meeting. An example is shown in Figure 6.4.

Especially important is that any and all actions, decisions, and agreements reached during the management review be fully documented. The example form provided has a table inserted to accomplish this. The management representative should review each action item at the end of the meeting prior to disbanding the team to ensure there is no misunderstanding or

Review Item	Champion	Time
☒ Follow-up actions from previous management reviews	EMS management rep	20 min.

Comments: All actions from the management review of December 2005 have been completed or will be completed as a result of this review.

☒ Results of EMS audits (internal and external)	Audit program manager	20 min.

Comments: Two external audits were completed in 2005, resulting in three NCs and four OFIs. The NCs covered objectives and targets, operational control (containers not labeled), and control of records (record listing and retention). All three NCs have been addressed and corrective actions accepted by the registrar. One internal audit was completed in April 2005 prior to the external audits. No NCs were recorded during this internal audit, but 12 OFIs were cited. It is considered that the NC found by the external auditor relating to container labeling was an isolated occurrence and is not reflective of the internal audit process; however, the audit team should have addressed the two other systematic NCs pointed out by our external registrar. This was regarded as a learning point for the internal auditors. It was noted that this was the first internal audit for most auditors.

☒ Results of EMS compliance reviews	EMS management rep	20 min.

Comments: An environmental compliance review was conducted by an outside consultant in April 2005 and included all regulatory requirements applicable to API. We were found to be substantially compliant in all areas, with some weaknesses in the SWPPP. A new SWPPP has been drafted and is in the process of being finalized by an outside consulting firm. Internal approval is still required, as is confirmation that all conditions required by the plan can be met. Action items were assigned to ensure actions are completed.

☒ Summary of EMS communications		
☒ From external parties	EMS management rep	10 min.

Comments: No external communications were received since implementation of the revised system (reference the communication log).

Figure 6.4   Use of the agenda to record the results of the management review.   *(Continued)*

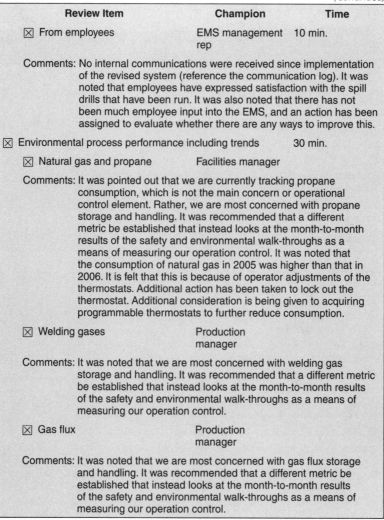

(Continued)

Review Item	Champion	Time
☒ From employees	EMS management rep	10 min.

Comments: No internal communications were received since implementation of the revised system (reference the communication log). It was noted that employees have expressed satisfaction with the spill drills that have been run. It was also noted that there has not been much employee input into the EMS, and an action has been assigned to evaluate whether there are any ways to improve this.

☒ Environmental process performance including trends   30 min.

| ☒ Natural gas and propane | Facilities manager | |

Comments: It was pointed out that we are currently tracking propane consumption, which is not the main concern or operational control element. Rather, we are most concerned with propane storage and handling. It was recommended that a different metric be established that instead looks at the month-to-month results of the safety and environmental walk-throughs as a means of measuring our operation control. It was noted that the consumption of natural gas in 2005 was higher than that in 2006. It is felt that this is because of operator adjustments of the thermostats. Additional action has been taken to lock out the thermostat. Additional consideration is being given to acquiring programmable thermostats to further reduce consumption.

| ☒ Welding gases | Production manager | |

Comments: It was noted that we are most concerned with welding gas storage and handling. It was recommended that a different metric be established that instead looks at the month-to-month results of the safety and environmental walk-throughs as a means of measuring our operation control.

| ☒ Gas flux | Production manager | |

Comments: It was noted that we are most concerned with gas flux storage and handling. It was recommended that a different metric be established that instead looks at the month-to-month results of the safety and environmental walk-throughs as a means of measuring our operation control.

Figure 6.4   (Continued)

miscommunication as to who will do what by when. Again, the purpose of the review is to drive action. Make sure everyone agrees on these actions and who will be responsible for them.

The final section of the agenda-turned-record is the action matrix at the bottom of the form. The action matrix for this review might look as shown in Figure 6.5.

Summary of Actions and Agreements Reached			
Action	**Who**	**By When**	**Date Completed**
Receive final approval of SWPPP	Bob	March 2006	
Verify that all conditions of SWPPP are in place	Tom	April 2006	
Evaluate methods for increasing employee input into the EMS	Chris	April 2006	
Establish a new metric for monitoring propane tank storage and handling	Karen	April 2006	
Establish a new metric for monitoring welding gas cylinder storage and handling	Karen	April 2006	
Establish a new metric for monitoring gas flux container storage and handling	Karen	April 2006	
Modify the monthly safety and environmental checklist to include monitoring of the new metrics	Chris	April 2006	
Investigate feasibility of local disposal of transformer condensation wastewater	Tom	April 2006	
Modify EMS Planning Workbook to denote cardboard, pallets, and shrink-wrap no longer significant	Chris	March 2006	
Establish actions and dates for the objective "Eliminate oil from tools stored outside from reaching storm water drains"	Tom	March 2006	

Figure 6.5   Action matrix for the management review.

You may have noticed that we have not discussed the evaluation of performance in achieving environmental objectives and targets or the identification of new objectives or targets. These absolutely should be a part of the management review, but the importance of the topic warrants a separate section.

ENVIRONMENTAL OBJECTIVES, TARGETS, AND MANAGEMENT PROGRAMS

We are now ready to put the last link into the circular chain that is our EMS. Keep in mind that the actions discussed in this section are in fact happening during the management review. Although it is possible to have a separate review for objectives, targets, and management programs, the management review provides an excellent time to evaluate and set new objectives because the performance of the overall EMS has just been analyzed and discussed, and opportunities to improve it have been identified. With this background, identifying new environmental objectives should be relatively straightforward.

The example management review provided was from an EMS that had already been developed and was undergoing significant modification to make it more effective. For a new EMS, no objectives will have been set, so a review of performance in achieving the objectives will not be needed. The discussion that follows focuses therefore on setting initial objectives and targets and developing management programs to ensure their achievement.

When setting the environmental objectives and targets, keep in mind the requirements of the standard and the discussion provided in Chapter 2 regarding the alignment of the objectives, targets, policy commitments, and significant aspects. As noted in Chapter 2, the standard requires that the following items be considered as part of setting objectives and targets:

- The commitments the organization made in its policy statement

- The organization's legal and other requirements

- The organization's significant environmental aspects

- The organization's financial, business, and operational requirements

- The views of interested parties

Each of these items should have been thoroughly covered during the earlier topics of the management review. The challenge now is to identify meaningful objectives that will drive environmental performance beyond compliance. Remember that the environmental objective is a broad overall goal, while the targets are detailed performance requirements that must be met to achieve the environmental objective. The linkage between environmental objectives and targets and the organization's policy commitments and significant environmental aspects was shown in Figure 2.7 in Chapter 2 and is reproduced here as Figure 6.6.

Now that the organization has several months' worth of data, it should be in a position to select meaningful objectives and targets. Let us assume that the organization has decided to reduce its energy consumption. This is directly related to its commitment to conserve the planet's natural resources. It will also reduce the amount of air pollutants and greenhouse gas emissions released to the environment, and in so doing it will support the commitment to the prevention of pollution. Finally, with energy costs skyrocketing, the management team felt that it would improve its financial

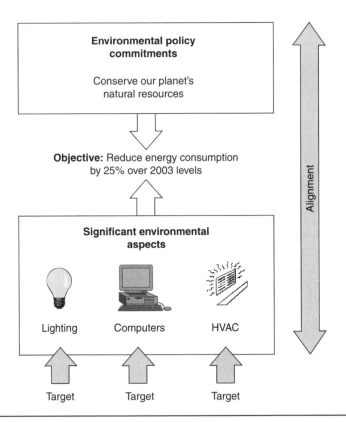

Figure 6.6   Environmental objectives, targets, and aspects.

and business condition and provide a rapid return on investment if significant improvements in energy efficiency could be realized.

The first question is, by how much should the organization plan to reduce its energy consumption? The company felt that 25 percent would be a challenging but achievable goal on the basis of reports published by various government and industry groups. The next question is, by when? The team felt that most of the techniques used to raise energy efficiency are well known and can be put into the next fiscal year's budget, so it set the completion date for the end of the next fiscal year.

Now that a goal has been set and a timetable for achieving the goal identified, the focus can turn to what will need to be done to accomplish the goal. Targets for action can be identified that will support the overall environmental objective that has been set. Many of these targets will be directly associated with the organization's significant environmental aspects. In our example, the aspects associated with energy are:

- The energy used in lighting

- The energy used for heating, cooling, and ventilating the building

- The energy used for office and production equipment

With these targets identified, the team can now develop detailed action plans for reducing the energy consumption from each of the targeted areas. For example, for lighting, the company might identify the following actions:

- Relamp 100 percent of the administrative areas and 20 percent of the production areas with energy-efficient lighting by June 30, 2007.

- Install motion sensors in all conference rooms and restrooms by September 1, 2007.

- Evaluate overall lighting needs throughout the facility and identify areas where lighting can be safely reduced. Complete the survey and recommend actions by March 30, 2007.

Note that these targeted actions are themselves quantified and include timing for completion. For the relamping target there would be a need to identify alternative energy-efficient lighting sources, establish the cost, procure the new lighting, establish a schedule for the relamping, and actually replace the lighting. Additional actions would be identified for each of the targeted actions along with specific responsibilities. When complete, this collection of objectives, targeted actions, time frames, and responsibilities will form a management program suitable for planning and monitoring the actions needed to achieve the overall environmental objective. These management programs could take the form of a Microsoft Project plan or a Microsoft Excel spreadsheet. There is no specified format that must be used for the management program. An example of a simple format is provided in the Environmental Planning Workbook provided on the CD and is shown in Figure 6.7. The important thing to keep in mind is that the management program must provide sufficient detail to allow monitoring of performance in achieving the objective. This means that several intermediate milestone actions should be identified.

Normally, the details of the management program, including actions, responsibilities, and intermediate milestone dates, would be developed after the management review was completed. The goal of the management review is to simply agree with the senior management team on what the overall environmental objectives should be for the coming period. Once the management programs have been developed, the objectives would be funded and monitored during other periodic reviews. The importance of scheduling the management review and setting environmental objectives prior to the annual strategic planning and budgeting process should now be obvious,

Objective	Affected Aspect	Targets	Action	Responsibility	Due Date	Comp. Date
Reduce energy consumption by 25% in CY 2007 from CY 2006 levels	Energy consumption	Re-lamp 100% of the administrative areas and 20% of the production areas with energy efficient lighting by June 30, 2007	Identify alternative energy efficient	M. Jacoby	1/15/2007	
			Establish cost and budget	M. Jacoby	1/30/2007	
			Procure the new lighting	M. Jacoby, C. Sheehan	3/30/2007	
			Establish a schedule for the re-lamping	M. Jacoby	3/30/2007	
			Replace the lighting	T. Tomlines	6/30/2007	
		Install motion sensors in all conference rooms and restrooms by September 1, 2007	Develop list of locations for sensors	B. Smith	1/30/2007	
			Screen sensors and suppliers	B. Smith	3/30/2007	
			Choose a supplier	B. Smith, C. Sheehan	5/15/2007	
			Procure sensors	C. Sheehan	7/1/2007	
			Install sensors	B. Smith	9/1/2007	
		Evaluate overall lighting needs and identify areas where lighting can be safely reduced by March 30, 2007	Plan the survey	M. Jacoby	1/30/2007	
			Conduct the survey	M. Jacoby	2/10/2007	
			Evaluate survey results	M. Jacoby	2/28/2007	
			Recommend actions	M. Jacoby	3/7/2007	
			Carry out actions	M. Jacoby	3/30/2007	

Figure 6.7   Environmental management program using Microsoft Excel.

as several of the objectives will require funding to accomplish. With the senior management team's heavy involvement in selecting the objectives, this funding should be easier to obtain.

SUMMARY

We have now completed the design, deployment, and planning for the initial round of improvements of our EMS. We understand how the system is performing and where improvements are needed, and we set objectives and targets to move beyond compliance. The next chapter focuses on the details of performing EMS audits as the basis for ongoing improvement of the EMS.

7

Conducting EMS Audits

ISO 14001 REVISITED

As noted in Chapter 2, the ISO 14001:2004 standard is based on five primary clauses, as shown in Figure 7.1.

These five clauses can be grouped into five operational components as follows:

- *A planning component.* In ISO 14001 planning is represented by the initial and ongoing identification of significant environmental aspects and legal requirements associated with the organization's products, services, and activities and the identification of appropriate methods to control them. Planning for unexpected events is captured by the emergency preparedness and control requirements. Planning is centered around the establishment of an organizational policy that declares the company's commitments for environmental performance.

- *An operational component.* In ISO 14001, requirements focused on operation and maintenance of the system are specified in the requirements for operational control.

- *A monitoring and corrective action component.* In ISO 14001 these activities are defined in monitoring and measurement, evaluation of compliance, nonconformance and corrective and preventive action, and the EMS audit clauses.

- *An improvement process.* Improvement is embedded in the requirements for setting environmental objectives and conducting management reviews.

- *Key support processes.* These activities support the overall EMS and include document and record control; structure and responsibility; communication; and training, awareness, and competence.

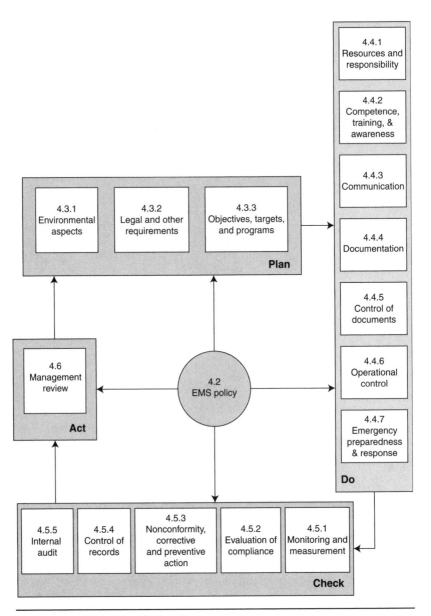

Figure 7.1   ISO 14001:2004 EMS.

In Figure 7.2 the organization's core business activities are shown by the shaded boxes and dashed lines. They represent the things we do (activities) and things that we make (products) or provide (services). The ISO 14001:2004 components that monitor and control the environmental impact of these activities are shown interacting with these core business activities.

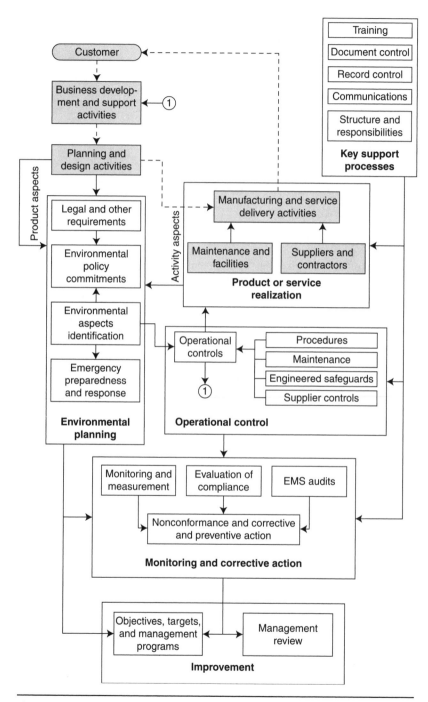

Figure 7.2 ISO 14001:2004 process flow.

AUDIT SCOPE

It is recommended that the ISO 14001 components be grouped together where appropriate for two reasons. First, it provides for a more efficient and effective audit. The grouped elements are closely related, and it can be hard to evaluate one without evaluating the others in the group. Second, and just as important, it is then possible to apply process approach popularized by ISO 9001 to the EMS audits. By grouping these elements together, you form natural processes where the output from one process becomes the input into a related process. The recommended audit groupings are a little different from the operational groupings shown in Figure 7.2, as is discussed in the following section.

Environmental Planning Components

The environmental planning components are normally evaluated first because the proper identification of significant environmental aspects and legal requirements that apply to the organization is central to all other components within the EMS. In Figure 7.2 inputs into the environmental planning process include the organization's planning and design activities (environmental aspects of products), product realization (environmental aspects of activities), and/or service realization (environmental aspects of services and activities that provide them). Identifying legal and other requirements and preparing for emergencies are also key to planning. All these activities are folded around the environmental policy statement.

A slight departure from Figure 7.2 is recommended in that it is also efficient to review evaluation of compliance to legal requirements during the audit of the planning components. This is because there is a natural audit flow that arises from identifying legal and other requirements and evaluating compliance together. This flow will be presented when we discuss evaluation of the environmental planning components.

Operational Control

The operational control component verifies that the controls associated with the organization's significant aspects are in place and are being used and maintained. It is similar to the production audit of a QMS. It answers the question, are we doing what we said we would do? In any organization there will be multiple activities that need to be controlled, and there could be multiple controls for each activity. These audits will evaluate these controls. Note the use of the plural case, "audits," because there may be multiple audits throughout the year, focused around operational control.

The auditor should also evaluate a portion of the monitoring and measurement component during operational control evaluations and may also spot-check compliance to regulatory requirements. If the organization has trained internal auditors who are knowledgeable of environmental regulatory requirements, the environmental compliance reviews could be folded into these operational control audits *almost* entirely.

During these reviews the auditor will also be checking on the control of documents and records associated with the activities being evaluated, the training and competency of the personnel performing these activities, and their knowledge of their roles and responsibilities for properly conducting the activities without harm to the environment.

Monitoring and Corrective Action

The monitoring and corrective action component evaluates the overall monitoring and performance of the EMS. It includes an analysis of trends in environmental performance and actions taken to correct any adverse trends. It also evaluates the internal audit program and the follow-up on any weaknesses noted during these audits. Both of these components feed into the nonconformance and corrective and preventive action system, which will also be reviewed during this evaluation.

Improvement

The evaluation of improvement activities focuses on setting environmental objectives and establishing environmental management programs to achieve them. Performance toward meeting these objectives will be assessed along with any actions being taken to ensure they are met if performance is lacking. The management review process will also be examined.

Key Support Processes

The centralized activities for key support processes such as document and record control are evaluated in this audit. Only the common, or centralized, control portions of these systems need be evaluated because many of the outputs from these activities (accurate documents located where needed, legible and complete records, and so on) will be assessed during the other audits. Other items included in this review are roles and responsibilities of key functions, communications, and training.

KEY AUDIT POINTS

The remainder of this chapter focuses on strategies for conducting audits of these groupings. The audit checklists provided on the CD accompanying this handbook have been structured along these groupings. You are encouraged to review these checklists as you read the discussions that follow.

ENVIRONMENTAL PLANNING

The environmental planning process forms the heart of the EMS. The activities that form this process are shown in Figure 7.3. This figure also outlines the key audit points that will be examined during the evaluation.

It is important that the auditor keep in mind the purpose of the environmental planning process, which is to identify those activities that must

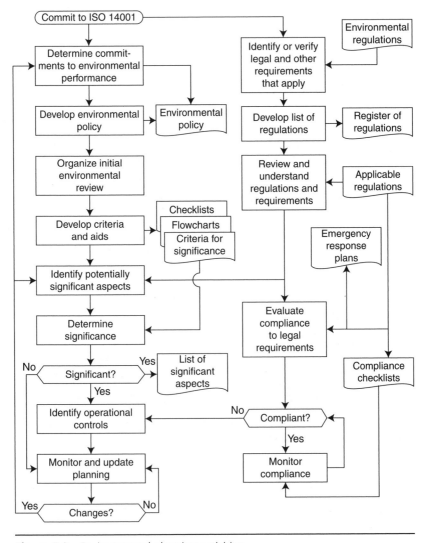

Figure 7.3   Environmental planning activities.

be controlled to maintain and improve the organization's environmental performance. The goal is to move beyond regulatory compliance. Many organizations focus almost exclusively on compliance to environmental regulations when they design their system. While important, compliance to environmental laws and statutes will not achieve the goal of ISO 14001 of achieving a level of sustainable development. The United States' contributions to the growing problems of global warming, depletion of natural resources, ozone depletion, and loss of biodiversity, despite the most stringent environmental regulations in the world, give testament to this. The auditor should verify that nonregulatory-based environmental aspects were considered during the initial and ongoing environmental reviews.

Note the parallel path through the environmental planning process. The ISO 14001 standard, although focused on moving beyond compliance, does require an organization to meet its regulatory obligations. In the course of implementing ISO 14001 the company will have to demonstrate that it understands what environmental regulations it must meet, that it has access to what those regulations require, and that it is performing reviews to ensure it is meeting those requirements. For many small-to-medium-sized companies without environmental specialists on staff, this may be the first time that they have systematically evaluated their environmental compliance posture. What they learn must be incorporated into the planning for the EMS. This environmental compliance review may be done prior to the identification of significant aspects, or it may be performed as part of the initial environmental review. The key audit point is that it must be done as part of the planning of the EMS and any deficiencies corrected or prevented through the application of corrective action and operational controls.

AUDIT STRATEGY AND KEY AUDIT POINTS

This section defines a general audit flow and strategy that can be used to evaluate the environmental planning process. The components of this process are presented in the order in which the auditor would normally evaluate them.

Environmental Policy

The auditor should begin by examining the environmental policy statement. The policy statement (or more importantly, the commitments within the policy) forms the heart of the planning process, which in turn forms the heart of the EMS. Rather than evaluating simple compliance to the standard, the auditor should determine whether the policy and its development meet the intent of the standard. Compliance to the intent of the ISO 14001:2004 standard can be evaluated by examining the following key audit points.

Who was involved in the development of the policy statement?

The standard requires top management's involvement in the development of the environmental policy statement. There is no hard and fast definition of who makes up top management, but a general rule of thumb is that top management comprises the senior person present at a facility and his or her direct reports.

This involvement should be more than simply signing off on a policy developed by the environmental management representative or consultant. It should include active debate about what environmental stewardship means to the organization and what commitments it is willing to make. Later on, the company will be required to establish improvement objectives focused on meeting its commitments in the policy statement. Most improvement projects require some initial allocation of time, money, and other resources. Management should not make commitments that it is not willing to back up with sufficient resources. The auditor can assess the level of top management involvement by asking senior management how the policy was developed. If management's involvement was simply a signoff, and it admits to this, then the auditor should consider issuance of an OFI. Engaging top management in the development of the environmental policy helps ensure the alignment and support needed for real environmental performance improvement.

What is included in the scope of the EMS and what is not?

The 2004 version of ISO 14001 added wording to indicate that the organization should define and document the scope of the EMS. The scope defines what is included and what is not. The auditor should ask to see the documented scope. It may be a separate document, or it may be embedded in an environmental policy manual. The auditor should use the defined scope to help evaluate the response to the next question.

Is the policy statement appropriate, given the nature, scale, and environmental impacts of its activities, products, and services?

This is a difficult requirement to evaluate because it is somewhat subjective. While the auditor should not try to second-guess the wording of a reasonable policy statement, he or she should challenge policy statements and related commitments that have absolutely nothing to do with the activities the organization performs. It makes no sense for a service organization that does not generate or handle hazardous materials or wastes to have a policy commitment to minimize or reduce the quantity of hazardous wastes it generates.

Instead of challenging what *is* in the policy statement, the auditor should focus on what *is not* reflected in the policy statement that should be or could be. As an example, a company heavily involved in the design, development, and launch of new products should somehow reflect its commitment to the design of environmentally friendly products for the marketplace. The design of a product normally has a far greater overall impact on the environment than does its manufacturing. The auditor could issue an OFI in this situation, assuming that the design of products is within the scope of the organization's EMS.

Review of Environmental Policy Commitments

Environmental policy commitments form the core of the policy statement. They represent what the organization feels is important regarding its environmental performance and stewardship. They form the framework for environmental objectives and targets, and they can also provide the framework for developing the criteria used to determine the significance of the organization's environmental aspects.

Unfortunately, most organizations do little more than embed the three mandatory commitments from the ISO 14001 standard into their policy. While technically the organizations meet the requirements of the standard, they fall far short of meeting its intent. The three mandatory commitments—continual improvement, prevention of pollution, and compliance to legal and other requirements—are too broad to provide any focus on what's really important to the organization. And they fail to provide a framework for setting environmental objectives and targets because *any* objective could fit within one of the three mandatory commitments. What we want to do is use the policy commitments to help focus on what's most important to *this* organization.

The auditor should, of course, verify that the three mandatory commitments are found somewhere in the policy statement, in some form. Ideally, these mandatory commitments will not be stated verbatim as they appear in the ISO 14001 standard. Instead, the auditor should hope to find that they have been reworded to be more appropriate to the nature of the organization's environmental aspects and related impacts or that additional, more specific commitments have been added beyond the three mandatory ones to drive performance in areas that really matter. Some examples of specific commitments include:

- *We are committed to the ongoing reduction in our emissions of airborne pollutants and hazardous solid wastes.* This commitment would be appropriate for an organization whose most significant aspects involve air emissions and hazardous waste generation.

- *We are committed to the protection of our lakes, streams, and the local ecosystem.* This commitment would be appropriate for an organization that operates near a local waterway or wetlands and that has point-source discharges to these waterways; it would also be appropriate for an organization that operates in a rural area surrounded by wildlife areas or forests.

- *We are committed to the use of environmentally friendly design principles in our products.* This commitment would be appropriate for an engineering design firm that has little in the way of air, water, or hazardous waste emissions.

- *We are committed to the involvement of our employees and the local community in the improvement of our EMS.* This commitment may be appropriate for an organization that operates in the midst of a local community where there are concerns about the company's operations. It can be especially important if the company is trying to improve its reputation in the community.

- *We are committed to the concepts of natural resource conservation, including the ongoing reduction in the materials and resources consumed, including energy.* This commitment would be appropriate for almost any organization because all companies use energy, but it would be especially important to those that consume large amounts of paper, wood, water, minerals, oil, and natural gas or other natural resources, such as steel manufacturers, the construction industry, and printers.

These are but a few of the specific commitments that might be offered up in the environmental policy statement. Their usefulness is in their ability to focus environmental objectives and targets toward specific improvements that have a large and real effect on the organization's environmental performance. They point to where an organization can really make a difference. Lacking this kind of specificity, companies often establish objectives to improve their recycling of aluminum cans, paper, and scrap wood pallets that, while helpful, do little to really make a significant improvement to the environment.

In Chapter 1 we discussed the evolution and maturing of an organization's management system. The evolution of a company's environmental policy is often one of the first areas where this maturing is seen. Many companies initially develop a policy around the three mandatory policy commitments. As the system matures, it should be expected that the policy will gradually evolve to include some of these more specific and more focused commitments to drive improvements in areas of environmental importance. As an auditor I evaluate the policy statement in terms of this evolution. If the system is new, I may simply accept the environmental policy as is, at most adding an OFI to consider commitments that more properly reflect the organization's activities, products, and services. If the system has been in place for a while, I also look at the organization's performance in making improvements in areas relating to its significant environmental aspects. If I find improvement is lacking, I make the case more strongly, possibly tying the general nature of the policy statement into a finding relating to the lack of environmental performance improvement.

To summarize, the auditor should verify that the mandatory commitments are embedded within the policy statement. Failure to embed these commitments in the policy statement should result in a nonconformance. The auditor should also evaluate how well the policy commitments reflect the nature of the organization's products, services, and activities, taking into account the organization's maturity and current environmental performance improvement. If the results are found lacking, the auditor should issue an OFI. The auditor will also evaluate whether the organization is meeting the intent of the standard and not just the requirements.

Review of Documentation, Implementation, and Communication of the Policy within the Organization and to the General Public

All policy statements are documented, or at least I haven't found one yet that wasn't. Implementation and maintenance will be reflected in its maturing and/or modification, as stated earlier, and in its success in driving environmental performance improvement, also discussed earlier. Communication within the organization, including to individuals working on behalf of the organization, will be evaluated during other audits. This leaves communication to the general public.

The auditor should ask how the policy is made available to the general public. He or she might pose the question, If my aunt Betty, who drives by the plant every day and sees the ISO 14001 flag flying, calls and asks about the environmental policy, what would you tell her? Answers may be that she would be directed to the company Web site, where the policy is listed; she would be faxed a copy; or that the call would be directed to the environmental management representative, who would send her a copy or read it over the phone. The key is that there has to be a process to make it available to the public. Almost every company has a Web site, which makes posting the policy one of the easiest and most effective ways of communicating to the public. The auditor should issue an OFI if the process for communicating the policy is cumbersome or inconvenient. For example, if the answer to the question was, "Well, we would tell her to stop by and come into the lobby. It's posted there," the company should find a better way to make the policy available to the public, as this approach is neither practical nor realistic.

Making the policy available to the public is important because it makes top management more accountable to follow through on the commitments it has made. If the general public is aware that the organization is committed to involving the community in environmental performance improvement, you can bet they will want to know when, where, and how they can become involved. Likewise, if the organization has committed to reductions in its emissions of hazardous air pollutants, it is reasonable to expect local citizens to review the publicly available Toxic Release Inventories and to call management out if it doesn't follow through on its commitments.

You're probably thinking that I've killed quite a few trees expanding on the environmental policy statement, and you'd be right. I do so because the policy statement truly is the key to the entire EMS to a much greater degree than in QMSs or safety and health management systems. Unfortunately, the legacy of slapping together a nice, flowery policy statement that looks good on the wall but does little to drive improvement remains rampant, especially in companies that have had QMS experience prior to implementing ISO 14001. I am hopeful that this discussion on the policy statement will give auditors insight on not only how to evaluate this critical document but also why it's important.

Environmental Aspects

If the policy is the heart of the EMS, then the identification of significant environmental aspects is the head. The goal of this process is to identify those activities that must be controlled to prevent harming the environment, or to actually improve it. Even though we will consider the environmental aspects of our products, services, and activities, we can control only the activities. This awareness is important because many organizations list only the significant aspects they identify, neglecting the activities that produce them. Significant environmental aspects should be associated with the activities that relate to the aspects for control to have any practical meaning.

A second consideration is whether the audit is performed on a newly installed EMS or one that has been in place for some time. A review of the process used to identify and determine significance of a new EMS is more involved than one that is focused primarily on the updating of the significant environmental aspects for changes to the organization's products, activities, and services. Both are discussed in the strategy that follows.

The auditor should start by asking to see the procedure for identifying significant environmental aspects. The standard requires that an organization have a procedure, but it doesn't necessarily have to be documented (although I certainly recommend it). If the process has been documented, the auditor should ask the environmental management representative or process owner to walk him or her through the procedure, stopping at key points as outlined in the following section. If it hasn't been documented, the auditor should still ask the auditee to walk him or her through the process, paying close attention to the key activities and making notes to follow up on when asking to see the objective evidence. The auditor will have to rely more on the standard and on the checklist in this situation.

During the walk-through, the auditor should verify the following key elements of the process.

Was the evaluation of potential aspects comprehensive?

The auditor should verify that all areas, core activities, and products within the scope of the EMS were included in the evaluation. Many organizations conduct the review by portioning the plant into areas such as production, administration, outside facilities and grounds, and auxiliary areas such as tank farms, pumps, and boilers. The auditor can look for evidence that each of these areas was included in the review. The auditor should inquire about any areas where there is no evidence, typically identified by their lack of inclusion on the list of potential or resulting significant aspects. If it becomes clear that major areas were not included in the review, the auditor should generate an NC.

Another important item to consider relates to the review of the environmental aspects associated with the organization's products. This is especially important if the company designs the products that it sells. In this situation the organization has significant influence over the environmental impacts of its products and can control them through proper design. I have evaluated many companies where the organization designs its products but has never considered the environmental aspects of its products or how it might minimize the negative impact of its products on the environment through design controls and practices. I have even evaluated the research and development business unit of a major global corporation where product design was not considered, even though this was the organization's primary activity. While properly controlling the acids, solvents, and wastes generated as a result of product testing is important, minimizing the hazardous materials used in the product design, optimizing the product's ability to be disassembled, reused, or recycled, and optimizing its energy efficiency are much more important.

The design of a product almost always has more overall impact on the environment than does its manufacture. The auditor should verify that product materials, weight, energy efficiency, and ability to be disassembled, recycled, reused, or otherwise properly disposed of are considered during the identification of significant environmental aspects. The auditor should issue an NC if there is no evidence of product review and the company is responsible for the design.

A final consideration is whether the evaluation included nonroutine as well as routine activities. Nonroutine activities could include bulk liquid loading and unloading, maintenance of equipment and facilities (whether performed by the organization or by contractors), and facility modification, expansion, or renovation. For facility modifications, the auditor may want to verify that the organization has a process to evaluate such modifications for their environmental impact before they are initiated, because each modification is unique and there may not have been any major facility projects under way when the initial environmental review was performed.

Were the reviews thorough?

Once the auditor is satisfied that the scope of the review was adequate, he or she may wish to verify that the team that performed the review knew what to look for. The auditor may ask what training the team received prior to conducting the review. He or she may also ask to see any checklists used to guide the team in what to look for. Some companies like to use flowcharts of production activities to help identify potentially significant aspects. They document the inputs (materials and natural resources) and outputs (wastes and emissions) on the flowchart to help identify aspects. The auditor should ask to see the flowcharts.

Related to this topic is the evaluation of who was involved in the review. Ideally, the review is performed by a CFT with representatives from each of the areas evaluated. This can be especially important in identifying the nonroutine activities that should be considered but that may not be occurring when the walk-through is performed. If the auditor discovers that the review was performed by one person, he or she should more aggressively evaluate the comprehensive and thoroughness of the review by examining the evidence already cited. Nothing in the standard *requires* that a CFT be used to conduct the review, but it is highly unlikely that one person can do the job adequately. Because it is possible that one individual is the source of all knowledge, however, the auditor must focus on the results. If the auditor finds evidence that the review failed to consider important activities, or that the review did not include obvious aspects such as materials, wastes, emissions, resource usage, or products, he or she should issue an NC.

How was the significance of the environmental aspects determined?

The auditor should examine the rationale used to determine significance of the aspects identified during the initial environmental review. In

Chapter 5 the methodology used was to ask a series of questions, such as, Does this activity result in the generation of significant quantities of hazardous materials? Is this aspect regulated? Does the activity consume significant quantities of natural resources, including energy? Other companies like to use a failure mode and effects methodology, evaluating the severity of the impacts and their likelihood of occurrence. Most companies use some form of quantification or ranking to help identify those that are significant and those that are not. Ideally, the criteria used to determine significance will be related to the organization's policy commitments, as was discussed in Chapter 5. As an example, consider several of the following specific commitments presented in the discussion on the environmental policy:

Commitment: We are committed to the ongoing reduction in our emissions of airborne pollutants and hazardous solid wastes.

Criterion: Does this activity result in the release of emissions to the air or the generation of hazardous wastes?

Commitment: We are committed to the protection of our lakes, streams, and the local ecosystem.

Criterion: Can this activity result in the release of wastes or pollutants to the local environment?

Commitment: We are committed to the use of environmentally friendly design principles in our products.

Criterion: Does this activity impact on the ability to design environmentally responsible principles into our products?

Commitment: We are committed to the involvement of our employees and the local community in the improvement of our EMS.

Criterion: Does the activity result in any significant odor, noise, dust, or other local concern to the community or our employees?

Commitment: We are committed to the concepts of natural resource conservation, including the ongoing reduction in the materials and resources consumed, including energy.

Criterion: Does this activity consume significant amounts of water, energy, or other natural resources?

Because one of the mandatory commitments in the policy statement is a commitment to comply with regulatory requirements, it is common to include criteria relating to the regulated or nonregulated status of the aspect. By including specific commitments in the policy statement and then using these commitments to determine the criteria used to identify significance, the organization creates an EMS that is aligned from top to bottom.

The key audit point is that the methods used to determine what is and what isn't significant should be reproducible. There should be a consistent process in place. A team evaluating the same environmental aspects next year should come to roughly the same conclusions as to what is significant and must be controlled. Consistency is important because the EMS functions within a dynamic system. Processes, products, and facilities change. Environmental concerns change. Perhaps even our criteria will change, but even so, such changes must be carefully reviewed and must have some basis. A consistent set of criteria helps provide the basis for these changes.

The auditor should ask how the determination was made as to which aspects are significant. The auditor may ask why one aspect was deemed to be significant while another was not, and he or she should verify that there is some method to the determination. If there was no rationale at all, the auditor should generate an NC, citing the lack of a procedure (that is, process). If there was some reasonable rationale, but it was not formalized or applied consistently, the auditor should consider generating an OFI.

Finally, the auditor should verify that the significant aspects are somehow linked to the activities that generate or control them. As noted in the introduction to this section, organizations control the activities in order to minimize the impact of the aspects. Just citing "energy consumption" does not allow for control of this aspect. Citing energy consumption from lighting; energy consumption from heating, ventilation, and air conditioning; and energy consumption from production machinery operation allows for the application of real controls for these activities. The auditor should generate an OFI if the auditee cannot relate the significant aspects to the activities that produce or control them.

How is the information kept up to date?

For audits performed well after the EMS has been in place and certified, this question of how to keep the information up to date becomes the focus of the evaluation. Up to this point the audit flow has focused on new management systems. For an existing system, the auditor should have confidence that the methods used to identify environmental aspects and their related significance have been verified to be adequate. The main question for an existing system, therefore, is whether these methods are being applied to product, process, and facility changes. The key questions are how are those responsible for reviewing new products, services, and activities made aware of the need to perform an evaluation, and is the evaluation conducted prior to the implementation of the changes.

The auditor should begin by first identifying new or modified products, services, or activities and facility modifications that have taken place since the last audit. If the auditor does not know what these are, he or she should first talk to the production manager, maintenance manager, or engineering manager to help generate a list of recent modifications or introductions. The auditor should try to select major modifications or new products that are significantly different from existing products. These items will become the auditor's samples for later verification during the interview.

The auditor should then interview the management representative about the methods used to keep the list of significant aspects current. Some organizations reperform the initial environmental review periodically to ensure that they identify any new significant aspects. While I generally accept such reviews, I don't necessarily like this strategy, primarily because it is reactionary versus proactive. An organization could operate for many months without proper controls under such a system, pending completion of the annual or semiannual review. Instead, I prefer an approach that uses existing controls to manage change, modified to include the consideration of potential environmental aspects and/or impacts and to identify the need for a review. Many organizations use a "management of change" process to control and plan for new products, processes, and products. Others have an advanced product quality planning process. Some organizations use a management of change process and an annual review to ensure that new significant aspects are identified. The auditor should thoroughly understand the methods used by asking questions and by asking to see the documents, checklists, and other aids used to control changes. The absence of any consistent method to keep the significant aspects list updated should obviously result in an NC.

Once the auditor fully understands the methods used to stay up to date, he or she should test the application of the methods by asking to see the results of the reviews for the items selected prior to the audit. If a management of change process was used, the auditor should ask to see the checklist completed for the facility or process modification made two months ago. Assuming that new environmental aspects were identified for the change, the auditor should ask to see the results of their review for significance. If the auditor finds that the process was not followed, or that the management representative was not even aware of significant changes to the company's products, services, activities, or facilities when he or she should have been, the auditor should issue an NC.

Staying aware of changes to processes that could impact on the EMS is important from a regulatory standpoint as well as an environmental performance perspective. Assume your company is a conditionally exempt, small-quantity generator of hazardous wastes. Due to a new product or a product modification, you now have to apply a glue and adhesive that is hazardous. As a result, your generation of hazardous waste triples to over 100 kilograms per month. While in the past you were exempt from most of the regulations governing the control of hazardous wastes, you are now required to implement additional requirements relating to employee training, manifesting, inspecting, and reporting. Not doing so would be in violation of federal and state environmental regulations. Being made aware of this impending change allows you to put the additional controls in place before you become a violator, or possibly even to find a nonhazardous glue and adhesive that would avoid the whole issue of having to put new controls in place. Heaven forbid you fail to identify the change and it results in sufficient waste to put you over the threshold into a large-quantity generator.

The bottom line is that the auditor should verify that methods are in place and are being used to keep the organization's listing of significant environmental aspects current.

Were operational controls identified?

The auditor also needs to verify that the organization has taken its significant environmental aspects into account in the design, implementation, and operation of its EMS. This can be evidenced by identifying and implementing appropriate controls to minimize negative environmental impacts or maximize those activities that benefit the environment. The auditor can ask how each of its significant environmental aspects is controlled. At the planning stage, the auditor is most concerned that appropriate controls have been identified. The operational control audits will confirm that they were properly implemented and are being maintained.

Legal and Other Requirements, Evaluation of Compliance

One of the first areas where organizations see a significant improvement after implementing ISO 14001 is in their environmental compliance posture. This is especially true in small-to-medium-sized firms that do not have environmental professionals on staff. In these organizations, identifying the legal requirement that applies to their activities may require more effort than implementing the EMS itself. Even so, it is critically important that the organization not only identify the regulatory requirements it must meet, but also understand them and ensure that it meets them. This portion of the environmental planning audit focuses on verifying that the organization is meeting its policy commitment to comply with legal and other requirements.

"Other requirements" in this sense means requirements imposed by the management system design itself, by customers, and by voluntary adoption of environmental protocols such as the Business Charter for Sustainable

Development and Responsible Care. Internal requirements will be called out in the organization's policies and procedures. Customer requirements will be called out in contracts and specifications. Voluntary protocols, like the Business Charter for Sustainable Development, should be listed along with the legal requirements that the organization must meet.

The auditor should begin by asking the management representative or individual responsible for environmental compliance for a listing of the regulations and other requirements that apply to the organization. While the standard does not require a listing, or register of regulations as it is often called, typically there are far too many to commit to memory. As a result, a listing of some type is necessary. Once the auditor has this list, he or she should verify conformance to the standard by asking the questions in the following sections.

Is the listing comprehensive and complete?

The auditor should verify that the listing includes federal, state, and local requirements. Most states have the authority to implement the federal requirements and do so by enacting state statutes that must be followed. If the state has the authority to implement the federal regulations, listing the state statutes and public acts may be sufficient because they must be at least as restrictive as the federal regulations, and sometimes they are more stringent. Local requirements may include sewage and drinking water standards, laws, and permits. I also look to see if significant voluntary requirements like Responsible Care are listed, assuming they apply.

Is the listing sufficiently detailed?

Simply listing the Clean Air Act or the Resource Conservation and Recovery Act doesn't provide evidence that the organization understands the legal requirements it must meet. The auditor should ask the auditee, Which titles of the Clean Air Act apply to us? or What parts of 40 CFR 260–279 must we comply with? All too often organizations simply list the name of the law or CFR that contains the requirements. Some of the regulations are hundreds of pages long but contain only a few sections that apply to the organization.

The auditor can evaluate whether the auditee has sufficiently researched the regulations by asking the auditee to show him or her the requirements that apply. I normally pick three or four regulations from the list to sample. This question—is the listing sufficiently detailed?—evaluates two critical prerequisites of environmental compliance: does the organization have access to the regulations it must meet (also a standard requirement), and does the organization understand what they require? Often when I ask this question I get a blank stare, or the auditee pulls up 40 CFR 260–279 and tries to find his or her way through the regulation for the first time. You don't stand much of a chance of meeting the requirements if you don't know what they say.

Many organizations now use hyperlinks to the federal or state Web site where the regulations are maintained. I strongly endorse this practice because it is practical and greatly simplifies staying up to date with regulatory changes. Local regulations and laws normally have to be retained in hard-copy format. If the organization meets the access requirements of ISO 14001 by keeping hard copies, the auditor should verify that these documents are controlled and kept up to date. One of the challenges of using hard copies of the CFRs is keeping them current. They are revised on an annual basis and can be expensive.

Is there evidence that the organization considered its legal and other requirements during the design and implementation of its EMS?

The auditor has already reviewed the listing of significant environmental aspects, so he or she should know if the company considered its regulatory obligations during the identification of its environmental aspects. If the auditor did not conduct a review of environmental aspects identification as part of the audit, he or she should review the list to verify that significant regulatory obligations were embedded within the reviews and criteria for determining significance.

Is there evidence that the organization is evaluating its compliance to regulatory and other requirements?

Other requirements, such as Responsible Care, are normally evaluated during other evaluations. Compliance to regulatory requirements is typically verified through the use of environmental compliance reviews. Although it is possible to fold these reviews into other audits, they are typically performed by personnel with specialized knowledge of the environmental regulations. The auditor should ask the auditee about the processes used to conduct environmental compliance reviews and reviews of compliance to other, non–ISO 14001 requirements that the organization has adopted. If a documented procedure is available, the auditor should have the auditee walk him or her through it. The auditor should pay attention to the frequency of the audits, who performs them, how they are reported, and how any actions coming out of the review are tracked.

One of the reasons why I evaluate compliance to legal and other requirements now, instead of folding it into the monitoring and corrective action audit, is that it fits well with the audit strategy. At this point I have seen the listing of the requirements that apply to us, and I have asked for and been presented with a copy of a number of the requirements themselves. It is now a simple matter to ask the auditee to provide me with evidence that we have evaluated our compliance to the requirements that I have in front of me. The auditee might provide me with a compliance report, completed checklists, or a consultant's evaluation. What I want to do now is evaluate the thoroughness of the review. Because I have the requirements in front of me, I can easily scan the records of the review to see if there is evidence that the requirements were evaluated. The evidence may be in the form of statements or conclusions in the compliance report or questions on the checklist, but what I want to know is did we do a thorough job of evaluating our compliance to *all* the requirements. This is where management system audits differ from regulatory compliance reviews. Whereas management system audits sample compliance to important requirements, compliance reviews should verify conformance to all requirements.

If the records of the compliance review are very general, stating, for example, "The review verified compliance to the Resource Conservation and Recovery Act, the Clean Air Act, and the Clean Water Act," I generate a finding, typically in the form of an OFI, that notes that the detail in the compliance records could be expanded to provide more assurance that the organization is meeting its regulatory requirements. If my other audits find regulatory violations, I cite the issue as an NC, using a lack of sufficient evidence and my own findings as the basis for the NC.

Some organizations rely on outside consultants or corporate staff to conduct their compliance reviews. I have no concern with this as long as the records of the review provide sufficient evidence of compliance monitoring.

Now, you may be thinking that you are not an environmental specialist and therefore cannot evaluate the regulatory compliance sections of the standard. Take heart—you don't have to be an environmental expert to do a credible job. If you note the audit strategy presented, there is nothing that requires an extensive knowledge of environmental regulations on your part. All you have to do is ask the right questions and use the answers or evidence provided to guide you. The auditee will provide the list of regulations, which has already been evaluated, assuming you are certified, by the outside registrar auditor, who is knowledgeable in environmental regulations. From that list you picked several regulations and said "show me." The auditee then pulls down the regulations for you or prints off a copy. Next you ask the auditee to explain how compliance reviews are conducted and then again say "show me" when you ask for records of reviews for the regulations he or she printed off. When he or she gives you copies of the reviews, you can easily scan the records to see if there are questions or statements relating to the requirements you have in your hands. If you can't find them, you say, of course, "show me." Environmental expertise is required to do the compliance review but not to verify that the review was done.

Were weaknesses identified in the compliance reviews acted on?

If violations or weaknesses were noted in the compliance reviews, the auditor should verify that actions were taken or have been implemented to address the deficiencies. The auditor should check with corporate policy on how to cite the findings in this case.

Emergency Preparedness and Response

The last topic of the environmental planning audit is to verify that the organization has the appropriate procedures and plans to respond to or to prevent environmental accidents and emergencies. I review this during the planning audit because, first, this should be a planning activity and not a routine occurrence; and second, in the United States many of the plans and procedures are required by law and are therefore part of the regulatory framework.

The auditor can evaluate this area by asking for copies of the emergency response plans the organization maintains. Common plans include the following:

- Spill prevention, countermeasures, and controls plan

- Storm water pollution and prevention plan

- Pollution prevention plan

- Fire and evacuation plan

Which plans are maintained by the organization depends on the nature of the organization's products, services, and activities. When the plans are presented, the auditor can ask the auditee to show him or her the requirements that describe what must be in the plan and where the plan is required by law. With the regulatory requirements in hand, the auditor can spot-check the plans for their content and currentness. I commonly find deficiencies in these plans when compared with their regulatory requirements. In addition, some of these plans focus on specific types of accidents, like spills of oil. The auditor should inquire about other types of accidents, like spills of solvents or ammonia, if the auditor's review of the organization's significant aspects shows that these aspects are present. If there is no plan for responding to these other emergencies, the auditor should generate an OFI. Note that many of these plans focus not just on response but also on prevention. Therefore, the number of actual incidents or emergencies is an indirect measure of the quality of these plans.

The auditor should also verify that the plans are up to date. Some plans must be submitted to and approved by government agencies at specified periodicities. In addition, it is not at all uncommon to find that personnel named as emergency responders or coordinators no longer work at the facility. It doesn't do any good to call someone in the middle of the night during an emergency if that individual no longer works at the facility.

The auditor should ask for a list of incidents, accidents, and spills or other uncontrolled releases that occurred since the last audit. It helps if the auditor already knows about some of these events, which is likely if this is an internal audit. The auditor should verify that reviews were held after these occurrences and that the adequacy of the response, and the organization's response plans and procedures, were evaluated as part of these reviews. If no evidence of any review can be provided, the auditor should generate an NC.

Finally, the auditor should verify that some form of drill, test, or walk-through was conducted to evaluate the adequacy of the procedures and plans and to familiarize those responsible for action. The organization is required to establish periodicity requirements for these tests, and the auditor should confirm they are being conducted as required. Failure to conduct the drills or tests should result in an NC.

Performance Indicators

The auditor may expect to find the following indicators associated with the environmental planning components. The auditor should review these indicators where they exist to help evaluate overall performance and effectiveness and to help focus the audit. Areas of poor performance, as identified by the indicators, should be evaluated for actions to correct the performance. The lack of any action to address significant performance issues can serve as the basis for an NC citing ineffective implementation. Note that the majority of the performance indicators will be associated with other components of the EMS:

- Percentage of environmental compliance reviews completed to schedule

- Number of violations found during compliance reviews

- Number of violations found by outside agencies (Oops! Not a good thing)

- Percentage or number of violations corrected

- Percentage or number of emergency response tests/drills conducted

OPERATIONAL CONTROL

Operational control implements the actions and safeguards needed to minimize any adverse environmental impacts associated with the significant aspects identified during environmental planning. Operational controls can include procedures, practices, engineered safeguards, maintenance, and protective equipment and devices. They could also include requirements passed down to suppliers and contractors.

The process that organizations use to implement the operational controls normally looks something like that shown in Figure 7.4.

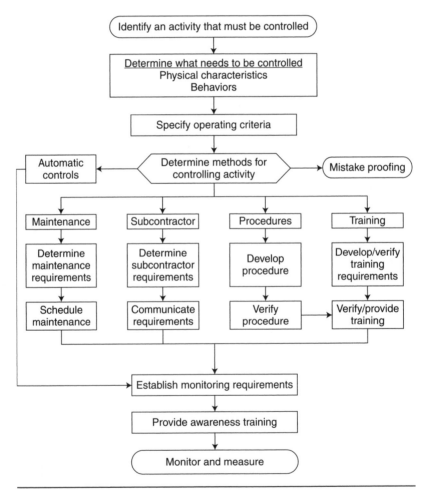

Figure 7.4 Establishing operational controls.

The controls themselves are normally defined as part of the environmental planning process. Most organizations find that many of the controls are already in place, although they may not have been formalized yet. Formalizing the controls in documented procedures and instructions is part of the process of developing operational controls. The mistake-proofing control shown in Figure 7.4 includes actions taken to ensure that the adverse impact cannot occur. An example would be to specify a nonhazardous substance for parts cleaning in place of the current hazardous substance. In many cases the aspect (cleaning fluid for part washing) would cease to be significant after the mistake-proofing solution was implemented, therefore the stop symbol.

Although the process flow shown in Figure 7.4 is useful for understanding the method used to determine operational controls, I generally prefer to use the process flow shown in Figure 7.5 to illustrate the strategy used. Remember that this process would be repeated for each activity associated with a significant environmental aspect. Rather than conduct one audit of operational control, it is normally more efficient and effective to conduct multiple audits, with each series of audits focused on different processes, activities, or areas. This provides a more continuous evaluation of operational controls throughout the organization and allows easy integration with quality management and safety and health management system audits, if desired.

Note that the evaluation of operational control will also assess the outputs from some of the key support activities, including training and awareness of employee roles, responsibilities, and authorities. The auditor should also examine the control of any environmental documents and records associated with the process, as well as the calibration of any environmental monitoring devices found to be in use. As noted in the introduction to this chapter, the auditor should also verify that any monitoring of key characteristics and operating criteria is being performed as needed to maintain the environmental controls. When performed in this fashion, the operational control audit becomes a process-based audit similar to the process-based audits conducted on an organization's QMS. The benefits of process-based versus element-based audits have been discussed in numerous sections of this handbook, but suffice it to say, it allows for a more effective and efficient audit. The checklists on the CD have been structured around the evaluation of processes.

As an alternative to auditing by activities, the audit program manager could instead choose to audit by significant aspect category. This might be advantageous for aspects that involve numerous activities throughout the organization. An example might be an audit of the organization's recycling program or energy conservation program. Both of these aspects will reach into many different areas of the organization, some of which might not be

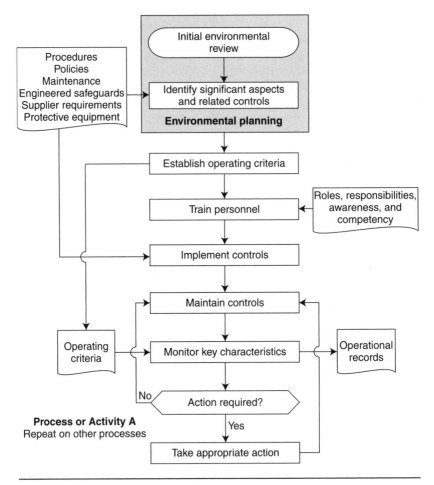

Figure 7.5 Operational control activities.

examined during routine process-based audits. This approach also works well in organizations without QMSs or where the EMS and the QMS are maintained as separate systems. Specific checklists for these audits would need to be developed based on the organization's procedures and policies for implementing these programs.

Audit Strategy and Key Audit Points

The auditor should begin by examining the list of significant aspects and their associated activities and controls. If the auditor has been assigned to evaluate a process, he or she should identify all significant aspects associated with that process. For a manufacturing process there may be three or four aspects. The auditor should note on the checklists how these aspects are controlled.

If the auditor has been assigned to evaluate an aspect, he or she should review the listing of significant aspects and identify the activities associated with the aspect. The auditor may identify four or five areas where hazardous waste is handled, a dozen key points for nonhazardous industrial wastes, or the entire facility may need to be reviewed if assigned energy consumption and conservation.

Because many operational controls take the form of procedures, the auditor should obtain any procedures that relate to the control of the activities or significant aspects that he or she has been assigned to audit. Examples include waste handling procedures, energy conservation guidelines, and material handling instructions. Operating permits also fall into the category of procedures because they contain the controls and monitoring that must be maintained. The auditor should prepare for the audit by reviewing these procedures and modifying and/or developing checklists of questions and key audit points. Audit planning was covered in detail in Chapter 5.

With a list of significant aspects for the process and an understanding of how they should be controlled, the auditor is now ready to conduct the review. The auditor will be talking to the process operator. The auditor should introduce himself or herself, set the auditee at ease, and begin by asking, "Is there anything that we do here that could harm the environment, if not done correctly?" The auditor is verifying operator awareness of the significant environmental aspects of his or her job. The standard requires that operators have such an awareness, along with knowing the consequences to the environment if they do not follow procedures, for good reason. The procedures tell the operator *what* to do; awareness tells them *why* it is important. Win the heart, and you will eventually win the mind.

Note that I do not ask, "Are you aware of any significant environmental aspects associated with this process?" If you ask the question like that, you're just as likely to get a serious look of confusion from the auditee. Stay away from terms like "significant aspects" because most employees will not know what you mean. Unfortunately, I've also run into a few environmental management representatives who didn't know what that meant, either, but that's another story.

Once the auditee replies, the auditor can ask about the effects to the environment if the procedures are not done properly. Typical answers might be "it could pollute the air" or "it could put oil in the creek." The auditor is ensuring that the auditee understands why it is important to control the activity. The auditor can then ask how these activities are controlled. During the auditee's response the auditor can verify that the activity is being properly controlled in accordance with company policies and procedures. The auditor should verify that controls are in place and operating (for example, filters installed, ventilation systems operating, advanced power management system features on computers enabled) and should ask to see any records required to be maintained by the operator.

The auditor is now verifying that monitoring of key attributes of the activity is being performed as required by local procedures and practices. For example, if the control of air emissions from a glue and adhesive operation is through the use of filtered ventilation, and the procedure requires hourly monitoring of the differential pressure across the filter, the auditor should verify that the hourly monitoring is being conducted. The differential pressure is in essence an operating criterion, and the hourly check is a monitoring requirement. Assume that the procedure for controlling this activity requires the operator to notify maintenance when the differential pressure reaches 2 psid so that the filter can be replaced. The auditor should ask the operator, "Are we required to do anything when the differential pressure increases? What do we do, and at what pressure?" Notice how the auditor is also verifying the operator's understanding of his or her roles and responsibilities relating to control of the aspect, along with knowledge and understanding of what he or she must do (that is, training and competency). For specific tasks such as waste handling, the auditor may also want to jot down the auditee's name for later verification of training.

For activities such as hazardous waste handling, packaging, labeling, and bulk liquid unloading, it is desirable to also observe the activity being performed. This requires careful coordination with area management, normally through the audit program manager, because these activities may not be performed all that often. Their nonroutine nature makes it all that much more important to actually observe them if possible. People are normally fairly competent in the performance of routine activities; it is usually the nonroutine activities that bite them. If the operators have specific responsibilities for emergency response relating to the activity or significant aspect, the auditor can also question them on these responsibilities.

The auditor should pay particular attention to operating criteria in procedures and operating permits. These criteria are normally specified to ensure the operation has minimal impact on the environment. Examples include flowrates, temperatures, and pressures. Operating a plating bath at a higher temperature than required increases the air emissions and could lower the filtration effectiveness.

During the audit the auditor should note the revision date of any EMS procedures or instructions found in the area for later comparison with the master list of documents. He or she should also review any monitoring records for legibility and completeness. Any environmental monitoring equipment in use in the process should be checked for calibration. He or she should also verify that proper maintenance is performed on equipment and facilities used in the process when maintenance has been identified as a means of operational control.

If the organization has established any improvement objectives or targets relating to this activity or its significant aspects, I also like to ask the operator if he or she is aware of the objectives. Communication of improvement objectives should flow down to those most directly involved in meeting them, and that is the employee most directly involved in the activity. I normally issue an OFI if I find that employees are not aware of improvement objectives and targets associated with their activities or areas.

Behavior controls are more difficult to assess. Behavior controls include things like properly disposing of batteries and fluorescent bulbs, turning off lights when not in the office, and recycling paper, cardboard, and aluminum cans. Awareness is the key. The auditor should interview numerous employees to verify that the level of awareness is as it should be. The auditor can spot-check waste storage areas, of course, but the chances of finding systematic deficiencies are slim, and I'm not going to go diving into the dumpster in the back of the plant. I prefer to use the monthly safety walk-throughs to spot-check compliance to behavior controls and to review the results of those walk-throughs to assess how well personnel are complying with the policies. Awareness is still the key, however. Employees need to understand not only what they should do but also why they should do it.

If the auditor is evaluating an engineering process such as design and development, he or she should pick several of the company's products and ask how elements of DfE were factored into the design of these products. The auditor should ask to see design review records and other documents that substantiate the auditee's responses. The auditor should absolutely note the names of those involved in the design to verify that they have received training in DfE.

Performance Indicators

The auditor should expect to find performance indicators for the operational controls being evaluated. The auditor should review these indicators to help evaluate overall performance and effectiveness and to help focus the audit. Areas of poor performance, as identified by the indicators, should be evaluated for actions to correct the performance. The lack of any action to address significant performance issues can serve as the basis for an NC citing ineffective implementation. The following are some examples of performance indicators used to measure how well we are controlling our significant environmental aspects:

- Amount disposed of or amount consumed (materials and wastes), normalized for production volume

- Amount in inventory (solvents and other hazardous materials, chemicals)

- Operating hours (reuse of chemical baths, cleaning agents)

- Energy usage, normalized to production volume

- Amount recycled

- Percentage recyclable (product design)

- Energy efficiency ratings (product design) or survey results (facilities)

Monitoring and Corrective Action

Monitoring and corrective action focuses on measuring the performance of the EMS and on the implementation of actions when it is not performing as it should. Note that some components of monitoring have been incorporated into other audits—monitoring of regulatory compliance was reviewed during the environmental planning audit, and monitoring of operational control characteristics during the operational control audits. Likewise, corrective action for violations to regulatory requirements arising out of the environmental compliance reviews was evaluated during the environmental planning audit. The focus of this evaluation will be on the overall monitoring of environmental performance and on the corrective and preventive action program.

The general process of monitoring and corrective action looks something like that shown in Figure 7.6. Interrelationships with the environmental planning, operational controls, and improvement processes are shown in the shaded boxes. While there is a possibility of some overlap between the components, and therefore some redundancy between the audits, the audit does not take a large amount of time, and the redundancy is minimal.

Some audit program managers may want to combine this evaluation with the evaluation of the improvement process. The improvement process includes a review of the setting of environmental objectives, management programs, and the conduct of the management review. There is a natural linkage between that audit and the evaluation of monitoring and corrective action. They were split into separate reviews because the interviewees will be different—the environmental management representative for the audit of monitoring and corrective action, and executive management in the case of improvement. Even so, it may still make sense to combine the audits, realizing that an audit plan may be required to support the multiple interviews.

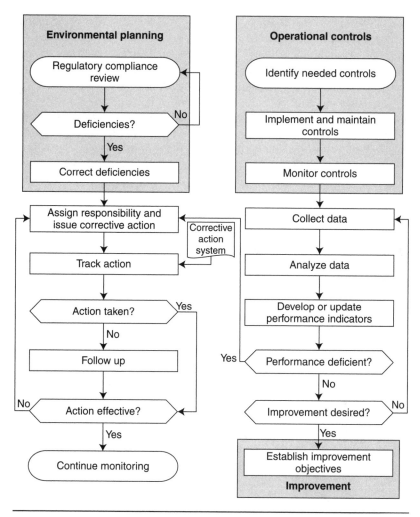

Figure 7.6 EMS monitoring and corrective action.

AUDIT STRATEGY AND KEY AUDIT POINTS

Monitoring

The auditor should begin by asking the auditee (typically the environmental management representative) how overall performance of the EMS is monitored. The auditor should ask to see the performance measures. During the review, the auditor should look for trends and performance to defined goals, where they have been established. The auditor should question any areas where performance is not meeting the goal or the trend is going in the wrong direction. For sustained negative trends, or performance far below the goal, the auditor should ask what actions are being taken to correct the performance. Failure to take action for significantly poor performance is the basis for an NC. If the period-to-period performance cannot be assessed because of changes in operations (for example, large increases in production activity), an OFI should be issued stating that monitoring could be improved through normalization of the data. Normalization means adjusting the indicator to account for the volume fluctuations, usually due to production activity. Keep in mind the goal of this monitoring is to evaluate environmental performance improvement. If the indicators fail to provide useful data in this regard, they should be modified.

Areas where performance is satisfactory but where additional improvement is desired would normally become improvement objectives. If the audit program manager has combined this audit with the improvement audit, the auditor could flow into an evaluation of the improvement objectives now. Otherwise, the auditor would move into an evaluation of the internal audit program.

EMS Audits

The auditor should commence the audit by interviewing the audit program manager. The auditor should:

- Ask to see the audit procedure and the audit schedule

- Walk through the process with the audit program manager

- Inquire about the rationale for the scheduling of the audits

- Verify that status and importance of processes are considered during audit scheduling

It would be reasonable to expect additional audits of areas associated with nonconformities, a history of problems, areas key to the achievement of environmental objectives, or areas with indications of poor environmental performance. If the auditor notes that all areas/topics are scheduled once per year, the auditor should consider issuing an OFI if significant problem areas exist.

The auditor can then examine audit performance. He or she should find out if audits are completed on schedule and probe into the reasons for any significant slippages to the schedule. Insufficient numbers of trained auditors or difficulty getting part-time auditors released to perform audits may explain the inability to get the audits done. Note that some rearrangement of the audit schedule should be expected if the audit program manager is responsive to the status and importance when scheduling audits.

The auditor should compare the systematic weaknesses noted in these audit reports with external audits of the same areas or processes. If external audits found systematic weaknesses in areas where internal audits did not, this may indicate a lack of effectiveness of the internal audit process. The internal audit must have been performed prior to the external audit and around the same period of time for this comparison to be valid.

The auditor can also evaluate the completeness of the audit reports and timeliness of their issuance against local requirements. The auditor may also want to verify auditor training and independence, if not known.

Audit findings should be reviewed. The auditor should evaluate whether the audit findings contain sufficient detail to fully understand the nonconformity, opportunity, or best practice. Any NCRs or CARs should get special attention. If the auditor cannot understand the issue from reading the finding, there is a high likelihood the auditee may not either. If the auditor finds numerous poorly worded or incomplete write-ups, a finding should be generated.

The auditor should now ask to see the tracking system used to monitor the status of actions associated with audit nonconformances. The audit program manager may have a separate tracking system or may use the corrective action system. The auditor should check on the status of any audit nonconformances and evaluate whether action to correct the finding is proceeding. Any instances of overdue, outstanding corrective action should be investigated. Unless there is additional evidence of actions being taken to resolve the problem, the auditor should issue an NC. Audits provide no value if action is not taken to resolve the deficiencies they find. The auditor should also confirm that verification of action taken is being performed, and that audits are being used to verify the long-term effectiveness of actions taken to address nonconformities identified during previous audits.

Finally, the auditor should confirm that the final audit file contains the information required by the local procedure. Typically, this includes the audit report and any checklists used. Maintaining the checklists is not mandatory unless required by local procedures, but it is strongly recommended.

Nonconformance, Corrective and Preventive Action

Armed with information on overall EMS performance and the results of the internal EMS audits, the auditor can now evaluate the corrective and preventive action system. The auditor should begin by asking to see the procedure(s) for nonconformance and corrective and preventive action. The program coordinator should walk the auditor through the process, and the auditor should stop to ask questions and to view evidence for the following key points. During the review, the auditor should verify through an evaluation of the log, database, and corrective and preventive actions that information and timing requirements mandated by local procedures are being met.

Corrective Action Use

It is often found that the only time a corrective action is issued is after an audit nonconformity is received. This indicates a lack of understanding of the corrective action process, or a lack of commitment to invest the time required to identify the true root cause and the actions to prevent recurrence. The corrective action program should be used anytime a problem or nonconformity occurs that requires a root cause determination and action to prevent recurrence. While some isolated problems may not require corrective action, repetitive or significant problems do. Problems involving poor waste management, potential violations to regulatory requirements, and repeated disregard of the organization's energy conservation policies are a few examples where corrective action is warranted. Informally taking care of these problems forgoes the benefits a disciplined problem-solving methodology enacted through the corrective action process provides. Problems are likely to recur, but failure to identify them using the corrective action process makes them hard to monitor. The auditor should issue an OFI if he or she finds that all or a majority of the CARs were generated through the audit process.

Corrective and Preventive Action Tracking

The auditor should verify that the program coordinator is actively monitoring the status of outstanding corrective and preventive actions. Outstanding, overdue corrective actions should be bumped up to more senior management if the follow-up is not successful in getting action to occur.

Quality of the Action Taken

Did the action taken to resolve the problem address immediate and containment actions, any short-term or temporary actions, long-term action to eliminate the cause and prevent recurrence, or any remedial action that may have been necessary? These same action categories apply to nonaudit corrective and preventive actions. The following lists provide an explanation and an example of each of these types of action.

Immediate or Emergency Action

- Contains the problem

- Mitigates any environmental impact

  Example: *The electrostatic paint line cleaning operation was immediately shut down.*

Short-Term or Temporary Corrective Action

- Allows operations to continue

- Provides a Band-Aid fix

Example: *A temporary catch tank was connected to the system to contain the hazardous rinse water until the wastewater treatment system can be restored.*

Long-Term or Preventive Action

- Eliminates the root cause

- Permanently corrects the problem

Example: *The wastewater treatment system was restored to full normal operation. Additionally, a daily system check was added to the preventive maintenance schedule to verify proper system operation.*

Remedial Action

- Provides recovery from the effect of the problem

- Cleans up the mess

Example: *Monitoring of the ditch and creek downstream of the plant was immediately performed. No effluent escaped the plant. All residue inside the plant was cleaned up and appropriate reports filed.*

Improvement

The improvement process includes setting environmental objectives and targets, establishing management programs to ensure achievement of these objectives, and performing periodic management reviews. The general flow of the improvement process is shown in Figure 7.7. Interrelationships with other core activities are shown in shaded boxes.

Environmental Objectives and Targets

Many companies review and set environmental objectives during the management review process. In this case, this topic should be discussed during the evaluation of the management review. General comments on the evaluation of objectives can be found in the "Environmental Objectives, Targets, and Management Programs" section of Chapter 6. Additional specific audit points unique to the EMS are presented here.

The ISO 14001 standard requires setting environmental objectives and targets. There is a lot of confusion about what an objective is and what a target is. The ISO 14001 standard defines an environmental objective as:

An overall environmental goal, consistent with the environmental policy, that an organization sets itself to achieve.

An environmental target is defined in the standard as:

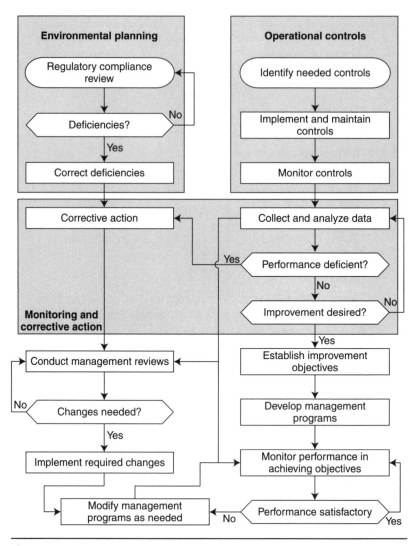

Figure 7.7   Improvement process.

A detailed performance requirement, applicable to the organization or parts thereof, that arises from the environmental objectives and that needs to be set and met in order to achieve those objectives.

Clause 4.3.3 of the standard states that both objectives and targets should be measurable where practicable.

Many organizations define the objective in global terms (for example, "reduce air emissions") and the target in terms of amount (for example, "by 20 percent"). I prefer to think of the target as the actions that must be accomplished in order to support the overall objective. For example, the objectives and targets to improve energy conservation might be as follows:

> *Environmental objective:* Reduce energy usage by 25 percent over 2003 levels by the end of 2005.

The objective is measurable and has a timeframe associated with it. To accomplish this objective, the organization may target the following activities:

> *Target 1:* Relamp the production area with high-efficiency lighting by June 2004 (this target is also measurable and has a time frame)

> *Target 2:* Install motion sensors in all conference rooms by March 2004

> *Target 3:* Conduct an energy survey of the facilities in the first quarter of 2004

> *Target 4:* Evaluate, select, and install an energy management system for the main building by June 2004

> *Target 5:* Evaluate the use of variable speed motors for the oil transfer system during the first quarter of 2004

> *Target 6:* Provide refresher training on the energy conservation guidelines to all personnel in January 2004

I prefer this method of defining objectives and targets because it provides more specific measurable goals that must be met by the various functions and levels of the organization. Each target would then have its own required set of actions. Taken together, achieving the targets should allow the organization to meet its overall objective of a 25 percent reduction in energy usage. When defined as suggested here, the objective is derived from the policy commitments, and the targets focus on the activities related to the significant aspects that must be improved to meet the objective. This alignment of policy, objectives, targets, and aspects looks something like Figure 7.8.

Detailed Audit Strategy and Key Audit Points

The auditor should ask to see the objectives and associated programs established for the current period. During this review, the auditor should ask how these objectives were determined. If the auditor has recently completed the audit of the monitoring and corrective action process, he or she should be familiar with the overall performance of the EMS and where improvement objectives may be warranted. In particular, the auditor should verify that the views of interested parties were considered during the setting of objectives (the ISO 14001 standard requires this).

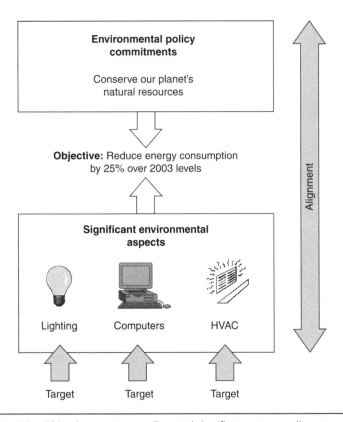

Figure 7.8 Objectives, targets, policy, and significant aspects alignment.

Interested parties include outside organizations like community residents, government agencies, and the organization's stockholders and employees. The auditor should inspect the communication log to see if there were any concerns or opinions expressed by interested parties, and if there were, that these were considered.

The auditor should compare the objectives with the management programs set up, to help ensure their achievement. These management programs, or action plans, must contain details on what has to be done, who is responsible for doing it, and when it should be done. The auditor can use the actions and time frames to evaluate performance in achieving the objectives. Some form of tracking progress should be in place. If no tracking of performance in meeting objectives is evident, other than during an annual or semiannual management review, the auditor should consider issuing an OFI. Such infrequent monitoring does not allow sufficient time for recovery actions if progress is deficient.

Communication of improvement objectives is also important. The auditor may ask the auditee about the methods used to communicate objectives throughout the organization. Note that the operational control audits evaluate the effectiveness of these methods by asking employees about any objectives established for their departments or activities. The auditor may want to issue an OFI if no formal means of communicating objectives has been established.

Of course, the most important item to verify is the organization's performance in meeting its objectives and targets. With the performance objectives and management programs in hand, the auditor should be able to establish whether the management programs have been effective in supporting achievement of the environmental objectives and related targets. The auditor should question any areas where performance is not meeting the defined targets. For sustained negative trends, or performance far below the target milestone, the auditor should ask what actions are being taken to correct the performance. Failure to take action for significantly poor performance is the basis for an NC.

Management Review

The purpose of the management review is to drive action. The auditor must always keep this in mind because many organizations have evolved their management review to little more than a short status review. The management review is the key forum for management to get active and engaged in improving the EMS's performance and for driving action that leads to performance improvement. While management should demonstrate its overall commitment and support on a routine, day-to-day basis, the management review is somewhat like a strategic planning session, where high-level decisions and actions on what the organization needs to do are generated and then deployed. Management reviews should be major events in the life cycle of the EMS. However, the opposite is often true—the management review is a short, one- or two-hour report out once a year that must be endured, versus anticipated.

Unfortunately, there may be little that the audit program can do in this situation, other than to verify that the minimum requirements of the standard are being met. This section discusses how to verify that the management review meets these minimum requirements. Beyond that, the audit program manager may want to have senior management review Chapters 1 and 8 to help foster a more positive attitude toward the EMS in general and the management review as a tool to drive improvements in the EMS.

I normally like to interview the senior manager or executive during the evaluation of the management review process. If a procedure is available, I follow along as the manager describes the process used to conduct the review. I also ask for the records from the last two management reviews conducted. The following requirements should be verified by the auditor as he or she evaluates the management review process:

- *Who attends?* The management review is a top-level review. Most auditors consider top management to consist of the senior person at a facility and his or her direct staff. While not everyone has to be there, a majority should attend. If the organization has a procedure that provides guidance on who should attend, the auditor should audit to that guidance.

- *How often are management reviews held?* The management review must be held at planned intervals. How long should that interval be? That really depends on the maturity and status of the EMS. Most auditors consider annual reviews to be the minimum frequency. If the management system is relatively new, or if performance indicators show major problems with the organization's processes or performance in achieving its objectives, then more frequent reviews are probably appropriate. Put it this way—if audits and performance trends indicate that the management system is in shambles, and the management review is still only held once a year, then a finding is warranted.

- *How long does the review take?* While there is no required duration for the management review, the auditor should use what he or she has learned from the evaluations of other improvement processes to determine whether sufficient time is being provided to conduct a thorough review. If a global review and analysis of data were performed prior to the review, performance information could be summarized, shortening the time for the review. If the analysis of data will be performed as part of the review, then more time will be required. I find it hard to believe that an annual management review could be conducted in less than two or three hours under any circumstances. I could see an hour-long review if it were held monthly, as is the case in some companies where a portion of the system is evaluated at each review. Because there is no stated duration for the review, and because it is hard to tie duration directly to effectiveness, I do not issue findings relating to duration. I do use the auditee's answer to evaluate how deeply I research into other aspects of the review, however.

- *What sources of information are included in the review?* The auditor should look for evidence that the key inputs into the review are evaluated. These include:

  – The results of internal and external management system audits

  – The results of environmental compliance reviews

−Process performance indicators associated with activities related to significant environmental aspects

−Status of corrective and preventive actions

−Follow-up actions from previous reviews (this is why I ask to see records of the last two reviews)

−Changes that could affect the EMS (for example, new technologies, new processes, new or changed environmental regulations, and new facilities)

−Recommendations for improvement, including changes to the environmental policy, the organization's procedures, and objectives and targets

There should be solid evidence that these items were included in the review, preferably as discussion points in the records or meeting minutes from the review. If the only evidence is that they showed up on the agenda, the auditor should look for evidence of their review in the actions arising from the review, or ask the auditee to summarize the results presented for these items. If all show up on the agenda but some have no discussion in the records, I generally accept the evidence on the agenda. If there is no evidence for these items, or if the only evidence is the agenda (that is, there are no actions or discussion of the items in the records or meeting minutes, or the auditee can't remember the specifics of what was discussed), then I issue an NC. The standard requires that records of the management review, and any actions arising from it, be maintained.

- *What actions resulted from the review?* Clearly, the intent of such a high-level review is to drive action. The auditor should check the records of the review to determine if actions are an output from the review. If my examination of the last two management reviews fails to identify any actions or decisions arising from the review, then I issue an NC or an OFI, depending on my knowledge of the EMS status. If the audit reports, regulatory citations, and process performance data indicate that the EMS is falling down around our ears, I issue an NC. If these indicators show that the EMS is in reasonably good shape, I issue an OFI. If the system is in great shape, I may not issue a finding. The key to being able to generate a finding is to tie it into system status.

- *How are the actions tracked?* If there were actions arising from the review, the auditor should ask how these actions are tracked. The auditor should use the records from the last management review to determine whether the actions arising from the review were completed and/or discussed during the most current review. I normally issue an OFI if I find that there is no formal system for tracking actions arising from the review other than going back and looking at the review records from a year ago.

The auditor must use ample tact and perspective when evaluating the management review process. Senior managers may support findings in other areas of the company, but now the auditor is hitting closer to home. The auditor should:

- Point out the benefits that a robust management review should provide, without pushing too hard

- Tie findings into other problems noted during earlier audits

- Reinforce the consequences of system failures, where known

- Encourage management to spend the time to do a thorough review

KEY SUPPORT PROCESSES

The final group of activities is the key support processes. These activities support all components of the management system. They have been grouped together for convenience and to allow for an efficient audit. Portions of these activities will be evaluated during other audits. This audit will evaluate only the centralized elements of these processes.

Audit Strategy and Key Audit Points

Document Control

The auditor should ask to see the document control procedure. The auditor should ask the auditee to walk through the procedure and show the components of the system, such as the master list, files of archived documents, and so on, as they come to them in the procedure. During the reviews of these elements, the auditor should verify that they are being maintained. The auditor may want to select a few documents to verify that only authorized personnel reviewed and/or approved the documents. If this is checked during other process-based audits, this step may not be necessary.

For the most part, the auditor is verifying that there is a system to locate and distribute documents, a system that establishes the appropriate revision status, and a system to properly archive and safeguard obsolete documents. The auditor may also want to evaluate the backlog of document change requests to determine whether resources supplied are sufficient to allow timely document preparation and issue.

The auditor should also verify proper control of environmental regulations and assurance that there is a method to stay aware of changes to them. Many companies rely on subscription services, links to government Web sites where changes are announced, and corporate staff to maintain this awareness. The auditor should verify that some method is in place and is being used. Note that this review may also be performed during the environmental planning audit when evaluating legal and other requirements.

Record Control

The auditor should ask to see the record control procedure and the records matrix. The auditor can select several records from the matrix and verify that these records are stored and retained as indicated in the matrix. Records in long-term storage should be properly indexed and protected against deterioration and loss. If the records matrix identified a retention time of one year, the auditor could ask for a record generated six months ago to see if the records management system can retrieve the record. If record retention is decentralized, this may not be practical. If records are stored electronically, the auditor should verify that records are properly backed up and are password protected. Finally, if the organization has a record disposal policy, the auditor may want to verify that records are disposed of as required by local procedures.

Keep in mind that many of the environmental records that must be maintained have legal retention requirements. Most, but not all, regulatory records must be retained for at least three years. The auditor may want to have the auditee show him or her the legal retention requirement for the records if doubt exists.

Training

Like many other activities discussed in this section, training and competency should be evaluated during every process-based audit. The focus of this evaluation is on the centralized training functions.

Especially important is the process for identifying competency requirements. Auditors may find that personnel have met all the defined competencies, and have training records to prove it, but if the critical competencies are not correctly defined in the first place, the results will be poor performance, nonconformities, and potentially regulatory violations. It should also be noted that competency identification is not a one-time evolution—competency requirements change over time as new methods and technologies are adapted by the organization. For this reason, the audit of the centralized training activities focuses on the identification and communication of required competencies.

Another area in which training programs are often deficient is in the verification of training effectiveness. Although tests, pre- and posttraining quizzes, and student feedback forms provide some information on the effectiveness of training delivery, the real test is whether personnel can properly do their job. This requires actual observation and ongoing monitoring. Training departments can and should use the results of internal audits, internal and external problem reports, and posttraining feedback to evaluate how effective the training program is.

The auditor can begin the evaluation by asking to see a copy of the training procedure, if one has been developed. Most procedures are laid out along the natural flow of the process, which in this case would be identification of competency requirements, delivery of training, and verification of training effectiveness. The auditee should walk the auditor through the process, and the auditor should pay particular attention to the following items.

Competency Requirements   The auditor should ask to see the competency matrix or its equivalent that identifies the competencies that must be achieved. Some organizations use job descriptions to identify competency requirements. Although I don't necessarily like this method, if the job descriptions adequately define the required competencies and are maintained, I will accept them. The auditor should use his or her knowledge of the tasks performed within the organization to evaluate several functions for review. It helps if the audit program manager selects more experienced auditors to do this evaluation because, as a result of their previous audits, they will have a better idea of the types of competencies required to perform functional tasks. As an alternative, this review could be added to other audit checklists. Although it would add to the time required to perform these audits, it would result in a more thorough and penetrating evaluation because the auditor would be very familiar with the types of competencies required, having just evaluated the process. It would also result in better coverage than could be attained from a sampling of functional duties performed here.

The auditor should also ask how competency requirements are updated and maintained. In the dynamic business environment of today, new technologies, new materials, and new processes are constantly being introduced. Some method of reevaluation and adjustment of competencies should be in place to respond to these dynamics. The training matrices or job descriptions should be controlled documents, and the auditor should be able to identify updates and modifications. If the training matrices have been in use for some time and have never been updated, the auditor should probe this area. The auditor should verify that some method is in use or otherwise issue an OFI.

Finally, note that identifying required competencies requires the support of the various departments and process owners who know the tasks best. Human resources can't really do a credible job without their input. Some type of formal or informal task analysis is required. Because so many different owners are involved in determining competency requirements, there is often a wide variance in the level of detail and quality of the output (the competency requirements). Auditors should be sensitive to this variation and should note functions where it doesn't look like much effort was put into defining the required competencies.

Competency Attainment The next task is to verify that adequate progress is being made to attain the mandatory competencies. The auditor can ask how competency attainment is monitored. Competency attainment may be indicated on the competency matrix or on an individual's training plans. If the organization has criteria for training, such as "basic required skills must be attained during the initial three-month probationary period," the auditor can sample several recently hired (between three and six months ago) employees to see if the policy is being followed. Normally the auditor will select records of personnel hired since the training procedure or program was established. Employees working at the organization prior to that time are often grandfathered in on the basis of their previous demonstrated skills or experience. I accept this as long as there is some evidence that a review of the employees' current skills against the newly identified competencies was performed and they weren't just signed off en masse as being competent. The evidence, if not in writing, may be in the form of an interview with the functional head of the department responsible for identifying and verifying current competencies.

The auditor now looks to see if competency gaps have been identified and if actions to close those gaps are being taken, normally through the scheduling of training for an individual. The auditor also indirectly monitors the deployment of resources in support of training. In today's lean and cost-conscious business environment, it is not uncommon to find that the first thing cut is the training budget. Failure to meet established training goals or recurring delays in providing required training due to resource limitations should be noted as findings. Delays in providing optional training can be justified; delays in providing mandatory training cannot. If the auditor finds that mandatory training is not being provided, he or she should inquire as to what additional safeguards are being taken to protect the employee and the environment pending provision of the training. The auditor is primarily looking for trends and broad issues with competency attainment because the training and competency of employees should be reviewed during other audits.

Verification of Training Effectiveness   Training verification should confirm that employees can actually do their jobs as a result of the training. Most verification instead evaluates training delivery and is highly biased toward the presentation skills of the trainer, the quality of the visual aids, or the trainer's skill in prepping the trainees for the posttraining quiz. Effective verification normally requires observation of the individual performing the task, evaluation of indicators that the individual can or cannot perform the task correctly, or feedback from the individual *after* he or she has tried to apply the training on the job. Direct observation works well for tasks with little variety. Tasks that may be hard to completely define, such as most service activities, as well as engineering (for example, DfE), need additional means of verification. This can come from reviews of performance data, audit results, and compliance reviews.

During the review of training, the auditor must be aware that some organizations have a legal obligation to provide certain types of training, such as hazardous waste training for employees who handle hazardous wastes, and storm water operator training if the organization is operating under a storm water permit. The auditor may want to question the training coordinator or management representative on how these mandatory training requirements were identified, in addition to verifying that the training was provided.

The auditor should also ensure that contract and agency personnel are made aware of the organization's environmental policies and practices, to the extent the policies apply to the work they are involved with.

Control of Purchased Products and Contractors (Purchasing)

In the EMS, we are most concerned with two things relating to our suppliers and contractors. First, we need to ensure that any relevant environmental policies and requirements are communicated to suppliers and contractors. This can be done through passing down the requirements (for example, passing down any restricted or prohibited material lists) or by briefings before the contractor commences work on-site. Most organizations have a fairly robust process to do this. The auditor should verify that the process is being followed during the audit.

The second consideration, more often lacking, is obtaining information from the supplier or contractor regarding its activities and any significant environmental aspects arising from these activities. For suppliers of materials and products, this is often accomplished through receipt of the MSDS. The auditor should ensure that the MSDS for new products is reviewed for any environmental (or safety) concerns that may need to be addressed before using the new chemical or material. For contractors, an environmental survey is often used. The survey asks questions regarding the types of materials and chemicals to be used, the types and amounts of wastes expected to be generated, and what is done with the wastes. The auditor should verify that methods are in place to address these two considerations and that they are being used.

Roles and Responsibilities

Roles and responsibilities connected with defined activities associated with significant environmental aspects will be evaluated during operational control audits. In this audit the auditor focuses on the definition, communication, and awareness of roles; the responsibilities and authorities of key individuals; and the functions needed to support the EMS. These include the management representative, internal EMS auditors, emergency response coordinators, and the CFT assigned responsibilities for identifying environmental aspects and determining their significance. If these roles are examined during other audits, they do not need to be reviewed here.

Communications

The final evaluation examines the process used to communicate important environmental information within the organization and to outside interested parties. Communication of key information internally, such as roles and responsibilities, awareness, and improvement objectives, will be continually evaluated during other audits. I usually like to ask how concerns, issues, and improvement suggestions are communicated up the ladder, however. I often find that no formal system exists for upward communication from employees. This will damage the support for the EMS and will result in losing ideas that could significantly improve environmental performance. The auditor should issue a finding if no formal system to support upward communication from the workforce exists. If a system does exist, the auditor can test its effectiveness by asking to see the log or file of concerns, issues, or suggestions provided by employees. A blank file or log should tell the auditor that something isn't working.

The primary focus of this evaluation is on external communication. ISO 14001 requires that a system for receiving, documenting, and responding to inquiries or concerns relating to the EMS exists. This is almost universally met by the maintenance of some type of communication log. The auditor should ask about the methods used to respond to outside inquiries, including who receives them, how they are handled, and who responds to them. The auditor should also ask to see the log. In the case where there are no entries in the log, indicating no outside inquiries, the auditor should verify that a system is in place to handle them if any come in. If the auditor wanted to be sly and find out whether outside inquiries are logged, he or she could have Aunt Betty call in and request a copy of the environmental policy. Just don't say I told you to.

This concludes our review of how to evaluate an EMS. You may have seen many similarities between audits of a QMS and an audit of an EMS. Indeed, there are many similarities, to the point where it is not only possible but even desirable to jointly audit the QMS and the EMS.

SUMMARY

In this chapter we presented strategies for an audit of an EMS. These strategies were developed to make the audit process more efficient and more effective at finding the weaknesses that exist in any management system. The audit program is a key tool for ensuring that the EMS is meeting its performance expectations, and this consideration drove the detail provided in this chapter. Additional audit resources in the form of audit checklists are provided on the CD.

8

Moving beyond Compliance

Your EMS is now in place and operating. You have conducted your first and maybe second round of audits and are working toward achievement of your first set of environmental improvement objectives. You have achieved certification, if so desired. Now what? The goal from this point forward is to substantially improve your environmental performance. By this we mean taking actions to go beyond compliance to regulatory requirements and the minimum requirements of ISO 14001 toward sustainable development. Sustainable development means modifying your products, services, and activities so that you can meet the needs of this generation without harming the ability of future generations to meet their needs. Considering the long list of environmental concerns discussed in Chapter 1, our society has a long way to go to reach a state of sustainable development.

As was noted previously, mandating ever-more-stringent regulations can help, but this will not be sufficient to reduce and/or prevent many of the serious environmental effects currently impacting our planet. Indeed, in the United States we have seen that concern over the economic impacts of additional regulation frequently inhibits the passage of much-needed regulatory reform. This is not to be critical of government in that the economic well-being of its citizens is always a top priority, and the passage of stricter environmental regulations does indeed cause negative economic impact in many cases. The whole intent of the ISO 14001 standard was to provide a model whereby corporations, municipalities, and industries could systematically and voluntarily take steps that would lessen their environmental impacts. These steps, which focus on source reduction versus pollution treatment, do not necessitate the passage of new laws or more aggressive enforcement; rather, they depend on making sensible and conscious decisions regarding the nature and operation of our products and processes. A significant side benefit of these actions is that unlike treatment methodologies (which can cost thousands or millions of dollars to install and maintain), these actions can actually save the company money and improve the bottom line.

This chapter examines many of the options that can help an organization move beyond compliance. Most of these programs also provide long-term cost savings. Many of these programs are supported by the federal government or industry groups that provide "how to" assistance to get the program running. While some are industry specific, many are generic and can be adopted by any type of organization in any industry. In addition, we will show several examples of beyond-compliance improvements that were bubbled up through the internal organization to provide a sense of what can be achieved once the entire organization is focused on pollution prevention.

The programs described in this chapter interface with the ISO 14001 EMS in several ways. First, major initiatives can be folded into the organization's environmental policy statement to provide more focused attention and improvement. Examples include DfE and the EPA's Energy Star program. An example of one such statement was provided in Figure 3.5 in Chapter 3. Second, these programs can be used to help control or minimize the negative environmental impacts of the organization's significant aspects. The components of these programs can form the basis for some of the operational controls associated with these aspects. Third, the programs can be used as a framework for environmental objectives and targets in that they provide guidance on the steps and/or actions needed to achieve performance improvement within the scope of the program. In all cases, they provide insight into what an organization can accomplish and how it can improve its environmental performance using source reduction concepts.

POLLUTION PREVENTION

The general framework established for pollution prevention is as follows:

1. Reduce the amount of hazardous material, waste, or emission generated prior to any recycling, treatment, or disposal (that is, source reduction)

2. Reduce the amount of hazardous material, waste, or emission released to the environment through recycling and reuse

3. Properly treat any hazardous waste or emission to reduce its impact on the environment prior to release

4. Properly dispose of any hazardous waste or emission to minimize its impact on the environment

This framework represents a hierarchy of actions, ranked according to beneficial impacts on the environment. In essence, it provides a flowchart of actions that should be considered in the following order:

1. Prevention

2. Recycling and reuse

3. Treatment

4. Proper disposal

Option 1 should always be considered before option 2, option 2 prior to option 3, and option 3 before option 4. Option 4 is always the least preferred option, but it may be necessary in some situations. Pollution prevention as described in this chapter focuses on option 1 (prevention) and to a limited extent option 2. Simply put, to achieve sustainable development we must focus on source reduction.

The current regulatory structure primarily focuses on options 3 and 4. The problem with treatment, although it is necessary in many cases, is that it does not remove pollution. Instead, treatment generally just changes the form of the pollutant to make it suitable for proper disposal. For example, the treatment of air emissions from a coal-fired utility involves electrostatic precipitators, separators, baghouses, and scrubbers to remove hazardous air pollutants from the emissions. While this process results in cleaner air, it does so at the expense of creating solid hazardous wastes that must then be controlled and properly disposed of. There is still an environmental impact associated with this activity that must be addressed.

The second problem with treatment and disposal is the additional costs. It is estimated that over $200 billion is spent annually by U.S. businesses on maintaining regulatory compliance, primarily in the form of treatment and disposal. This represents more than 2 percent of the U.S. gross domestic product and only represents the direct costs of regulatory compliance. The indirect costs are probably even larger. Consider that most of this money is not spent on eliminating pollution; rather, it changes its form so that it can be more safely disposed of with less environmental impact. Source reduction, on the other hand, eliminates the pollutant at its source, and in so doing it avoids the costs of compliance to regulatory requirements, which include:

- The costs of acquiring and installing precipitators, separators, baghouses, scrubbers, or other equipment needed to treat the pollutant

- The costs of operating and maintaining the equipment

- The costs of applying for certain types of permits

- The costs of properly handling and packaging the wastes

- The costs of disposing of the wastes

- The costs of manifesting and documenting the wastes

- The costs of providing specialized training in how to properly handle the wastes and respond to incidents or emergencies associated with the wastes

- The costs of preparing and generating various reports associated with hazardous wastes and certain types of emissions

- The costs associated with responding to regulatory nonconformities (for example, fines, audits, and inspections)

This is not a complete list of all the direct and indirect costs an organization will incur in order to properly control its hazardous wastes and emissions, but it does illustrate the point that dealing with pollutants (hazardous wastes, hazardous air pollutants, contaminated wastewater, and so on) is expensive. And in most cases it does not completely eliminate the pollutant or its eventual impact on the environment.

Source reduction, on the other hand, not only removes the source of pollution (thereby eliminating its impact) but also eliminates most, if not all, of the costs noted earlier. When considered in this light, it only makes economic and business sense to focus first on prevention.

This chapter will now discuss several pollution prevention programs that can be used to achieve source reduction. Much of the information regarding these programs has been obtained from the U.S. EPA. The information in most cases has been reproduced here as it appears on the EPA Web site. Additional information on many of these programs is provided on the CD in this book. Keep in mind that these programs do not represent a complete package of source reduction opportunities; rather, they demonstrate mature programs with clearly defined action protocols that can be implemented within almost any company.

EPA WASTEWISE PROGRAM

(Taken from http://www.epa.gov/wastewise)

General Description

WasteWise is a free, voluntary EPA program through which organizations eliminate costly municipal solid waste and select industrial wastes, benefiting their bottom line and the environment. WasteWise is a flexible program that allows partners to design their own waste reduction programs tailored to their needs. All organizations within the United States may join the program. Large and small businesses from any industry sector are welcome to participate. Institutions such as hospitals and universities, nonprofits, and other organizations, as well as state, local, and tribal governments, are also eligible to participate in WasteWise.

Waste reduction makes good business sense because it can save your organization money through reduced purchasing and waste disposal costs. WasteWise provides free technical assistance to help you develop, implement, and measure your waste reduction activities. WasteWise offers publicity to organizations that are successful in reducing waste through EPA publications, case studies, and national and regional events. These events also provide networking opportunities for organizations to share waste reduction ideas and success stories.

There is no fee for membership in WasteWise. EPA designed Waste-Wise to be a free, voluntary, and flexible program. The amount of time and money you invest is up to you! You are free to set goals that are the most feasible and cost-effective for your organization. In the long run, waste reduction can save your organization money. Registration can be accomplished by completing an online registration form or by calling the Waste-Wise Helpline at (800) EPA-WISE.

Benefits

Technical Assistance

EPA established a toll-free helpline to communicate with WasteWise partners and others interested in the program. Staffed by WasteWise information specialists, the WasteWise Helpline can answer both general program questions and specific technical questions on solid waste reduction. Helpline staff have access to an extensive library as well as a compendium containing current information about waste reduction resources nationwide.

The WasteWise Technical Assistance Team is available to provide individual assistance to partners. The WasteWise Technical Assistance Team can help partners complete the WasteWise Assessment Form for baseline and annual data, assist them in setting goals, and provide technical assistance in waste reduction issues.

The WasteWise Onsite Visit Program enables partners to meet with WasteWise representatives and receive assistance in developing and implementing quantifiable waste reduction programs. Onsite visits enhance the quality of our service by reinforcing our commitment to active partners. Likewise, the Onsite Visit Program enables WasteWise to build stronger relationships with partners that have significant waste reduction potential, but have encountered barriers to enhancing their waste reduction programs.

Common components of a WasteWise onsite visit include informal roundtable discussions and facility tours, which enable WasteWise representatives to provide tailored, personal recommendations for partners. To date, WasteWise representatives have conducted onsite visits for Colonial Pipeline Company, Canon USA, BGF Industries, Siemens Automotive Corporation, Commonwealth of Massachusetts, and Fresh Fields Whole Foods Market.

The WasteWise program has produced dozens of publications for distribution to partners and other interested parties. Partners have access to a variety of waste reduction publications, including tip sheets, WasteWise Updates and Bulletins, waste reduction guides, directories, and other Waste-Wise publications.

Public Recognition

Each year, EPA recognizes outstanding achievements of our partners by presenting "Partner of the Year" awards in several categories, including business, government, and educational sectors. To qualify, partners must submit complete annual reporting forms that detail tonnage of waste reduced, associated cost savings, and promotion of the WasteWise program to employees, customers, and suppliers. EPA also offers "Challenge Partner of the Year" awards to commend exemplary performance in meeting the WasteWise Challenge and "Endorser of the Year" awards to recognize outstanding endorser efforts in promoting WasteWise to other organizations.

EPA established the "Hall of Fame" to recognize exemplary partners that have made significant contributions to the WasteWise program for years. To be considered for the Hall of Fame, partners must report significant waste reduction results, win multiple WasteWise awards, and promote the program to other organizations.

In addition to the national forum, EPA sponsors regional forums to recognize the waste reduction efforts of existing partners and to welcome new partners. The meetings are held in cities across the country to help prospective partners learn about program requirements and the benefits of membership. These forums also provide partners an opportunity to network with others in their local area.

Case Studies

EPA recognizes the efforts of individual WasteWise partners by featuring their waste reduction successes, in the form of case studies, in a number of WasteWise venues. Past features ranged from speaking engagements at program workshops to publicity in documents such as annual reports and the WasteWise *Update*.

EPA publicizes the WasteWise program to help the public understand the significance of an organization's participation in WasteWise. Working with a wide range of business and trade publications, EPA provides information about WasteWise activities and major program events, benefits of membership, program accomplishments, and where to go for more information. *WasteAge Magazine* and *MSW Management Magazine* recently featured the WasteWise Climate Campaign in articles. EPA has encouraged further public recognition of the program by placing public service announcements in such well-known journals as *Fortune, U.S. News and World Report*, and *BusinessWeek*.

CASE STUDY

BETHLEHEM STEEL CORP.

Bethlehem Steel Corporation's experience with WasteWise has been very positive. The program created an awareness of resource conservation and recycling among our employees. WasteWise assisted us in establishing a baseline to measure the success of waste reduction activities, evaluate current programs, and discover new waste reduction opportunities.
—Rama Chaturvedi, Senior Environmental Engineer

Bethlehem Steel joined WasteWise as a charter partner in 1994 and was a Program Champion in 1998. Since joining WasteWise, Bethlehem Steel has achieved impressive success in waste prevention and recycling. The company also uses recycled metals in its manufacturing operations, which has saved millions of dollars since the program's inception.

- Reduced waste of furniture, computers, and disposable kitchen products by more than 14 tons. This effort saved the company more than $16,700.

- Reduced office paper use by more than 9 tons by using electronic communication methods, duplex copying, and scrap paper. As part of this policy, Bethlehem Steel saved more than $1 million in 1999.

- Used 700 pounds of remanufactured toner cartridges.

- Recycled more than 406 tons of materials in 1999.

- Used more than 36,500 tons of recycled steel and nonferrous metals in the manufacturing process. This action saved the company more than $1.8 million in 1999.

C A S E   S T U D Y

AIRPAX CORPORATION

WasteWise provided a way to systematically identify solid waste reduction opportunities and translate pounds reduced into dollars saved. The partner meetings, list server, and technical support make it easy to succeed.

—Scott H. Shapleigh, Environmental Coordinator

Airpax Corporation, an electronics manufacturer located in Cambridge and Frederick, Maryland, has a well-rounded waste reduction program, with quantified results in waste prevention, recycling collection, and buying recycled. These efforts helped it gain recognition as a WasteWise Program Champion in 1999. The company's recent waste prevention activities focused on transport packaging and office paper reduction.

- Conserved nearly 2 tons of wood through reusing pallets

- Reduced paper use by nearly 2 tons by making purchase order forms shorter and increasing use of e-mail for customer service communications

- Saved an estimated $24,000 in avoided disposal costs by recycling more than 220 tons of materials, including paper, corrugated, plastics, metals, glass, and wood

- Encouraged the purchase of recycled-content products through an in-house office supply preferred list and spent $12,000 on these products

C A S E   S T U D Y

MOTOROLA

The world has gracefully stepped into a new millennium and we at Motorola are moving forward on the journey to a sustainable world. We must each have the courage to face our individual contribution to the current state of the earth and be willing to change.

—Robert L. Growney, President and Chief Operating Officer

Motorola was named a WasteWise 2000 Partner of the Year for reducing more than 1,000 tons of waste in 1999. It continues to implement an aggressive waste reduction program focused on donating equipment and supplies, working with suppliers to take back packaging materials for reuse, and reducing the packaging used to ship products to customers.

- Conserved 154 tons of waste pallets, plastic, and cardboard by switching to reusable packaging.

- Collected 72 tons of clean room booties and gloves for reprocessing and reuse.

- Focused on new product lines to reduce the disposable corrugated packaging used to ship products to customers. In 1999, five new returnable packaging systems were implemented.

- Collected 103 tons of used computers, cell phones, electronic equipment, furniture, and office supplies to be donated to schools and charities where possible and otherwise recycled.

- Spent nearly $1 million on recycled-content products, including 44 tons of towels with an average 55 percent postconsumer content and 18 tons of napkins with an average 100 percent postconsumer content.

- Established a partnership with the facility office supply vendor to promote the use of recycled-content office products as the default choice from its catalog, conducted a Lunch and Learn meeting regarding recycled-content purchasing goals, and formed a cross-functional team to promote the use of recycled-content office supplies.

CASE STUDY

PITNEY BOWES

Knowing that the generation of waste is a reflection of operating inefficiency, Pitney Bowes continues to work diligently to eliminate the generation of solid waste. Through EPA's WasteWise Program, company initiatives to further reduce business-related solid waste are addressed comprehensively and aggressively.

—Don Offinger, Senior Corporate Environmental Engineer

Pitney Bowes discovered that simply reusing waste materials can reap financial rewards. By implementing programs to reuse waste plastics, resins, and cardboard, the company has saved hundreds of thousands of dollars. In addition, Pitney Bowes has realized waste prevention gains through the WasteWise Transport Packaging Challenge and was recognized as a Program Champion in 1998, 1999, and 2000.

- Reused more than 22 tons of waste plastics and resins, saving $113,400

- Purchased more than 1.5 tons of remanufactured toner cartridges

- Reused more than 114 tons of corrugated from interfacility shipping as packing material, saving more than $100,000

- Collected 5,750 tons of recyclable materials in 1999, which resulted in cost savings of more than $230,000

- Spent more than $243,000 to purchase 120 tons of recycled-content materials such as paper and cafeteria supplies

Regional Forums

WasteWise holds regional forums across the country. These meetings provide an opportunity for partners to interact with colleagues, discuss waste reduction issues, and share successful strategies with peers in their geographic area. Through the regional forums, EPA has established seven partner networks across the country, including the Chicago area, Dallas area, Northern California/San Francisco area, Southern California/Los Angeles area, New England area, New York/Tristate area, and Washington, DC/Mid-Atlantic area.

Sample Results

WasteWise partners eliminated more than 583,000 tons of material and saved millions of dollars through waste prevention activities in 1999. The following list provides some examples of WasteWise partner achievements in waste prevention.

Source Reduction

- Allergan achieved a 32 percent reduction in cardboard and plastic waste by improving process efficiency. This effort conserved more than 544,000 pounds of these materials combined and saved more than $43,000.

- Calgene conserved 400 pounds of paper, Styrofoam, and plastic by switching from disposable to reusable cafeteria supplies.

- Lucent Technologies eliminated more than 475,000 pounds of paper by increasing the use of electronic commerce and reducing hard-copy communications, saving more than $200,000.

- Herman Miller reduced fabric waste by more than 165,000 pounds by streamlining the manufacturing process, saving the company more than $498,800. The furniture manufacturer also reduced leather use and further decreased manufacturing waste by 8,800 pounds.

Recycling and Reuse

- Allchem Services reused 200 pounds of plastic packaging material as filler for outgoing shipments, saving $500.

- Eastern Illinois University reused more than 9,000 pounds of computer equipment and 25,000 pounds of coated paper office supplies through an internal employee exchange, saving nearly $7,000.

- Guardian Industries laundered and reused gloves and wiping cloths, which reduced waste by more than 12,000 pounds and saved the company almost $30,000.

Donate/Exchange

- The Walt Disney World Company donated more than 350,000 pounds of building materials to local nonprofit organizations and affordable housing projects and nearly 3,000 pounds of office supplies to a local program called "A Gift for Teaching."

- Polk County, Iowa, reused 10,500 pounds of furniture and saved $50,000 through auctions and an equipment-sharing program. The county also created an equipment-sharing catalog for all county agencies and departments to encourage sharing equipment by departments to fill anticipated, intermittent, and short-term needs.

- Accent Construction saved $35,000 by donating more than 12,000 pounds of excess building materials.

- Battelle Memorial Institute donated or resold more than 286,600 pounds of used equipment to local organizations. Additionally, Battelle gave scrap print shop supplies to an artists' organization and gave used computer equipment, office furniture, and books to local schools and nonprofits. Combined, these actions saved Battelle more than $674,500.

Employee Education

• The Grand Traverse Band of Ottawa and Chippewa Indians developed an office recycling procedures packet for the human resources department to distribute to new Tribal employees. Other employee education activities included adding recycling and buying recycled messages to pay stubs, sending out recycling reminders to all employees, and including environmental articles in the monthly newsletters that are distributed to all Tribal members and offices.

• The U.S. Postal Service–Alabama District developed a team of recycling coordinators to train employees on recycling practices prior to implementing recycling programs in district post offices. Training continues to be an ongoing process as new technologies are introduced and new employees join the postal service.

EPA ENERGY STAR PROGRAM

(Taken from http://www.energystar.gov)

ENERGY STAR is a government-backed program helping businesses and individuals protect the environment through superior energy efficiency.

Results are already adding up. Americans, with the help of ENERGY STAR, saved enough energy in 2005 alone to avoid greenhouse gas emissions equivalent to those from 23 million cars—all while saving $12 billion on their utility bills.

For the Home

Energy-efficient choices can save families about a third on their energy bill with similar savings of greenhouse gas emissions, without sacrificing features, style, or comfort. ENERGY STAR helps you make the energy-efficient choice.

For Business

Because a strategic approach to energy management can produce twice the savings—for the bottom line and the environment—as typical approaches,

EPA's ENERGY STAR partnership offers a proven energy management strategy that helps in measuring current energy performance, setting goals, tracking savings, and rewarding improvements. EPA provides an innovative energy performance rating system that businesses have already used for more than 26,000 buildings across the country. EPA also recognizes top-performing buildings with the ENERGY STAR. To partner with ENERGY STAR, your CEO, CFO, or top administrator must sign the partnership letter, committing your organization to continuous improvement of your energy efficiency. As part of this commitment, you agree to:

- Measure, track, and benchmark your energy performance

- Develop and implement a plan to improve your energy performance, adopting the ENERGY STAR strategy

- Educate your staff and the public about your partnership and achievements with ENERGY STAR

The EPA also maintains a Directory of Energy Efficiency Programs. The Directory can help you identify organizations in your state that sponsor energy efficiency programs that are partnered with ENERGY STAR. These offerings can include financial and technical assistance to improve the energy efficiency of your business. Program sponsor Partners include regulated utilities, publicly owned utilities, and energy delivery companies; national, regional, state, or local government entities; other organizations involved in coordinating or administering energy efficiency or environmental education programs that promote ENERGY STAR.

Guidelines for Energy Management

Superior energy management is good business. Recent research suggests that leaders in energy management are able to achieve superior financial performance. Whether your business is commercial, industrial, or institutional, energy is part of your value chain, and managing it strengthens your bottom line.

EPA offers a proven strategy for superior energy management with tools and resources to help each step of the way. Based on the successful practices of ENERGY STAR partners, these guidelines for energy management can assist your organization in improving its energy and financial performance while distinguishing your organization as an environmental leader.

Use the following diagram to navigate the steps of ENERGY STAR's Guidelines for Energy Management and learn more about what leading organizations are doing to achieve results.

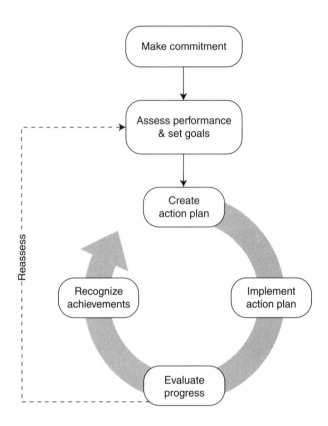

Purchasing and Procurement

Purchasing efficient products reduces energy costs without compromising quality. Successful energy management programs adopt a procurement policy as a key element for their overall strategy. Instituting an effective policy can be as easy as asking procurement officials to specify ENERGY STAR qualified products, such as office equipment, in their contracts or purchase orders. For products not covered under ENERGY STAR, EPA provides links to the Department of Energy's recommended efficient products used by federal government procurement officials.

> **Example:** Computers—An ENERGY STAR qualified computer uses 70 percent less electricity than computers without enabled power management features. If left inactive, ENERGY STAR qualified computers enter a low-power mode and use 15 watts or less. New chip technologies make power management features more reliable, dependable, and user-friendly than even just a few years ago. Spending a large portion of time in low-power mode not only saves

energy, but helps equipment run cooler and last longer. Businesses that use ENERGY STAR enabled office equipment may realize additional savings on air conditioning and maintenance. Over its lifetime, ENERGY STAR qualified equipment in a single home office (for example, computer, monitor, printer, and fax) can save enough electricity to light an entire home for more than 4 years. Because most computer equipment is left on 24 hours a day, power management features are important for saving energy and are an easy way to reduce air pollution.

Example: Light Commercial Heating & Cooling—Space cooling accounts for roughly 15 percent of electricity used in commercial buildings, second only to lighting. ENERGY STAR qualified light commercial HVAC equipment is designed to reduce energy waste and save money on your utility bills.

Earning the ENERGY STAR means products meet strict energy efficiency guidelines set by the EPA and the Department of Energy. ENERGY STAR qualified light commercial HVAC equipment uses 7–10 percent less energy than standard equipment. These products can save your business approximately $3–4 per square foot over the life of the equipment. For example, a 12,000 square foot building using an ENERGY STAR qualified HVAC product could save $36,000 to $48,000.

By choosing ENERGY STAR and taking steps to optimize the performance of your heating and cooling equipment, you are helping to prevent global warming and promoting cleaner air while enhancing the comfort of your home. You may be interested to know that, according to the Consortium of Energy Efficiency, at least 25 percent of all rooftop HVAC units are oversized, resulting in increased energy costs and equipment wear. Properly sized equipment dramatically cuts energy costs, increases the life of the equipment, and reduces pollution.

Example: Commercial Transformers—Commercial and industrial transformers are low-voltage dry-type transformers used to decrease the voltage of electricity received from the utility to the levels used to power lights, computers, and other electric-operated equipment. ENERGY STAR qualified commercial and industrial transformers are designed to help save money on utility bills and reduce energy waste. Depending on the size of the transformer, an ENERGY STAR qualified transformer can save $100–300 each year at an electricity rate of $0.075 cents per kWh. A typical large commercial facility will have 6–10 low-voltage transformers, and thus can save between $600 and $3,000 per year. ENERGY STAR qualified transformers are distributed locally and are NEMA TP-1 compliant.

ENERGY STAR Qualified Products	
Products in more than 40 categories are eligible for the ENERGY STAR. They use less energy, save money, and help protect the environment.	
Appliances	
Battery chargers Clothes washers Dehumidifiers Dishwashers	Refrigerators and freezers Room air conditioners Room air cleaners Water coolers
Heating and Cooling	
Air-source heat pumps Boilers Central air conditioning Ceiling fans Dehumidifiers Furnaces	Geothermal heat pumps Home sealing (insulation) Light commercial Programmable thermostats Room air conditioner Ventilating fans
Home Envelope	
Home sealing (insulation and air sealing) Roof products	Windows, doors, and skylights
Home Electronics	
Battery charging systems Cordless phones Combination units DVD products	External power adapters Home audio Televisions VCRs
Office Equipment	
Computers Copiers External power adapters Fax machines Laptops	Mailing machines Monitors Multifunction devices Printers Scanners
Lighting	
Compact fluorescent light bulbs (CFLs) Residential light fixtures	Ceiling fans Exit signs Traffic signals
Commercial Food Service	
Commercial fryers Commercial hot food holding cabinets	Commercial solid door refrigerators and freezers Commercial steam cookers
Other Commercial Products	
Battery charging systems Exit signs External power adapters Roof products	Traffic signals Transformers Vending machines Water coolers

Results

Small-Business Success Stories

- **A.O.K. Auto Body** saves over $5,500 annually by upgrading its lighting and using commonsense savings.

- **Boulder Books** saves $4,800 annually by upgrading its lighting and installing energy-efficient windows.

- **Subway Sandwiches** saves up to $20,000 annually by replacing its lighting and using energy-efficient air conditioning, keeping its customers comfortable.

- **Thomas Mott Bed & Breakfast** saves over $10,000 annually through renovation and installation of energy-efficient heating systems.

- **Vic's Market** saves over $38,000 annually by upgrading its lighting and using energy-efficient freezers.

Program Results for 2005

Americans, with the help of ENERGY STAR, prevented 35 million metric tons of greenhouse gas emissions in 2005 alone—equivalent to the annual emissions from 23 million vehicles—and saved about $12 billion on their utility bills. They also saved a significant amount of energy in 2005—150 billion kilowatt hours (kWh) or 4 percent of total 2005 electricity demand. In addition, ENERGY STAR helped avoid 28,000 megawatts (MW) of peak power, equivalent to the generation capacity of more than 50 new power plants.

These benefits have grown by 15 percent from one year ago, now totaling more than twice the benefits achieved in 2000. Savings are on track to nearly double again in 10 years as more households, businesses, and organizations rely on ENERGY STAR for guidance on investing in energy-efficient products and practices. The 2005 ENERGY STAR results represent about one-third of the total greenhouse gas emissions reductions from EPA's climate change programs.

Business Results for 2005

EPA launched the ENERGY STAR Challenge early in 2005, calling on U.S. businesses and institutions to reduce energy use by 10 percent or more in coordination with key associations and states. More than half of the states and the District of Columbia, along with over 20 major associations whose members manage many of the nation's office buildings, schools, hospitals, and other commercial buildings, are participating in the Challenge. A first step for organizations is to assess the energy use of their facilities and to set an energy savings target of 10 percent or more.

More than 2,500 buildings have earned the ENERGY STAR label for superior energy and environmental performance, representing 480 million square feet. These buildings consume about 40 percent less energy than typical buildings, while providing the required comfort and services. Their owners are saving an estimated $350 million annually on their energy bills relative to typical buildings. The number of buildings whose energy use has been assessed using EPA's energy performance rating system continues to grow, increasing by about 20 percent over 2004. The rating system has been used to evaluate about 26,000 buildings, including 38 percent of hospital space across the country, 25 percent of office building space, 24 percent of supermarket space, 15 percent of school space, and 14 percent of hotel space.

EPA launched ENERGY STAR Exchange Services to facilitate the hosting of its rating system by third parties, making it easier to benchmark customers' facilities using their own energy-tracking software. More than 3,000 benchmarked buildings were associated with the nine companies that hosted the system.

EPA also offered training, including benchmarking sessions, to several hundred Service and Product Provider partners. They assisted with rating more than 5,000 of the buildings benchmarked and helped label 45 percent of the buildings qualifying for the ENERGY STAR during the year.

The number of participating architecture and engineering (A&E) firms rose to 70—a fourfold increase in 3 years. Partners now use the "Designed to Earn the ENERGY STAR" graphic on their project drawings to show that the projects meet EPA energy performance criteria.

In the industrial sector, ENERGY STAR partnered with three new focus industries—food processing, glass manufacturing, and water/wastewater treatment—to develop standardized measurement tools and industry-specific best practices. EPA also advanced its energy efficiency efforts within its existing industry partnerships—automobile manufacturing, cement, pharmaceuticals, and corn and petroleum refining. Achievements in 2005 included:

1. Completing the first industrial plant energy performance indicator (EPI), which measures the energy efficiency of automobile assembly plants located in the United States

2. Bringing two additional EPIs for cement plants and corn refineries close to completion

3. Developing guidelines for how these industries can earn the first ENERGY STAR industrial plant labels for demonstrating superior energy and environmental performance

EPA GREEN POWER PARTNERSHIP

(Taken from http://www.epa.gov/greenpower)

General Program

Green power is an environmentally friendly electricity product that is generated from renewable energy sources. Green power is a marketing term for electricity that is partially or entirely generated from environmentally preferable renewable energy sources, such as solar, wind, geothermal, biomass, biogas, and low-impact hydro. Green power is sold to support the development of new renewable energy sources. Products made with green power always contain a higher percentage of electricity from renewable energy sources than conventional electrical service. Buying green power is easy, and it offers a number of environmental and economic benefits over conventional electricity. EPA's Green Power Partnership provides assistance and recognition to organizations that demonstrate environmental leadership by choosing green power.

Benefits

The primary benefit of buying green power is environmental protection. For many organizations, the electricity they purchase is a significant source of air pollution and greenhouse gas emissions. Voluntary green power consumers are making a real difference environmentally by supporting the development of new power plants that generate electricity with significantly less air pollution and no net increase in greenhouse gas emissions.

Organizations experienced in green power purchasing have found opportunities to capture strategic value by leveraging their purchases. In most cases, organizations do pay a premium for green power, but these organizations have found that the value frequently exceeds the cost of green power purchases.

Green power leaders have achieved numerous benefits from purchasing green power, including:

- Avoiding air pollution and greenhouse gas emissions
- Meeting organizational environmental objectives
- Providing a hedge against future electricity price instability
- Demonstrating civic leadership
- Generating positive publicity and enhancing public image
- Generating customer, investor, or stakeholder loyalty, and employee pride

- Stimulating local economies
- Stimulating long-term cost reductions for renewable energy
- Increasing domestic security through a more diverse fuel mix
- Reducing the vulnerability of our nation's energy infrastructure

EPA GREENSCAPES PROGRAM

(Taken from http://www.epa.gov/greenscapes)

Roads and highways, golf courses and ski resorts, commercial buildings and industrial sites—the widespread use of economically and environmentally costly landscaping is everywhere. By simply changing these landscapes to "GreenScapes," you can save money and prevent pollution.

The EPA's GreenScapes program provides cost-efficient and environmentally friendly solutions for large-scale landscaping. Designed to help preserve natural resources and prevent waste and pollution, GreenScapes encourages companies, government agencies, and other entities to make more holistic decisions regarding waste generation and disposal and the associated impacts on land, water, air, and energy use. By focusing on the "4 Rs"—reduce, reuse, recycle, and rebuy—you can help improve both your bottom line and the environment.

The GreenScapes Alliance is a partnership program that aims to combine government and industry into a powerful, unified influence over the reduction, reuse, and recycling of waste materials in large land-use applications. These land-use activities include four million miles of roadside landscaping, Brownfields land revitalization, and the beautification and maintenance of office complexes, golf courses, and parks. More than 100,000 businesses are involved in these land-use activities and are potential participants in the Alliance.

The new Alliance is another unique component of the Agency's Resource Conservation Challenge, which is a major EPA initiative that identifies and uses innovative, flexible, and protective ways to conserve natural resources and energy. The GreenScapes Alliance reinforces these goals by emphasizing a holistic multimedia view of environmental impacts and stewardship. In addition, the Alliance:

- Provides information about the cost savings that can be achieved from reducing material use and waste, resource conservation, and on the performance and durability of environmentally preferable products such as recycled-content and biobased products

- Educates land managers that environmentally beneficial landscaping efforts yield water and energy savings, conserve landfill space, and reduce greenhouse gas emissions

- Publicizes case studies, success stories, and technical assistance to help alleviate concerns regarding alternative practices and products

- Promotes market expansion and growth of recycled-content and bio-based products

- Awards organizations that achieve environmental excellence in reduction, reuse, recycling, and rebuying for waste prevention and pollution prevention

GreenScapes participants fall into two categories.

- *Partners:* businesses and agencies that will achieve actual pollution prevention results

- *Allies:* supportive industry associations that will advertise and promote GreenScapes philosophies to their membership and others

Benefits

Cost Savings

Following the principles of GreenScapes can be a great financial move for your organization. Green landscaping means buying fewer products and switching from the purchase of disposable ones to those that are long-lasting and reusable. Buying durable goods might be more expensive at the time of purchase, but over the life of your landscape, maintenance, repurchasing, and tipping costs will go down. These savings can give your business an edge over the competition.

There are also immediate cost savings you can recognize. By composting instead of disposing of your yard waste, for instance, you will save money on disposal costs. Compost adds disease-suppressing properties to soils, reducing your need for pesticides. Even a move as small as leaving grass clippings on your lawn after mowing can save big bucks—lowered disposal costs and, because decomposing grass pieces return valuable nutrients to the soil, lowered fertilizer costs.

Waste Reduction

Millions of tons of waste materials are hauled away, buried, or burned each day from landscaping and grounds-keeping operations—trees, shrubs, brush, lumber, asphalt, and concrete, to name only a few. Millions of gallons of excess water, pesticides, fuels, and oils are in use each and every day. Why pay to dispose of this waste when you can avoid it? Following the GreenScapes philosophies of *reduce, reuse, recycle,* and *rebuy* can lower your tipping fees and other costs related to disposal. All of this waste also impacts our environment. By reducing your landscape's consumption, you will be helping prevent greenhouse gases (GHGs), save landfill space, and preserve natural resources.

Water Conservation

Most large-scale landscapes use an incredible amount of water to keep plants green and healthy. There are various GreenScapes activities you can try to reduce your water use and keep your plants beautiful. Just maintaining an efficient irrigation system and adjusting the time of day that you water can save money. A longer-term adjustment can be made by bringing native plants to your landscapes. Vegetation that is native to your area will be naturally hardier and more tolerant to your weather conditions. Planting native vegetation will reward you with lower water, fertilizer, and pesticide bills.

There are also GreenScapes methods to reduce runoff of storm water and irrigation water that carry topsoils, fertilizers, and pesticides into local rivers and lakes. Drawing from storm retention ponds supplies irrigation applications, as does installing rain barrels or cisterns to catch free rainwater on and around buildings. These options save water and money while reducing runoff, erosion, and nonpoint source pollution.

Environmental Impact

The huge amounts of waste generated, water used, and energy consumed to maintain a large landscape have an incredible impact on our environment. Every piece of trash takes up room in a landfill and produces GHGs not only as it decomposes but during each step of its production and transportation. Energy is required to treat and transport water—energy that generally comes from nonrenewable, polluting sources. And toxic pesticides and fertilizers abound in a typical large landscape, leading to the pollution of local rivers and lakes. Landscaping by the philosophies of GreenScapes will help you to minimize or avoid these environmental issues, lessening your landscape's impact on the earth.

Energy Savings

Almost every material that you use on your landscape requires energy to reach you. Large amounts of energy are used in acquiring materials, manufacturing products, and shipping products to you. Energy is used to produce and ship soil additives, water, tools, machines, paints, and virtually every other material used in landscaping. By purchasing fewer, more durable goods, you are saving an untold amount of energy. Many green landscaping activities help reduce energy usage. Creating compost on-site not only reduces the energy needed to transport organic waste to a landfill, but it eliminates the need for the production and transportation of fertilizers and often pesticides. Compost also absorbs water, reducing the amount of irrigation necessary and the energy required to transport the water. Strategic planting of vegetation around buildings can reduce indoor heating and cooling needs by creating shade.

Climate Impact

Most materials used on landscapes have an impact on our climate. Every product you use emitted GHGs as it was manufactured and transported, and will continue to produce GHGs in a landfill as it decomposes. The constant buying and trashing of products regularly adds GHGs to our atmosphere and impacts the climate.

RESOURCE CONSERVATION CHALLENGE

(Taken from http://www.epa.gov/rcc)

The Resource Conservation Challenge (RCC) is a national effort to conserve natural resources and energy by managing materials more efficiently. We conserve energy and preserve natural resources by committing ourselves to:

- Reduce more waste
- Reuse and recycle more products
- Buy more recycled and recyclable products
- Reduce toxic chemicals in waste
- Making change happen

We are working with states, industry, businesses, and others to find smarter, faster ways to accomplish RCC goals. Whether we partner within the federal government, with major businesses, or with a town and its residents, we use approaches or principles that yield environmental results.

The RCC is working hard to reduce waste and increase the reuse and recycling of materials. We've targeted the nation's largest waste streams and set priorities for:

- Recycling municipal solid waste
- Reusing and recycling industrial materials
- Reducing priority and toxic chemicals in products and waste
- Promoting green initiatives, especially the safe design and recycling of electronics
- Reaching a 35 percent national recycling rate by 2008

We're reinvigorating the public's commitment to, and value placed on, recycling. We hope to help the nation achieve our 35 percent goal by focusing on:

- Paper
- Food scraps and yard trimmings
- Packaging/container materials

We're working with states, local governments, national recycling organizations, and recycling businesses to provide more opportunities for recycling at local levels. America's Marketplace Recycles! is one example of how we're cooperating with the commercial and municipal sectors that provide the greatest opportunities for success.

Reusing and Recycling Industrial Materials

Historically, Americans simply disposed of millions and millions of tons of industrial byproducts. Now, through the RCC we're trying to increase reuse and recycling of these industrial materials. We have opportunities to increase the use of coal ash, construction and demolition on debris, and foundry sands in highway, building, and other construction projects. When we safely use these materials we:

- Conserve virgin resources;
- Reduce energy use and associated greenhouse gas emissions; and
- Extend the useful life of landfills.

There are also economic advantages to the safe reuse of some industrial byproducts. We're aggressively looking for smart ways to use:

- Coal ash
- Construction and demolition debris
- Foundry sands

Protecting Health and Ecosystems by Reducing Risk from Toxic Chemicals

We're taking careful and deliberate steps to remove the worst chemicals, such as lead, mercury, and dioxins, from our environment. These chemicals, along with 28 others, are federal priorities because they are persistent, bioaccumulative, and highly toxic. We're trying to reduce risk from these chemicals.

Companies can produce less waste and thus lower their disposal costs by substituting, eliminating, or recycling certain chemicals in manufacturing processes. We ask companies to voluntarily:

- Substitute safer alternatives when they can

- Minimize the amount of priority chemicals they use, if they can't substitute for them

- Maximize their recycling efforts

- Design products to minimize exposure to, and release of, priority chemicals during manufacturing and use

Through the National Partnership for Environmental Priorities (NPEP), we're providing technical assistance and special recognition to help motivate companies to reduce both the risk from and the amount of priority chemicals they use.

Promoting and Practicing Environmental Stewardship for Electronic Products

Computers and other electronic products are one of the fastest-growing (and among the least recycled) components of America's waste stream. We estimate that we discard electronic products at the rate of 2 million a year. On top of that are millions of televisions, video games, CD players, telephones, and computers that are stored somewhere because their owners cannot, or do not know how to, reuse or recycle them.

Our national partners are collaborating with us to address environmental considerations along the entire life cycle of electronic products. Focusing initially on personal computers, televisions, and cell phones, we're striving to change the overall design, operation, reuse, recycling, and disposal of electronic equipment. We are committed to maintaining and building markets for recyclable electronics.

One way we're supporting markets is through the Federal Electronics Challenge (FEC), a voluntary effort by federal agencies to buy greener electronics and to manage used electronics in an environmentally responsible way. Our Plug-In To eCycling partners are working diligently to provide recycling services for used electronic equipment. Working with them, we plan to increase recycling services nationwide by 50 percent over the next two years.

Changing Our Lives

Accepting responsibility for improving our environment means changing our habits, processes, and practices. Everyone has a role. Businesses, consumers, and governments work together to ensure change across the whole supply chain—from designing better, less toxic products to ensuring easier product reuse and recyclability, to constructing millions of miles of highways using millions of tons of coal ash.

Our RCC partners understand these concepts and are our means to this end. Their innovative solutions point us toward an environmentally sustainable future, where waste is a concept of the past. Moving to an efficient and safe materials flow system is our ultimate goal. We acknowledge government and industry progress and the willingness to adopt a resource and energy conservation ethic. The RCC combines and strengthens many individual efforts into a unified force that:

- Conserves energy and materials

- Reduces risks from the use of toxic and priority chemicals in waste

- Prevents pollution and promotes materials reuse and recycling in all product life cycles

EPA'S DESIGN FOR THE ENVIRONMENT PROGRAM

(Taken from http://www.epa.gov/dfe)

The Design for the Environment (DfE) Program is one of EPA's premier partnership programs, working with individual industry sectors to compare and improve the performance and human health and environmental risks and costs of existing and alternative products, processes, and practices. DfE partnership projects promote integrating cleaner, cheaper, and smarter solutions into everyday business practices.

EPA also supports using "benign by design" principles in the design, manufacture, and use of chemicals and chemical processes—a concept known as "green chemistry." EPA's Green Chemistry Program promotes the research, development, and implementation of innovative chemical technologies that prevent pollution in both a scientifically sound and cost-effective manner. In addition, EPA's emerging Green Engineering Program strives to help academia introduce a "green" philosophy into undergraduate chemical engineering curricula. The DfE Program works with these and other related programs.

The DfE process promotes voluntary environmental improvement by addressing industries' need for key information on how to incorporate environmental concerns into business decisions. The process systematically:

- Identifies the array of technologies, products, and processes that can be used to perform a particular function within an industry and related pollution prevention opportunities

- Evaluates and compares the risk, performance, and cost tradeoffs of the alternatives

- Disseminates this information to the entire industry community

- Encourages and enables use of this information by providing mechanisms and incentives to institutionalize continuous environmental improvement

Why Design for the Environment?

DfE provides decision makers with information, tools, and incentives to make informed decisions that integrate risk, performance, and cost concerns. A DfE project potentially provides many benefits, including:

- Reduced health, safety, and ecological risks

- Increased efficiency and customer acceptance

- Improved worker morale and productivity

- Reduced regulatory burden

- Improved channels of communication, cooperation, and collaboration among stakeholder organizations

- Expanded business and market opportunities

INTERNAL ENVIRONMENTAL IMPROVEMENT PROJECTS

Not all pollution prevention opportunities stem from the adoption of a formal program such as those discussed earlier. Many will arise from the recognition of opportunities by those who understand the processes the best—that is, process owners and operators. The following five case studies have been drawn from the Web site of the Michigan Department of Environmental Quality (MDEQ) and represent the joint efforts of management and process owners in creating a better environment. Readers are encouraged to visit this Web site at http://www.michigan.gov/deq to see many additional case studies that demonstrate the power of organizational involvement in environmental performance improvement. Follow the links to the Pollution Prevention and Auto Project Case Studies Directory.

CASE STUDY

WARREN STAMPING PLANT—ADHESIVE WASTE REDUCTION

The DaimlerChrysler Warren Stamping Plant fabricates steel components for use at the Warren Truck Assembly Plant in the manufacture of Dodge trucks and for use at other Chrysler assembly plants in the United States, Canada, and Mexico. The plant receives steel, adhesives, and various ancillary machining materials such as paints, oils, and grease. Steel is formed into various shapes for assembly of light-duty trucks and automobiles. The plant uses over 400,000 tons of steel per year.

Warren Stamping Plant (WSP) uses adhesives in most of its subassembly operations as a bonding agent, sealer, and/or vibration dampening agent. The adhesive costs on average $42 per gallon, with prices expected to continue rising. In fact, during the past four years, adhesive costs have increased 144 percent. Inefficiencies in the adhesive pumping process resulted in the disposal of usable adhesive material. During 1995 alone, WSP disposed of 20,799 gallons of unused and expired adhesive material that cost approximately $850,000. The increasing cost of adhesives has made elimination of inefficiencies a priority issue for the plant.

The first step in identifying inefficiencies in the current adhesive process was to develop a data collection system. A tracking system was designed to identify wasteful lines within the plant and uncover process inefficiencies. Next, common process inefficiencies were identified among all production lines. Insufficient pumping practices and material expiration composed the majority of the problem. The largest inefficiency discovered through the process analysis involved the lack of a standard pumping limit; the quantity of adhesive disposed per drum ranged from 2 to 10 gallons of material. It was decided that a standard pumping limit of 1 inch from the bottom of every adhesive drum was the best solution. This was achieved through the use of limit switches, which are simple devices that stop a pump once the switch is engaged. Existing switches were recalibrated, and new switches were installed on those pumps that lacked the mechanism. In conjunction with the switches, automatic changeover systems are utilized to ensure continuous operation during production. In an automatic changeover system, when the limit switch is engaged, the primary pump will be turned off and its backup will be turned on, ensuring a continuous flow of adhesive to the line.

The expiration of material was also a substantial problem for WSP. Material was exceeding shelf life for two primary reasons: overpurchasing and poor stock rotation. To remedy the overpurchasing problem, a new system that involves a simple calculation using adhesive specifications along with the projected number of produced parts is being implemented. This will give an accurate view of the quantity of adhesive that is required to produce parts. To improve the stock rotation problem, a first-in-first-out (FIFO) stock rotation program was implemented using a color-coded stock rotation schedule.

Implementation of the adhesive waste management system will eliminate approximately 13,200 gallons of waste adhesive, saving WSP approximately $500,000 annually through the elimination of inefficiencies in the current process.

Substance(s) targeted: Waste adhesives.

Results and advantages: Elimination of 13,200 gallons of waste adhesive per year. The other advantages include reduced costs of approximately $500,000 per year and improved process efficiencies.

Objective: The objective of the project was to reduce the amount of usable adhesive WSP disposes of annually and increase process efficiency. The project was intended to:

– Identify wasteful areas within the facility

– Increase process efficiency through pumping optimization

– Properly utilize all adhesive material

– Reduce costs

Environmental hierarchy: Waste elimination.

Pollution prevention approach: Source reduction.

Environmental media: Reductions in land releases.

Capital investment: Minimal. Less than $1,000.

Barriers encountered: There were no real barriers encountered.

C A S E   S T U D Y

MCGRAW GLASS PLANT—GLASS GRINDING SWARF RECYCLING PROGRAM

The McGraw Glass Plant is located in Detroit, Michigan, where it sits on 18.2 acres with 803,581 square feet of manufacturing floor space. The plant employs 1189 people during full production. The McGraw facility was built for automotive manufacturing in 1936 and has been cutting, shaping, and tempering glass since 1960. The products fabricated at the plant include clear and tinted windshields, side glass, backlights, and liftgate glass.

McGraw receives glass in rectangular sheets that must be cut and shaped into the final glass product. During the course of manufacturing, the glass sheets are cut to size on diamond-tipped routers. Because of the abrasive properties of glass, and the need to keep the glass from breaking or "burning" from the friction of cutting, a water-based coolant is sprayed onto the cutting head during the operation. A second step involves running a diamond-coated grinder over the edge of the glass to remove any burrs and to eliminate any sharp edges. The coolant and resulting glass dust create "swarf." This swarf is collected at the bottom of the cutting and grinding equipment stations and pumped to a microseparator. The microseparator spins the swarf, trapping the solids on the outside walls and returning any coolant back into the system for reuse. The solids are then sent to a portable "buggy" underneath the microseparator, where it is collected until full.

Previous to 1998 McGraw Glass was sending glass-grinding swarf to a landfill. The glass is so abrasive, it was literally wearing through the bottom of 40-yard dumpsters while compacting (the compacting ram would rub it across the bottom and sides of the container). This also caused mechanical problems to the landfill equipment.

In 1998 McGraw Glass partnered with Dlubak Glass Company and began a recycling program to avoid unnecessary landfill disposal of the glass in cutting/grinding swarf. Because the resulting sludge consists primarily of glass and a small amount of water, it is of high-enough quality for recycling. Dlubak transports the sludge from McGraw to its site, where it is able to reprocess it into a recycled product for use in fiberglass materials and to a lesser extent, other glass items. Dlubak Glass's ability to recycle the glass is mutually beneficial from both an economical and an environmental standpoint.

Substance addressed: Landfill of dried glass swarf.

Reduction obtained: 324,000 pounds of material removed from the landfill waste stream and recycled into fiberglass.

Savings realized: Cost savings $14,000; credit $4,860.

Environmental impact

−Landfill avoidance

−Beneficial reuse

−Minimize use of raw materials

C A S E   S T U D Y

TRENTON ENGINE PLANT—WASTE OIL REDUCTION

Trenton Engine Plant (TEP) is Chrysler Corporation's largest producer of Chrysler-made car and minivan engines. Waste oil from machining operations at the plant is recovered at the facility's wastewater treatment plant and shipped off-site for commercial recycling. When the costs of lost raw material as well as treatment and disposal were totaled, hydraulic oil leaks from production equipment were costing the plant about $6.5 million every year. Losses of motor oil were costing the plant almost $700,000 a year. In addition, the City of Trenton's limits for fat, oil, and grease concentration in wastewater are unusually stringent at a monthly average of 50 ppm and daily maximum of 75 ppm.

Some engine oils also contain small amounts of zinc, which is a Great Lakes Persistent Toxic Substance (GLPTS). The oily wastewater also contains phosphates, which are targeted by the Trenton Publicly Owned Treatment Works (POTW) for reduction from the current 20 ppm limit to 2.02 ppm under a newly proposed ordinance. On March 17, 1997, a Product Quality Improvement (PQI) Action Team was formed to develop a plan to address these concerns.

The team included personnel from Chrysler Trenton Engine and Epp-Tech Oil, the plant's commodity distributor for oil products. The team's goal was to reduce waste oil at TEP from projected annual levels of 1.8 million gallons of oil to less than 1 million gallons. To accomplish this objective:

- A plantwide "Leaker-Seeker" program was developed to expand the effectiveness of identifying hydraulic oil leaks in the machinery and to get all TEP employees involved, by implementing a poster/tag program that would encourage workers to tag any leaks they identify for maintenance.

- Additional heat was added to the waste treatment–processing tanks, by the modification of existing piping, which increased the volume of live steam, thus enhancing separation and evaporation to increase the percentage of oil recovered from wastewater. Further heating possibilities are being looked into, such as tank insulation and covering as well as the use of gas-fired heaters to remove expensive condensate from the system.

- Control systems were implemented in various locations around the plant in order to regulate oil usage.

- A new waste oil handler was hired to re-refine TEP's waste oil for alternate reuse. This move reduced the yearly average cost per gallon from $.088 in 1996 to $.071.

TEP is also studying the potential to reuse some waste oils in the plant if collected before entering the waste treatment facility. In general, simple, commonsense techniques were used to reduce waste oil. Proven, reliable "best practices" were employed to sustain the program.

Objective: Identify current oil wastes of 1.8 million gallons/year and create an action plan to reduce to less than 1 million gallons/year.

Targeted reductions: Reduce oil leaks in machinery, increase percentage of oil recovered at the industrial waste treatment plant, and reduce average concentration of fats, oils, and greases in wastewater sent to the City of Trenton's wastewater treatment facility to under 50 ppm. These reductions directly led to reductions in zinc, a GLPTS, and phosphate releases, which are currently being targeted by the POTW for reduction from the current 20 ppm limit to 2.02 ppm under a newly proposed ordinance.

Environmental hierarchy: Pollution prevention (P2).

P2 approach: Waste prevention.

Environmental media: Reduction in material wasted/recycled.

Results since 1996 and financial analysis: Waste oil shipped out of the plant and cost have significantly decreased. Percentage of oil in the waste has also increased.

Barriers encountered: The largest problem with the plan, in fact still being implemented, was the difficulty of repairing leaks while the plant was operating at capacity.

C A S E   S T U D Y

FORD MOTOR COMPANY MANUFACTURING PLANTS

Ford paint spray booths use continuous conveyor systems to move units past stationary paint applicator equipment. Each assembly plant has several booths, ranging in length from 500 to 1000 lineal feet. Cars and trucks are primed and painted in controlled conditions of airflow, temperature, and humidity.

Most spray booths built in the last 30 years have utilized T-12 VHO fluorescent lamps enclosed in vaporproof fixtures. The initial light output for these lamps is very high, and the energy consumption is also very high. The lamps have extremely poor efficacy, lamp life, lumen depreciation, and color rendering index. Maintenance costs are high due to frequent replacements. Energy costs are high due to the efficacy. Quality and operator comfort are affected when lamps burn out.

New fluorescent lighting technology has advanced the development of T-8 lamps to about double the efficacy of T-12 VHO lamps. High-output versions of the T-8 lamps were compared with T-12 VHO lamps for energy consumption, light output, maintained lumen level, life, and light quality (color rendering index). A retrofit has been designed and installed in 11 of 21 Ford North American paint shops. Lighting energy costs are reduced by more than 50 percent. Initial light levels are lower, but since the depreciation is less, the maintained light level is equal. The color rendering index is higher, and the new lamps will last two to three times longer.

Substance addressed: Energy use.

Reduction obtained: 17,500,000 kWh/yr.

Savings (operational): $500,000/year.

Environmental hierarchy levels: Source reduction, waste stream elimination, and energy reduction.

CASE STUDY

NORFOLK ASSEMBLY PLANT—SOLVENT MANAGEMENT AND REDUCTION

The Ford Norfolk Assembly Plant, located in Norfolk, Virginia, was opened in 1925. The facility manufactures and paints the F-150 and F-250 trucks. Recently, the Norfolk Assembly Plant was awarded Ford's Total Productive Maintenance award for checkpoint "C," the first Ford facility globally to achieve such an award for proactive preventive maintenance. Also, in October 1996, the facility was approved for ISO 9000 certification.

The facility's total waste management supplier, as part of its contract, working with the paint area management, is responsible for reducing waste streams at the plant and is paid on a cost-per-unit basis. In the paint facility, waste streams relating to solvents are captured and recycled by the facility's solvent supplier. As part of the plant's ongoing effort to reduce costs, improve quality, and its commitment to reduce volatile organic compound (VOC) emissions, the paint area management asked the solvent supplier to review and improve, where possible, the current method of tracking solvent usage and also review the spray booth preventative maintenance cleaning procedure.

Solvent usage during nonproduction hours was studied and inventory taken on Friday after production and Monday before production. After several weeks of tracking usage it was determined that solvent was being used over the weekends, during nonproduction hours. The booth maintenance cleaning practices were also reviewed to determine if any improvements could be made to the existing procedure. After a series of meetings and employee awareness training programs, it was agreed that the solvent supply pumps would be shut off during nonproduction hours. The computer logic for the pumps was programmed to shut off the pumps 15 minutes after production and turn on the pumps 30 minutes before the normal Monday morning production start-up. This time frame allowed the booth maintenance staff time to obtain small quantities of material to hand clean equipment prior to their shift, thereby eliminating unnecessary usage. The existing booth cleaning procedure was updated to reflect the changes made on the computer logic for the solvent supply pumps.

Barriers: Employee awareness and training were addressed through small-group meetings with booth maintenance personnel. Small-group training sessions provided an emphasis on safety, cost-savings opportunities, and VOC reductions.

Savings realized or anticipated

– VOC solvent was reduced by 983.45 gallons per week

– Cost savings per year were $95,355.31 (based on a 48-week production schedule)

– VOC reduction of 342,713 lbs/year

Capital/operating investment: There was no capital investment required.

SMALL-BUSINESS EXAMPLE: OETIKER—USA

Oetiker—USA is the U.S. affiliate of the Oetiker Corporation, a provider of clamps and fittings to many different industries within several industrial sectors. Oetiker—USA is a small business, with approximately 120 employees and with facilities in Marlette, Michigan. Its main manufacturing processes include metal stamping, forming, and light assembly. It is ISO 9001, ISO/TS 16949, and ISO 14001 certified. Its EMS was implemented in 2002 and certified in 2004. Oetiker—USA is typical of many small businesses in that it does not have a large environmental footprint and would not appear, at first glance, to have many opportunities to go beyond compliance. Even so, Oetiker was determined to put in place a program that would do more than simply meet its regulatory commitments, but rather would drive its environmental performance beyond compliance while reducing the costs associated with its operations.

Oetiker—USA realized that in order to make meaningful improvements in its performance, it would need to get the entire organization involved in the environmental program. In order to promote this involvement, the executive team took several steps, with the full support of the parent corporation, including the following:

- Oetiker's significant environmental aspects were organized into natural categories. These categories included solid waste, liquid wastes, energy, air emissions, and noise emissions. Biannual improvement objectives were set for each category.

- Each of these categories was assigned to a team of between 5 and 7 employees. These multifunctional teams, which included both hourly and salaried employees, were then responsible for developing ideas and plans for achieving the objectives established for their category. Team members could rotate in and out of the teams. The result was a high level of direct participation (reported to be almost 60 percent) by the workforce in environmental performance improvement.

- Within each team, members were assigned specific responsibilities for one of the actions or responsibilities related to the significant environmental aspects within that category. This distribution of responsibilities within the team created a high level of accountability while minimizing the time spent in meetings. No overtime was necessary to effect the improvements implemented to support achievement of the objectives and targets.

- Senior managers' personal objectives and performance criteria, and therefore compensation, were directly tied into success in meeting the ISO management system objectives, thereby ensuring management's support of the programs.

- Team accomplishments were recognized both at the local level (Oetiker—USA) and at the corporate level in the form of an annual performance report that summarized performance in achieving the established environmental objectives and targets.

- Assistance was provided to each team where needed, such as the calculation of costs vs. benefits of proposed actions. Funding was provided to those projects that improved environmental performance and provided a positive return on investment. Indeed, a key to Oetiker's success was the recognition that good environmental management saves money, and the firm commitment on the part of the management team to show a positive return for the investments it would make in improving its environmental performance.

The results of these actions have been impressive and could not have been achieved without the support and involvement of the entire workforce. Many of the ideas for improvement came from hourly colleagues who normally operate the systems and know them the best. The following is an excerpt from Oetiker's 2005 EMS Performance Report. These gains were realized through many balanced improvements, including the use of variable speed motors (energy), closed loop water reuse (natural resources), and recycling (minimization of solid waste). Also note the investigation into the use of alternate power (Green Power) and the associated savings expected.

2005
Environmental Management System
Performance Report
Oetiker—USA[3]

1.1 Objectives & Targets (1 Jan. 2004–31 Dec. 2005)

Objectives & Targets established at the onset of the Environmental Management System implementation phase are identified below. Measurable results of each target are described within the Environmental Management Program Report for the 2004 & 2005 calendar years and revised for 2006–2007. We have eliminated the Air emissions team because we have accomplished everything we have set out to do for this team.

1.2 Objectives & Targets (1 Jan. 2005–31 Dec. 2006)

Objective 2004–2005	Target	Objective 2006–2007	Target
Minimize Solid Waste	5%	Minimize Solid Waste	5%
Minimize Energy Usage	5%	Minimize Energy Usage	5%
Minimize Liquid Waste	10%	Minimize Liquid Waste	5%
Minimize Air Emissions	5%	Minimize Noise Emissions	5%
Minimize Noise Emissions	5%		

2. Environmental

2.1 Minimize Solid Waste

> **Objective:** Reduce Solid Waste
> **Target:** 5% reduction by 2005
> 2000–2001 results: 504 cubic yards solid waste
> 2002–2003 results: 420 cubic yards solid waste
> 2004–2005 results: 210 cubic yards solid waste

A two-year benchmark was established to minimize variables that result within the business on an annual basis. The calendar years of 2004–2005 resulted in a 50% reduction vs. the calendar years of 2002 & 2003. Overall results were determined by the amount of cubic yards of solid waste that was legally disposed through Waste Management Services.

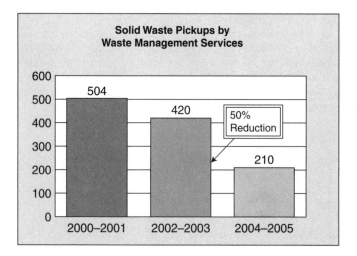

2.1.1 Recycling

2005 continued to be a prosperous year in regards to accomplishments by our Recycling Team. A total of 158,083 lbs of material, including material waste, was recycled in 2005. Material waste represented 80% with the remaining 20% from various plant input items within the facility. Due to the volume of material being recycled a paper/cardboard baler was added in 2005.

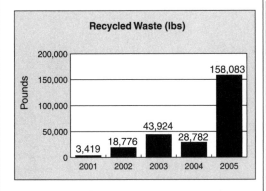

Recycled Waste (lbs)

Items currently recycled:
Plastic
Plastic wrap
Plastic bags
Rolled ribbon
Styrofoam
Metal
Glass
Paper
Cardboard
Batteries
Stainless & Z.P. Steel
Aluminum
Brass

2.2 Minimize Liquid Waste

Objective: Reduce Liquid Waste
Target: 10% reduction by 2005
2002 results: 3.42 gal./1,000 pcs
2003 results: 2.67 gal./1,000 pcs
2004 results: 1.94 gal./1,000 pcs
2005 results: 2.44 gal./1,000 pcs

2005 was a positive year for the Liquid Waste Reduction Program. Our 2004–2005 Program Goal of a 10% reduction in Total Water Usage per 1000 pieces Produced was exceeded with a 23% reduction over the previous 2002–2003 program period. This resulted in a savings of 305,304 gallons of water.

While our water usage per 1000 pieces produced rose slightly in 2005 versus the previous year, this was attributed to a reduction in Pieces Produced that resulted from an Inventory Reduction Program. Also, an increase in water usage for the TS01 Test Equipment was detected and resolved.

In addition to a reduction in overall water usage, we experienced significant improvement in Water Recycling capabilities for Parts Degreasing. An 83% reduction in Degreaser Water Usage resulted in an annual Cost Savings for Soap, Water and Waste Hauling of $45,087.

The conclusion of the 2 year Liquid Waste Reduction Program showed significant savings in both Resources and Costs. The Program saved 305,000 gallons of fresh water, 1700 gallons of soap and reduced our outgoing Liquid Waste Stream by more than 60%. The 2 year Cost Savings was $84,000. With the Oil Reduction Program doubling Degreaser bath life, Sales of non-degreased products increasing by 40% and continued improvements in recycling efficiencies, we anticipate continued Program success in 2006.

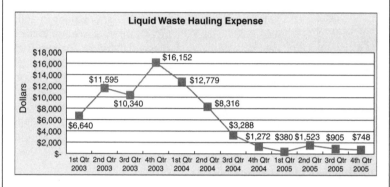

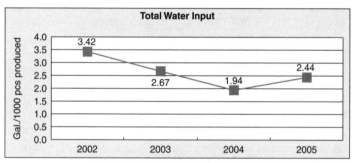

2.3 Minimize Energy Usage

Objective: Reduce Energy Usage

Target: 5% reduction by 2005

2001 results: 76 pieces per kwh

2002 results: 108 pieces per kwh

2003 results: 103 pieces per kwh

2004 results: 116 pieces per kwh

2005 results: 108 pieces per kwh

The energy committee completed five projects during the period of 2004–2005, which showed an annual savings of $7,592.20. Our budget was $35,850 and our actual costs were $33,731 which was also a savings of $2,119.

We installed a new 100hp air compressor and dryer late in the third quarter which is showing a savings of $1,500/quarter at this time. We estimated this could potentially save the company between $1,600 and $16,000/year. This will be monitored during 2006 to show a better picture of our savings.

Oetiker decided to switch to an alternate energy company in 2005 due to the substantial cost savings to our energy bills. We are looking at a potential cost savings of $26,000/yr to switch to First Energy. They also informed us about an additional savings of $24,090 in 2006 which may result from DTE's requested change in the PSCR (Power Supply Cost Recovery) part of their bill. This will be a total savings of $50,090 in 2006 due to an alternate energy source.

As you can see in the total Kwh chart we are showing a significant drop in Kwh usage in both plants due to shutting the lights off at 3:15 PM Monday–Thursday and at 9:45 AM on Fridays when the plant shuts down.

Our base unit has always been pieces produced divided by Kwh. Due to stocking levels being decreased by 30%, production was reduced by 39,000,000 pieces. This resulted in less production and an increase in the cost of energy per piece.

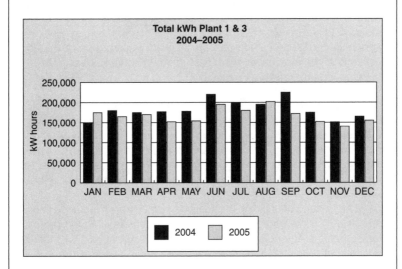

2.4 Minimize Air Emissions

Objective: Minimize Air Emissions
Target: 5% reduction by 2005

The achievements made in the reduction of aerosols in 2005 were maintained through the use of the Certification of New Materials/Services form. This form requires all purchases of new chemicals to be reviewed, accepted/denied, by the appropriate team leader and the Environment Rep.

An aerosol can depressurizing system was installed to prepare aerosol cans for recycling. This system uses an activated carbon cartridge to filter VOCs.

The impact of air emissions resulting from external transportation is being controlled by attempting to pack more shipments per truck using fewer carriers.

2.5 Minimize Noise Emissions

Objective: Reduce Noise Emissions
Target: 5% reduction by 2005

In June 2005, a representative from the MIOSHA training division conducted a noise study in plant 1 and plant 3. This noise study determined the level of noise exposure over an 8 hour period. The 8 hour average for employees in plant 1 was 82.4dBA and in plant 3 it was 84.5dBA. 85.0dBA is the criterion for having a hearing conservation program under MIOSHA standards. This program requires annual hearing testing and hearing conservation training for all employees exposed to 85.0dba and above levels.

Utilizing the information from the MIOSHA study and the machine noise study from the previous year, we targeted areas to lower the noise exposure to employees to under 84.0dBA. The noise emissions team reviewed the equipment once again to determine where more sound absorbing/dampening materials needed to added for optimum reductions. This project is well underway and should be completed within the second quarter of 2006. More testing is to be done in the first quarter to determine the progress made.

A significant reduction in the noise generated from the plant 3 HVAC system was achieved by installing noise attenuators in all the production area ducts. The noise was reduced from 84dBA to below 70dBA. A reduction of at least 14dBA or 16.7%.

2.6 Expenses Summary

Total 2005 Expenses tracked $67,413, which was down $51,512 from 2004.

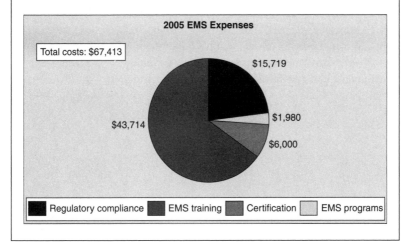

2005 EMS Expenses

Total costs: $67,413

$15,719

$1,980

$43,714

$6,000

■ Regulatory compliance ■ EMS training ■ Certification ☐ EMS programs

SUMMARY

The majority of the programs and case studies in this chapter were obtained from public information provided by the federal and state governments. The purpose of including them in this book is threefold. First, they provide concrete examples of what can be achieved when an organization focuses on moving beyond compliance. Second, they demonstrate the many resources that are publicly available to help organizations that wish to improve their environmental performance. Third, they should help generate interest in exploring the Web sites to find out more. One of the real advantages in implementing an effective EMS is that there is a wealth of information and assistance available for little to no charge. The case study of Oetiker—USA was provided to show that even a small business can achieve meaningful improvements in its environmental performance, and save money, by focusing on beyond compliance.

Your ISO 14001 EMS provides the foundation for making pollution prevention an ongoing and integral element of the organization's management system. The metrics established during the design phase provide indicators of where improvements are needed. The communications programs and training should provide the awareness of the organization's commitment to the environment and need for performance improvement. The process for setting environmental objectives, targets, and management programs provides the means to resource, track, and accomplish projects related to pollution prevention. Finally, management reviews provide insight on the organization's overall performance in preventing pollution. By thoughtfully and carefully considering each of these components and making them a dynamic element of the organization's business management process, you too can help drive performance toward sustainable development and save quite a bit of money while doing it.

Notes

1. ANSI/ISO/ASQ, *E14001-2004 Environmental management systems—Requirements with guidance for use* (Milwaukee, WI: ASQ Quality Press, 2004).
2. *One Planet, Many People: Atlas of Our Changing Environment,* United Nations Environment Programme, Nairobi, Kenya, 2005.
3. Oetiker—USA, *Environmental Management System Performance Report,* 2005. Used with permission.

Index